Josephine Community Libraries
Grants Pass, Oregon

Collection development
policies and procedures

NLLN

Collection Development Policies and Procedures

Third Edition

Josephine Community Libraries
Grants Pass, Oregon

Collection Development Policies and Procedures

Third Edition

Edited by Elizabeth Futas

A Neal-Schuman Professional Book

Formerly titled Library Acquisitions Policies and Procedures

Oryx Press
1995

The rare Arabian Oryx is believed to have inspired the myth of the unicorn. This desert antelope became virtually extinct in the early 1960s. At that time several groups of international conservationists arranged to have 9 animals sent to the Phoenix Zoo to be the nucleus of a captive breeding herd. Today the Oryx population is over 800 and nearly 400 have been returned to reserves in the Middle East.

© 1995 by Elizabeth Futas
Published by The Oryx Press
4041 North Central at Indian School Road
Phoenix, Arizona 85012-3397

Published simultaneously in Canada
Printed and Bound in the United States of America

∞ The paper used in this publication meets the minimum requirements of American National Standard for Information Science—Permanence of Paper for Printed Library Materials, ANSI Z39.48, 1984

Library of Congress Cataloging-in-Publication Data
Collection development policies and procedures / [edited] by Elizabeth Futas.
    p. cm.
Rev. ed. of: Library acquisition policies and procedures. 2nd ed. 1984.
Includes bibliographical references and index.
ISBN 0-89774-797-6
    1. Collection development (Libraries)—United States—Policy statements. 2. Academic libraries—Collection development—United States. 3. Public librar-ies—collection development—United States. 4. Library surveys—United States. I. Futas, Elizabeth. II. Library acquisition policies and procedures.
Z687.2.U6C65   1995
025.2'1'0973—dc20   94-34699
                                                                        CIP

CONTENTS

❈ ❈ ❈ ❈ ❈ ❈ ❈ ❈

PREFACE

* * * * * * * *

For the past several years, librarians and students of library science have been asking when the third edition of *Library Acquisition Policies and Procedures* would be published. This edition has required more time to produce than either of the other two (published in 1977 and 1984) simply because a great number of changes in collection development policies have occurred since the second edition. In hopes that these myriad changes in the building of library collections would have enough time to become part of the policy documents of the library, almost a decade was allowed to elapse between preparation of the second and third editions. In the cases of electronic sources, collection evaluation, and maintenance, for example, the elapsed time was sufficient; in other cases, such as cooperative and consortia arrangements affecting collections, preservation and conservation of collections, and disaster planning, the time period was long enough only to see these issues partially addressed. And in still other cases, such as the influence of the Internet on collection development, there has hardly been time enough for changes to begin to appear in policies. There comes a point when the profession needs information and guidelines for decision making and a volume with such information cannot continue to wait for the perfect moment. So this third edition offers a look at where the profession is at this time; where it will be in the future will have to wait for the next edition.

To reflect the complexity and sophistication of the policies now being written, the title of the volume has been changed to better represent the current language of the profession. In truth, both author and publisher struggled with the titling of the first edition. Because terminology was then in flux (as it still is today), the oldest words for the process of collection building were used, i.e. ,"library acquisitions." When the second edition was published in 1984, "collection development" was well established as correct terminology, but "collection management" was still vying for first place honors. Since no one could tell which would "win" out in the end, it was decided to keep the established title. This edition is titled to reflect the terminology used in the contents of the material presented here. Continuing to use the original title would be a disservice to the profession, especially to librarians unfamiliar with the first two editions, who might be misled as to the book's contents. The new title should serve to make all librarians aware that there is now more to acquisitions policies than one might suppose at first glance.

Practicing librarians and library science students continue to be the prime audience for this volume. With this edition, as with the first edition, you can use examples of other libraries' policy statements as guides to what you might include in the written statement of your library's collection development policy. The policies reprinted here are to be used as models, not copied verbatim. Many librarians will ignore this caveat and do so anyway, but they will thereby do themselves and their communities a disservice. Not all communities look alike, and not all policies should either. Therefore, the best way to use this volume is to consult it when you are developing your policy statement, so that it may help in brainstorming possible issues you might not have thought of yourself. In addition, the wording of statements can be used to describe similar processes from one library to another.

For use by the library science student, these policies have been selected to show how the policies of public and academic libraries come to be written; reading several policies can give a real idea of the values and principles of the libraries that wrote them. Reading these statements is also a lesson in the importance of good, clear writing and communication between the library and its staff, or the library and its patrons, or both. Writing policies is one of the "skills" that library educators try to impart to their students in the short amount of time the students are in library school. Collection development may be one of the few areas in our field where technology is coming slowly, and where the computer as a tool of that technology can be of real benefit to the librarian as well as the user. Strides are being made in interconnecting libraries so that information on collections can be shared. With the advent of full-text retrieval by telecommunications, cooperative collection development and shared resources may eventually become a reality. Although the profession clearly recognizes the need for this type of vision, the practicality of it is still in the future. Perhaps technology will be the force that finally allows it to flower.

Over 5,000 letters were sent to public and academic libraries in the United States and Canada in 1992 asking the recipients to fill out a survey questionnaire and to share with the author a copy of their latest collection policy statement. In all, 357 wrote back; not a particularly overwhelming return rate (7%). The survey, therefore, is certainly not scientific. It does, however, confirm for librarians the existence of trends and developments they knew were ongoing, even if it does not uncover any new or startling developments.

Of the policies that were sent, four were chosen to reprint in their entirety; they represent different types of libraries (public and academic) and different sizes of libraries (university, college, small and medium-sized public libraries). In the case of partial policies chosen, all sizes of libraries are represented. A total of 30 public libraries and 31 academic libraries are represented among the partial policies. A number of Canadian libraries, both public and academic, are among those used, and at least two fundamentalist Christian colleges with a different outlook on many parts of the collection building process are also included.

This edition continues the arrangement of the other two editions. Part 1 begins with an introduction that defines the overall setting for the policies, describes where the field of collection development is at this time, explores what the present promises for the future, and examines the direction, expected and unexpected, taken as a result of the trends identified in the last edition. Next, the 1992 survey is discussed, with results for public and academic libraries treated separately and then combined into the conclusion to Part 1. Trends and statistics gleaned from responses are presented, although no hard and fast conclusions can or be made.

Part 2 reprints four policy statements in full, representing two academic and two public libraries. The third edition reprints fewer policies in full than the previous two editions, not because there are fewer good policies, but because of time and size constraints on this edition.

Part 3 groups together parts of policies that might be models for librarians to use when writing or revising collection development documents. Users of this volume should feel free to digress from the arrangement of the topics in the policy sections (Part 3) and pick the organization that best suits their policies.

The selective bibliography is appended for those who wish further study on the topic of collection development policies or who need further help with the skills necessary to write these documents. The index will give added access to the documents and topics discussed in this book.

The differences between this edition and the earlier ones can be seen plainly in the answers given to survey questions and in the policies reprinted in this edition. The questions asked differed in some respects from the other two editions, and the policies that were returned seem somewhat more sophisticated. Fewer libraries indicated that they did not have policy statements, but since the return rate was low, this statistic may not indicate that a larger percentage now have such policies.

Comments still provided enjoyment. For instance, one librarian stated that s/he did not have any written policies in the library because they only "stirred up trouble," and several respondents wondered why they were asked about preservation in a survey about collection development—what had "one to do with the other?" Perhaps their lives will not be bothered by such questions, although one wonders about their vision of the field! This edition began with the hope that shared resources and cooperative collection development would be a reality. After all, many articles have been written about these ideas and visions of the future, and some have even been of the "how I did it good at my library" variety. Perhaps libraries that do it "good" are not willing to share with others, perhaps such cooperative ideas have not been written into collection development policy statements (so much else is not there, why not this?), or perhaps libraries are too busy accomplishing what they set out to do in those articles. In any case, none of them answered the survey or sent in a policy that recognized the value or need for such a cooperative venture.

There is a listserv (an informal discussion group via e-mail) on the Internet electronic network to which those of us interested in this field subscribe to with zeal. The issues brought up by the survey responses, and the role of the new technology in the area of collection building and management are often the focus of questions and answers. Recently, there was a call for Internet policy statements, which have now been collected and are available on the archive of that list. The librarian with vision explores all avenues of information so that the best and most up-to-date information available can be used in making important decisions. Library budgets are shrinking, and the days of protecting materials budgets are gone. Libraries have cut staff, service, and now are cutting materials. If we librarians are to continue doing our jobs as they need to be done, we must find a way to increase access without increasing costs. Technology is just one of the answers. Networking is another, by which is meant not the technology of connecting computers, but people-to-people networking, the sharing of ideals, values, and principles. In the field known for this kind of communication, such networking may be the salvation of our libraries and of ourselves.

ACKNOWLEDGMENTS

I am grateful to editors Anne Thompson, John Wagner, Julie Russ, and all the others at The Oryx Press for their generosity and their patience. At school, I am particularly grateful to a group of wonderful graduate student assistants who helped: Rebecca Armitage, Eric Barden, Sandy Cahillane, Julie Handren, Michelle Kelmsley, Pamela Lorenzo, Michele O'Malley, and Pamela Lorenzo. Student help is hard to find, but good student help is priceless. Working for us this past semester was Beth Hermelee, without whose assistance this never would have been done on time. To my faculty and staff—Jon, Fay, Herb, Gale, Cheryl and Donna, to Leena, Stew, and Linda, but most of all to Rosemary Northup, our administrative secretary, who accomplishes great things every day and makes life a little easier for all of us—thank you from the bottom of my heart.

PART
1

****

Introduction and Survey

INTRODUCTION

* * * * * * * *

Wh, hen the first edition of this volume was published in 1977, the terminology used to describe the processes of building a collection in a library and the policies derived from these collection processes were in flux. Consequently, *acquisitions policies*, the current term of the day, was used. By the time of the publication of the second edition of this book, in 1984, the terminology was changing, but there was still no definitive term for the entire process, with both *collection development* and *collection management* moving to the forefront, but no clear winner between them. There was more concern with the larger definition of the term *collection*, and many libraries by this time had some sort of selection policies in place, mostly public libraries, who were forced by state agencies into writing them before federal money was filtered into their budgets. Since that time, both the terminology and the processes themselves have significantly changed, and the terminology and processes for building and managing a library's collection have metamorphosed into *collection development and management*. Acquisitions, the purchasing of materials for the collection, has been relegated to just part of the overall process, which also includes goals and objectives, evaluation, planning, and selection criteria.

Changes in library resource management have been numerous; some show up in collection development policies, and some do not. One of the issues that has begun to appear in policies is maintenance of the collection. In past years, collection maintenance—the idea of binding, replacing, weeding, preserving, and protecting collections—was thought to be tangential to the real process of building collections. With the development of cost effectiveness concerns in the 1970s, the money crunch in the 1980s, and the understanding in the 1990s, finally, of the fact that the growth of a library's collection is not infinite, librarians are now realizing that existing library materials must be preserved so that limited funding resources can go for new information, to build better and not just bigger collections. This is what we as librarians are all about and what we shall continue to be all about.

Another issue beginning to appear in policies is criteria for electronic materials. These criteria relate to costs of electronic resources and to techno-logical trends, including selection of electronic sources in the area of reference, the continual upsurge in the use of audio and visual library materials, and the acknowledgment that accountability, which will always be with us, requires constant evaluation of these materials. These issues may or may not show up directly in collection development policies but each underlies some aspect of development policy, including allocation of funds, use of electronic sources in reference with CD-ROM products, and criteria for the purchase of both video and audio book materials separate from book, journal, and microform formats. Accountability for money spent shows up in a number of ways in development policy documents, but nowhere more substantially than in the evaluation of the collection.

Some areas being talked about on e-mail "listservs" on the Internet elec-tronic network, written about in journals, or spoken about at conferences and institutes have not yet appeared in any discernible number of policies. Among these areas are the collecting and archiving of electronic journals, the Internet and its relationship to collection building, cooperative efforts in collection development, and preservation of materials. Why these areas have yet to show up is somewhat perplexing since the library profession is certainly concerned about their impact on collection growth and development. However, it is possible that as a profession we are hesitant to create policies about something we do not yet have a handle on ourselves, or if we do have a handle, we aren't sure it's the right one. In cases of other library management issues not directly related to collections such as latch-key children, disruptive behavior, and sexual harassment, policies began to be instituted soon after these issues surfaced in the literature. However, this is not true for collection development issues. Electronic media (except for reference tools), the Internet, and coop-erative ventures are being recognized as alternative solutions to the money problem, but are not yet recognized as perhaps our best solutions. Librarians at many academic libraries and large public libraries find it increasingly difficult to give up control of their collections to consortium development, while librarians at smaller and perhaps less prestigious institutions are making great strides with smaller, but more successful, networks and consortia.

With the first edition of this book, few libraries even had acquisitions policies. The second edition showed that, for a variety of reasons, many libraries had begun to think about policy formation for their collections. With this new edition it becomes obvious that a great many libraries have instituted collection development policies. However, an examination of these docu-ments reveals that many policies were copied from existing collections of policies and published policy documents. As with most other areas of policy within an institution, the whole idea of developing policy is to start a process of self-discovery and self-awareness, not to copy words that seem appropriate from someone else's policy. Until we figure out that the process of developing these policies is at least as important as the policies we develop, we are never going to profit from this process or be able to develop realistic policies for our libraries to follow.

THE PROCESS

The policy development process begins with a group of people interested in the future of their library who get together to discuss how best to develop that library; to plan, to design, and to accomplish, so that optimum service is provided with the best and most judicious use of funding. No matter what kind of library—school, special, academic, or public—the plan for action begins with a first meeting. Although the impetus for this meeting may originate from several levels, the grassroots of staff or patron concerns, the directorial initiative, or even higher—from institutional necessity—the most usual stimulus comes from the director and/or management team getting together to do a strategic plan for the library's future (usually formulated in answer to a specific budget cycle or budget crisis). The strategic plan usually contains the acquisitions and collection development policy.

All good planning requires a number of "first things first" kind of actions. These actions include:

1. Setting down exactly what is to be accomplished in a "planning to plan" group,
2. Collecting the type and amount of information to make correct decisions,
3. Formulating and writing the final document, and
4. Determining what use is to be made of the final product—in other words, going from document to policy.

Planning to Plan

The first group that meets is the "planning to plan" group. They may set out in great detail or in sweeping brush strokes the areas of work to be done, who is to do it, the time frame within which it is to be accomplished, the amount of funding put aside for the project, and the selection of individuals to monitor the work that is being done. The planning to plan group sets up the structure and organization that they believe will yield the best results.

Out of this first group comes the working group, usually made up of a number of professionals from the library supplemented by interested patrons (from an active friends group, library faculty committee, students, or volunteer workers), members of the board (or its equivalent in academe), and at least one administrator or manager, not necessarily the director, who will guide the process and whose overview of the real situation and vision of the place of the library in its surroundings will help the group stay focused in their decision making. This group may choose to work together, or depending on their size, break up into smaller groups. Assignments may be made to people outside the group to work on parts of the policy. In all, as many people as possible should either be on this committee or involved in development of the policy document in ways that will provide satisfaction and elicit cooperation from them in the document's final outcome—adoption by board or institution.

With this accomplished, the next part of the process is to gather information from all sectors of the library's population, those served as well as those not served.

Collecting Information for Decision-Making

The second step is to start collecting information about those individuals and groups that the library is most concerned with, patrons and community, in order to make useful decisions. For planning research, whether strategic long range planning or simply the plan for next year, the sources which yield the greatest and most concentrated amount of information are the community and the library itself. From each source there are two kinds of information sought, primary and secondary. Primary information is collected directly with no analysis and no hearsay involved. Secondary information comes from other sources and may have to be analyzed for this project.

Primary Information about the Community. The primary information from the community consists of opinions, needs, evaluations, or any other points of knowledge that the community can comment upon or contribute to its relationship to the library. This can be done in any number of ways: surveys, interviews, focus groups, and large, community-wide meetings like town meetings for public libraries, or college- or university-wide meetings for academic libraries.

The survey is the most usual way that librarians find out opinions of patrons and communities. It is not easy to develop a questionnaire that will actually answer the information needed at the moment, but a few trial and error pretests should iron out most quirks and allow at least some of the questions to yield good and needed information. Direct interview has similar pitfalls in that sometimes interview questions lead to peculiar or unforeseen avenues of information; however these comments too may prove enlightening. Focus groups are useful for collecting information and opinions from specialized groups, and there are a number of trained facilitators prepared to develop focus group sessions. This process can be very illuminating if the group is arranged so that all participants are motivated by common interests, share a common terminology, and discussions are sharply focused. The last method of developing primary information from the community is one that is difficult to control, the town- or college-wide meeting. Very few groups will come out solely for discussions concerning the library, and given that only one or two questions can be insinuated into a long agenda which many people will simply turn off if they are not interested, large group meetings are the most difficult way of getting information. It is mentioned here because, although information is not easily obtained from such a group, it is easily disseminated through such a group, and that may be equally important in library decision making on such issues as shifting budgetary lines from monographs to journals, or cutting back on journal subscriptions.

Secondary Information about the Community. Secondary information is a collection of existing data on the community from written documents and studies. Most heavily relied upon in public libraries are census data, available at low or no cost to libraries from the U.S. government through census reports. These data tell a library about the demographics of its population—their gender, age, race, ethnic group, education and income level, to name a few areas. In an academic library, there are many sources of information about faculty and students from admission statistics, the college catalog, curriculum vitae of the faculty, syllabi from courses, information on faculty publications, and data on student finances. Information such as this and more is collected by colleges about their communities. It is important for the library to discover which statistics are being collected and to get on mailing lists to receive updates. Where individual faculty and courses are concerned, library personnel acting as liaisons to individual departments should keep abreast of any important new courses, degrees, programs, or faculty coming to the academic community and bring that information back to the library for action. Every academic institution has newsletters and other methods of communications within the community, and the library should be the archive for all of this. The archivist in charge should read all of this to keep others current on issues and trends on campus.

Primary Information about the Library. In terms of the library itself, there are many ways to collect primary information from patrons in the same ways they are collected from the community, including surveys of patrons as they walk through the door, focus groups of specifically targeted patron groups (for public libraries, groups such as the Friends, book discussion groups, storytelling groups, and small business leaders; and faculty, students, and other user groups in academic libraries), interviews with patrons, and finally, quasi-town meetings of library card holders. At the academic library, the same type of information can be obtained from students and faculty within the walls of the library itself. In most academic libraries, information collection is simplified because, except in a few areas, most members of an academic community are library users; therefore targeted patrons represent a closed set of individuals. Those who don't use the library still may be supporters. The difficulty is patrons, especially students, leave every four or so years, and there can be enormous changes in who the library exists for from decade to decade.

Secondary Information about the Library. In attempting to get secondary data from the library, we can now turn to many types of statistics collected as by-products from the library's own sophisticated computerized systems. It is not difficult to find statistical information about library systems. Circulation, interlibrary loan, acquisition, cataloging, reference, government documents, delivery systems, purchasing, publicity, administration, shared resources, and serials, to name some major areas, have substantial stores of statistics to deal with when searching for information from which to make decisions. For example, as a by-product of circulation systems reporting, information can be assembled on what in the collection is going out, and by inference what isn't; who is taking out materials, and who isn't; and when materials are taken out, and when they are not. This information can be broken down by format, classification number, subject headings, etc. We can use such data to directly influence what we buy, when we buy it, and how much of it we buy. These are very important bits of information to have when budgets are flattened.

With all the computers now in libraries, we are apt to forget that another good source of secondary information from the library is anecdotal. Anyone who deals with the public in any way is bound to have good stories to tell. Don't overlook this as a source of information. The people who work the circulation desk, those who tell stories to children, those who shelve materials, and especially those who answer reference questions for patrons often have experiences which can put many a library on the right track (or take them off the wrong track) of some new and important service that should be offered to their patrons, or, conversely, a service that should be dropped for lack of appeal or interest. Other issues that are dealt with well through anecdotal stories are collection deficiencies and areas where alternative formats might be needed.

The Document

The third part of the process is the actual writing of the policy statement itself. In the years since the first edition of this book, very little has been deleted from policy documents produced in the 1970s and earlier. Real changes in the content of policy documents are from additions and in procedural details developed to explicate the document to others. Collection development policies now are longer, more explicit, less general, more procedural, and better written than they were 15 to 25 years ago. What follows is a possible structure for the policy. It is not a hard-and-fast structure, however, and any arrangement is possible. What really matters most is using a structure that works best for your library's collection development document.

Mission Statements. The first part of most collection development policies presents the purpose of the document, description of the community, mission of the library (in the case of an academic institution how it is tied to the mission of its college or university), and goals and objectives. Whereas years ago, all of these issues might have been present, due to the length of some documents, many of these statements are being left out for purposes of length and perhaps readability. I think this a poor idea since it is on these statements that the entire theoretical underpinnings of the document are based. Without these introductory paragraphs, the rest of the document is only intelligible to the people who were part of the process of writing them, not those for whom it is basically intended—others on the library staff, patrons, and those in the community interested in library management issues. Most libraries will have some sort of introduction, but many skip directly to goals and objectives.

Goals and Objectives. To develop effective policy-making strategies, the proper use of mission, goals, and objectives must be understood. Often in a collection development policy, I find objectives that read more like goals, goals that read more like a mission, and no real objectives at all. Goals are broad statements of intentions, and objectives are narrower statements that show *how* these intentions are to be carried out. Objectives are measurable and tell you what actions must be completed to move forward in a particular goal. For instance, a goal for a public library might be:

to broaden the use of the library by the children of the community.

The objective which, if met, would show a movement toward this goal might be:

a rise in the number of children registered for library cards by the end of the year.

In this case, there is only one objective showing action toward the main goal; there may, however, be three or four others which provide action toward this main goal. There might also be two or three other goals, with objectives under each.

In the case of an academic library, a goal might read:

to increase the use of electronic media in the library.

while the objective that measures this in part might read:

develop bibliographic aids to introduce students to current electronic indexes and distribute them in each bibiliographic instruction class that comes through the library.

In each of the above cases, the objective is measurable and applies to the goal that it falls under. Just as in the public library sector, there may be other goals, and each goal should have its own objectives to measure progress and to provide for accountability to the funding source. And yet in practice, for many policy statements this is not true, and in some, the goals and objectives are not even tied together in any significant way.

Selection. A central part of the policy statement is usually where library materials selection is explained. In other words, who is responsible, who actually does it, how do they do it (criteria, aids, etc.), and what different formats of materials are selected (with any additional criteria explained under a discussion of the individual formats). An example of format is *video*, and additional criteria to be considered might be the issue of physical ease of handling or production values. Often with newer technologies (newer than plain print, that is) additional criteria are needed to judge other than content areas. In the case of audio and video materials, production criteria mean a lot to a library trying to decide about one piece of material over the other. In the case of electronic media or software packages, the hardware criteria needed to run these packages, or machine capacity needed to run the program are often taken into account when purchasing decisions are made. In addition the library needs to decide how much staff expertise is needed to explain the use of these materials to its patrons.

One of the areas which I failed to see addressed in any policy collected was the archiving of software usable only with certain older hardware, and with certain older issues of software programs. As yet, libraries have not dealt with these collection development issues just as they did not deal with similar issues in the last half century having to do with audio and video media. In the long run, this is an issue that some archive is going to have to deal with, and we are now better suited to do so after confronting and resolving other similar problem areas in the past. Unfortunately, these larger, universal resource management issues do not get the attention they deserve, as daily work schedules and crisis management consume librarians' attentions.

Clientele and Special Collections. Another area of collection development documents addresses clientele and special collections. In the case of the public library, this section discusses the collection as it relates to children, young adults, literacy programs, adult new readers, ethnic, racial and national groups, people with disabilities, the aging, and any other groups that are special within a particular community. In the case of academic libraries, this section deals with student and faculty differences, as well as any ties that an individual library may have with the community in which it is located.

As for special collections, these are too numerous to mention either here or within the text, so only examples have been given. Among those singled out for special consideration are archives, local history, rare books, reference, medicine, law, business, education, and other subject collections, as well as government documents, audio books, video, microform, and other formats collected.

Special Areas and Legal Issues. In addition to specialized collections, libraries should also mention areas in which they won't buy (such as textbooks or dissertations), or areas with which they are careful (such as gifts, exchanges, and multiple copies). In such cases, there may be procedural as well as policy statements that outline the library's parameters for patrons regarding materials acquisitions.

Often mentioned here are library legal issues. In the case of collections this usually consists of intellectual freedom and censorship, confidentiality, and copyright. This may in time expand to include policy matters related to insurance for disasters, which seem to have reached quite a peak in the last year or two in a number of areas around the country. In most of the last 20 years and even before, within collection development and selection policies, intellectual freedom and censorship issues consisted not only of policy statements, but also of all the procedures that went with them. For some reason these procedures made their way into policy statements very early on and stayed there, while procedures for confidentiality or copyright issues didn't appear. Confidentiality and copyright statements are evident in policies, but procedures to deal with infringement or upholding the policies often do not exist. Currently, procedures for many legal issues are beginning to be documented in policy statements instead of being only mentioned in procedural document manuals, which might or might not be included as part of the policy document.

Collection Maintenance. The issue of collection maintenance has blossomed in the past 10 years, and whole sections of documents have now been developed to institute both policies and procedures. Financial constraints of recent years have made us more aware of library resources currently in danger of being lost through neglect. Though parts of maintenance have always existed in policy documents, collection maintenance issues are now being consolidated under one heading and accorded a place of honor equal to selection in the document. This area consists of weeding, replacements, duplicates, binding, the controversy of hardbacks versus paperbacks, disaster planning, preservation programs, and collection evaluation policies and procedures.

Subjects. A large section of the document consists of a subject-by-subject analysis of the collection. Particularly appropriate for academic libraries, this section is increasingly found in public library collection development policies also. Subject analysis includes policies dealing with the collection intensity levels, including languages and formats collected, and any retrospective collection policies for each and every subject area in which the library is interested. For the academic library, analysis is provided for each discipline in which an undergraduate major (and sometimes a minor) is given, in addition to those areas in universities where advanced degrees are awarded. In a public library, the usual subject areas are covered with possible analysis of branch subject specialization. Policy statements for individual subject areas can run from a paragraph or a half page, to many pages (20 or more sometimes) and contain information on how and what is collected along with comments about specifics related to the library's particular collection of a particular subject. In addition to the individual subject treatment, the subject analysis section may encompass the use of approval plans, allocation formulas, and other divisions of funds.

Consortia, Cooperative Agreements, and Networking. One of the most important areas of concern in the policy document is consortium, networking, or cooperative contracts which have been made that impinge on a patron's use of the library's collection, a patron's use of another library's collection, or another library patron's use of this library's collection. All of the library's myriad of consortia agreements, which in any way affect the collection, should be in this document. This is the only way to ensure that patrons (and even future staff members) will know and understand why these agreements were and still are necessary and what a consortium agreement will do for patrons.

Promoting understanding is the job of the people producing the collection development policy, not only in this section but in the entire document. That is the very essence of writing the document and what the process is supposed to ensure. It is why using someone else's document seldom works to provide the kinds of statements necessary to really inform the public of the library's collection development policies. Since consortia agreements often allow for the use of an enlarged group of materials, they should rightly belong in that part of the document that concerns itself primarily with the building of the library's collection. How one builds this collection is not reduced to purchase, gift, exchanges, or any other one method of acquisitions. Even items borrowed or sent from another library constitute materials for your public and should be discussed in just that way. When librarians stop thinking about the collection as being what is contained in one (or more) buildings of a single library, perhaps our patrons will expand their concepts of what it means to be a library in the twenty-first century.

Revision Statement. The final part of the document is often overlooked. It is the revision statement for setting in motion the entire process of collection development. This statement is often explained (if at all) in terms of how often the library will review the document for necessary revisions. If the document states anywhere from three to five years, the product has become the end of the process, and the process is dead. Even if it states "constantly revised," or "revised every year," in practice this is difficult to achieve. No matter how much trouble is taken with the rest of the document, it will go for naught if the document isn't a living, breathing entity that is always thought of, always lived with, always tinkered with, and never quite finished. This can be achieved by separating procedures, processes, and policies into three documents so that only the policies require official approval. The processes and procedures can then be reviewed, revised, and updated constantly without the impediment of a formal approval process.

From Document to Policy

The fourth and perhaps most important aspect of the collection development policy procedure is the document's use. This means that the document must be prepared effectively for its end use. If the document is for the use, generally, of the library staff, then language can be jargon-filled, and format can be informal. But if, as is usually the case, the document is to be used for the public as well as for staff, then it must be one that explains with hardly a trace of jargon, in plain and simple language, what the library is about, and why and what this policy means in relation to the material that a patron will be able to find in the library, and sometimes by inference, what he or she won't be able to find. This last bit of information is very important as time goes by because money will remain tight, and libraries must economize on all things. What we buy, what we share, and how we share it must now be part of the document if a goal of the document is to explain to the community how they are being served and why. To ensure an understanding of the process and product, perhaps librarians should interject more introductory information into the document that is prepared for the entire community as contrasted to a document prepared, for the most part, for an internal audience.

Document Approval

Often the reason for writing the document is described within the document itself—the purpose of the policy. However, it is a rare document that ends up recording all the stages that the document goes through in order to become a policy. Public librarians know that unless the document passes its board of trustees it is simply just another document and not a policy. Academic libraries, for the most part, do not follow the same procedure. Whether not having any president, dean, faculty senate, or board of governors approve the document, with full knowledge and understanding of what they are doing, still allows an academic library to call this a policy, I don't know. Today's legal environment, however, demands that library policies must be officially approved and sanctioned by the library's highest authorities in order to be recognized as in force by the courts. The trouble is that many libraries won't find out that its "unapproved" policies will not be sufficient protection against lawsuits until something terrible happens; the library will reach for its policy protection, and find that it's just a library document, not an approved policy. Then, of course, it's too late.

S U R V E Y

* * * * * * * *

INTRODUCTION

As in previous editions of this book, a survey was sent out to a number of academic and public libraries listed in the *American Library Directory*. The survey was pretested and developed to get to the major problem facing libraries in the 1990s—declining budgets and rising prices.

An eight-question survey was sent out in 1992 to a group of academic and public libraries in the United States and Canada. A second mailing was sent to achieve the best possible return from a wide geographical area. This was achieved by late 1993, and both the answers to survey questions and sample policies came from libraries answering the survey.

The total number of libraries answering the survey was 384, of which 233 were public libraries and 151 were academic libraries. These libraries represent 47 states, 6 provinces of Canada, and Puerto Rico. Public libraries are represented from 43 states and 5 Canadian provinces; academic libraries are represented from 42 states, 5 Canadian provinces, and one from Puerto Rico. There is not a geographic area that does not have some representation, and library size ranges from the very smallest to the very largest.

The survey questions were selected by the author based on information collected from the first two editions. Additional questions were formulated to represent some new issues related to collection development. Among the "old" questions were ones on how materials are selected—always interesting to both librarians and publishers and usually very different from written policies. Also from the first two surveys were questions on the amount of the materials budget, written collection development policies, and policy revision. Among the new questions were percentage of changes in budgets during the previous three years; percentage of the budget allocated to different types of materials, formats, and subject areas; names and memberships in various consortia, networks, and cooperatives; and a query about disaster plans.

ACADEMIC LIBRARY SURVEY ANSWERS

The following section represents a compilation and analysis of the responses to these survey questions as written by academic librarians.

1. What size is your total materials budget (to the nearest thousand)?
The size of the budgets represented ranged from $10,000 to $6,330,000 per year. The range can best be shown in Graph 1 below (n = total number of represented libraries):

The largest group of academic libraries had materials budgets between $100,000 and $249,000 (37 or about 26%). Ninety-nine or almost 70% of libraries answering the survey had materials budgets over $100,000. The graph

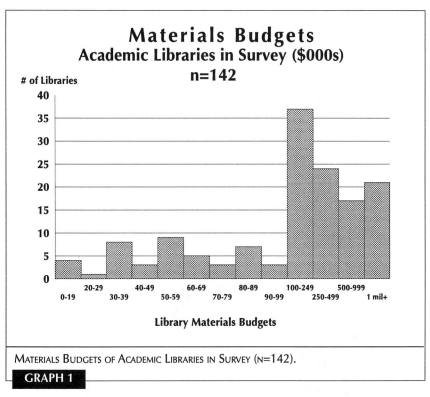

MATERIALS BUDGETS OF ACADEMIC LIBRARIES IN SURVEY (N=142).

GRAPH 1

looks very much as it did in the last edition, although there are more large libraries and fewer very small libraries represented. On the smaller end of the materials budget, once again, are community and junior colleges. On the higher end are the Association of Research Libraries, and Research Library Group members represented in the survey. Still, the survey encompasses large budgets as well as small ones, with the majority somewhere in the middle range. Of the libraries answering the survey, nine chose not to answer this question.

2. In the past three years (1990, 1991, and 1992), what percentage of its budget has the library spent on monographs, journals/serials, reference, audiovisual materials, electronic sources, and microforms?

This second question addressed two separate issues: first, what are the various percentages spent by the library on different formats of materials; and second, how has that percentage changed over time.

The object of this question was to see if the ratio of monographs to journals (and other newer types of formats) was changing over time, and if so, was it increasing or decreasing in comparison to the entire materials budget? So much has been heard about journal price increases and how academic libraries, in particular, were cancelling subscriptions. If this assumption is correct, it seems likely that the percentage of monograph spending would decrease or stay the same, while money spent on journals, electronic sources, and audiovisual material would increase, or if journal subscriptions were being cancelled, other formats would increase, and journal funds would decrease.

More than twice as many, or 70, libraries reported budget decreases in the percentage of monographs purchased than increases (34). The number of libraries reporting that monograph purchases remained constant was less than one-fifth, or 24, of the total libraries reporting. Therefore, the assumption can be made that libraries are spending less on their monographic purchases than before. See Graph 2 below.

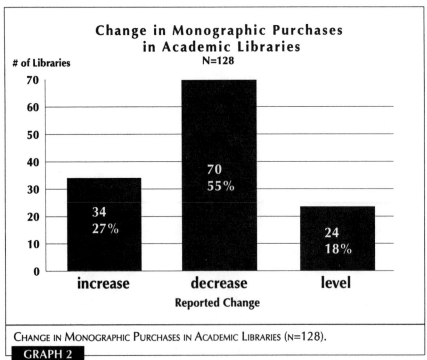

CHANGE IN MONOGRAPHIC PURCHASES IN ACADEMIC LIBRARIES (N=128).

GRAPH 2

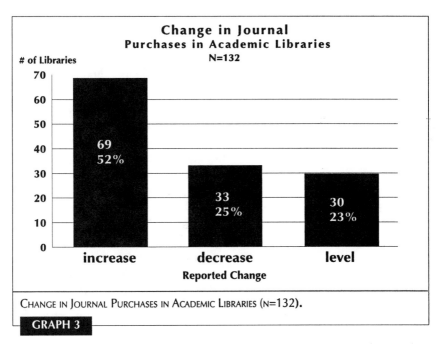

CHANGE IN JOURNAL PURCHASES IN ACADEMIC LIBRARIES (N=132).

GRAPH 3

For journals, not surprisingly, the reverse was true. Over twice the number of libraries reported increasing their expenditures on journals as compared with libraries reporting a decrease, though a slightly smaller number reported level spending. Since the price of journal subscriptions rose considerably during this period, the number of libraries reporting decreased budgets could be added to the number of libraries reporting level budgets (which might represent a decrease in real dollars for journal spending), for comparison to budgets that reported increased journal spending. The number of libraries showing a "real dollar" decrease in journal spending (63 or 48%) falls slightly short of the 69 (or 52%) libraries reporting an increase. So, even though journals were becoming more expensive during the early 1990s about half of the surveyed libraries chose to increase journal spending, and half of the journal budgets reflect a decline.

Reference Materials Budget. In the area of reference materials (which some libraries were unable to differentiate from other parts of their materials budget), 20% of the responding libraries reported an increase in reference materials budgets, 31% decreased, and 49% remained constant. It appears that for these academic libraries, reference materials budgets tended to remain constant. This may suggest a real decrease in dollars spent, since prices of reference materials were going up at this same time, or it may be that reference budget spending was shifting to other types of formats.

Audiovisual Materials Budgets. With audiovisual materials, 44% of library budgets remained constant, 27% decreased, while 29% increased. In this era of perceived decreases in funding levels, many libraries did hold percentage levels constant for different formats of materials. Although spending for both monographic and serial format has been changing (one increasing and the other decreasing), in this sample the trend for reference and audiovisual materials purchasing is flat.

Electronic Materials Budgets. In the area of electronic sources, 69% of the academic libraries reported increasing their percentage in budgets that were already tightening. Only 9% of the libraries answering this question decreased electronic sources, while 22% held the line and spent the same money over this financially restricting time period. It appears as if this format gained a great deal of influence over materials budgets during this time period.

Microforms Budgets. For microforms, 41% of the libraries increased their spending on microforms, while 40% remained at the same level; therefore, 81% were spending the same or more on microforms as they had before. Only 19% decreased their spending on microforms. One explanation of this trend could be that as journal subscriptions decreased, libraries bought more of these journals in micro formats, charging them to different budget lines.

	Increase		Decrease		Constant	
	#	%	#	%	#	%
Monographs (n=128)	34	27%	70	55%	24	18%
Journals (n=132)	69	52%	33	25%	30	23%
Reference (n=68)	14	20%	21	31%	33	49%
Audiovisual (n=78)	23	29%	21	27%	34	44%
Electronic Sources (n=75)	52	69%	7	9%	16	22%
Microforms (n=80)	33	41%	15	19%	32	40%

DIRECTION OF CHANGE IN ACADEMIC LIBRARY MATERIALS BUDGETS ALLOCATED TO SPECIFIC FORMATS (CONSOLIDATED RESULTS FOR SURVEY DATA FROM 1990, 1991, AND 1992; #=NUMBER OF LIBRARIES REPORTING ON THAT FORMAT).

CHART 1

3. In the past three years have you experienced decreased, increased, or level funding in your materials budget?

In 1990, the earliest year of survey data, a little over 60% of libraries indicated that their materials budgets had increased. Another 27% indicated that their budgets had level funding, while only 13% indicated decreased materials budgets for this period. In 1991, the middle year, almost 64% indicated increased materials budgets, while 20% indicated level funding, and 16% indicated decreased materials budgets. In 1992, the final year of the survey, the budget crunch seems finally to be felt in the materials budgets, with only 56% of the libraries indicating increased materials budgets, while 24% indicate decreasing budgets, and 20% indicate level funding. (See Chart 2, below.)

	Increase # %	Decrease # %	Constant # %
1990 (n=141)	85 60%	18 13%	38 27%
1991 (n=147)	94 64%	24 16%	29 20%
1992 (n=147)	83 56%	35 24%	29 20%

DIRECTION OF CHANGE IN ACADEMIC LIBRARY TOTAL MATERIALS BUDGET FUNDING.

CHART 2

What does this mean? We know for a fact that library budgets were generally decreasing during this entire period, and that prices of monographs, and especially journals were increasing. It could be speculated that libraries were possibly protecting their materials budgets from cuts by taking deeper cuts in services and staff; finally, toward the end of the three-year period when overall funding cuts were still being made each year, the libraries, although many still protecting their materials budgets, were forced to turn to them and start cutting. Still, during this three-year period, an average of more than half of the libraries increased their materials budgets. It appears that materials are still being protected at the cost of personnel, services, hours, and other services.

4. What selection aids do you use? (please rank by number; 1=highest)

Although asked to *rank* selection aids, librarians generally checked off all those that they used. From their responses it was hard to analyze what their favorite method of selection of materials was, although some indications are present.

	Ranked # 1	Ranked other than 1
Review media	76	68
Approval plans	19	42
Publishers' announcements	11	131
Ads	2	124
Jobbers' catalogs	1	84
Faculty		39
Other (salespeople, standing		
order Choice, BIP, newspapers,		
personal knowledge, bibliographies)		18

ACADEMIC LIBRARY SELECTION AIDS (N=144).

CHART 3

The number of libraries using review media first certainly far exceeds any other type of selection aid. However, just as in the first two surveys, both publishers' announcements and ads were used as selection aids. These choices reflect selection decisions not based on quality of materials, but rather on personal knowledge of the author, publisher, or subject, and does not necessarily denigrate them as purchasing tools. After all, many reviews come out so late that to wait for them to make a purchasing decision means either missing the material completely, or perhaps getting it into the collection too late for the current demand. In either case, most policies mention review media but few discuss the process of using ads or announcements.

5. Do you have a collection development policy in force? If so, when was it first written? When was it last reviewed? By whom?

For the first time the survey asked a question about whether the library had a collection development policy in force (not just written, but approved by some higher authority). Only three libraries chose not to answer this question. I assume they did not have a policy, but perhaps they felt, since most of the survey was on policy questions, it was a moot point. Although a large majority answered yes (72%), there are still 28% of academic libraries surveyed that do not have collection development policies in force as of 1993. The largest group of academic libraries surveyed without collection development policies are in the private sector (79% private and 21% public-without policies). A number of the librarians who answered that they did not have such a document responded that they were developing one, and some even responded that they had had one in the past but did not presently have one.

The majority of collection development policies were originally written in the 1980s (62%), and an almost equal percentage were written in the 1990s as were written in the 1970s. Since responses cover only 1990 through 1992, the number of policy documents written in this decade should surpass the percentage written in the 1970s, but perhaps not as many as written in the 1980s. The 1980s seem to have been the big push for the majority of libraries to produce these written policies. The reason for this is that state departments of education and academic administrations began to demand formal internal library policies to ensure accountability of funds. The fact that public academic institutions are more likely to have written collection development policies indicates a greater pressure on them from government (federal and state) agencies.

In academic libraries, the policies are reviewed almost exclusively by librarians, whether by committee, heads of departments, collection development personnel, or the director. Few policies are reviewed by faculty or faculty committees.

A number of libraries queried have reviewed their policies either annually or in the past three to five years. Other respondents have stated that it has been many years since their policies were reviewed, and still another group responded that they were about to review their development policies. There is no formal review policy in most documents, and probably few are reviewed as much as they should be.

6. **If you are a member of a consortium (network, etc.), please list name:**

   a. **approximate number of network members:**

   b. **types of library members:**

   c. **functions served:**

   d. **number of years of your membership:**

It is gratifying to see that 81% of the academic libraries answering this survey belong to one or more consortia. Over 25% belong to more than one. Only 5% indicated that they do not belong to a network, while 14% did not answer the question at all.

The size of the various networks of which academic libraries are members ranges from two libraries to hundreds, with the largest group of libraries participating in the largest consortium. For most academic libraries answering this question, OCLC and its various geographic vendors distributing this service (such as SOLINET, WLN, NELINET, and others) appear to be the large networks. There are others that are almost as big, but they still tend to broker cataloging services. The remaining groups in decreasing order are in the 10- to 24-member range, the 25- to 49-member range, the 2- to 9-member group, and finally the 50- to 99-member group. See Graph 4 next page.

In response to questions about the types of networks that have been developed, the largest group answered that the basis of their network was geographic (all in the same state, area of the state, region, etc.). Still, a large number of libraries belong to both multitype and academic-only consortia.

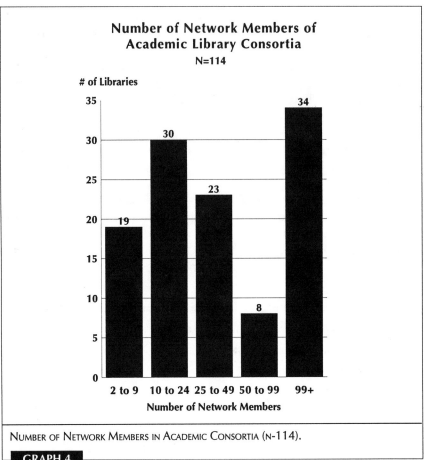

NUMBER OF NETWORK MEMBERS IN ACADEMIC CONSORTIA (N-114).

GRAPH 4

The single most popular function performed by these network or consortium agreements involves cataloging. The next largest function is interlibrary loan. After a wide gap and close together on the scale of functions satisfied, the next areas are reference, circulation, acquisitions/collection development, and education. A few networks are used mainly for shared resources, serials, and for delivery of materials. Finally, functions mentioned only a few times were publicity, administration, government documents, automation, grants, insurance, information systems, and advice and consultation.

Many of these consortia are not new; members have mainly belonged for 20 years or more, with a large group belonging for 15 to 19 years. There is almost equal division among each of the remaining membership term categories, with an almost equal number of members for 1 to 4 years, 5 to 9 years, and 10 to 14 years. One library said it had been a member of OCLC for 76 years. I'm still trying to find out if that is possible!

7. Is the consortium, network, etc. mentioned in your collection development policy?

It is my opinion that anything concerning the acquisition or disposal of materials should be included in the collection development policy. There are a number of things that should not be in this policy (personnel matters, facilities matters, much budgetary information perhaps), but processes that directly concern collections, such as networks, disaster planning, and preservation, should be in these policies. Are they? The answer is no. Of the 108 libraries who answered this question, 77 did not include any mention of consortium membership in their policies, and I got the idea from one or two respondents that they didn't think it belonged in such a policy. Since corsortia membership seeks to enlarge available materials for a library's patrons and for the patrons of fellow members, I am still wondering where does it belong? Where else would such a policy statement go if not here?

8. Does your library have a disaster plan? If so, is it mentioned in your collection development policy?

Only one respondent said that they had no policy—a fact stated in their policy statement (I am still pondering how to count that in the survey results). The others said overwhelmingly that they did not have a disaster plan. When this survey was sent out in late 1992, the disasters encountered in 1993 and 1994 (floods in the midwest, California earthquakes) were yet to happen. I think there might now be more answers that say, "We're working on it!" than there were in this survey. Sixty-nine percent of the libraries answering this survey do not have disaster plans. Of those who do have plans, 88% do not include it in the collection development policy statement. I don't know why, nor can I guess, although several respondents have suggested that it doesn't belong there. That may be true, since the procedures part of the disaster plan takes up many pages and would be inappropriate for a collection development policy statement. But, to have no mention of it or of network arrangements, both of which affect the materials collected in libraries, seems to me to be equally inappropriate.

PUBLIC LIBRARY SURVEY ANSWERS

Although somewhat different answers were obtained from the public libraries answering this survey, most were expected and show the differences between a public and academic library collection. The survey answers prove that written policies and the process of building a library collection are very different with different types of libraries.

1. What size is your total materials budget (to the nearest thousand)?

The size of the budgets ranged from $500 to $4,146,000. The range can best be shown in Graph 5 below:

The largest group of public libraries (31 or about 16%) had materials budgets between $100,000 and $249,000, which is similar to academic libraries, although the distribution range is very different. Almost 36% (or 69)of public libraries answering the survey had materials budgets over $100,000, almost 39% (or 75) had budgets of less than $50,000, and 25% (or 49) had budgets in between. The graph doesn't look much like the one in the last edition; there was a much flatter graph throughout the public library grouping. The current survey results show eight libraries whose materials budgets are below $10,000 (equal to the number that are above one million in this survey), which is vastly different from academic libraries. Of the libraries answering the survey, nine chose not to answer this question.

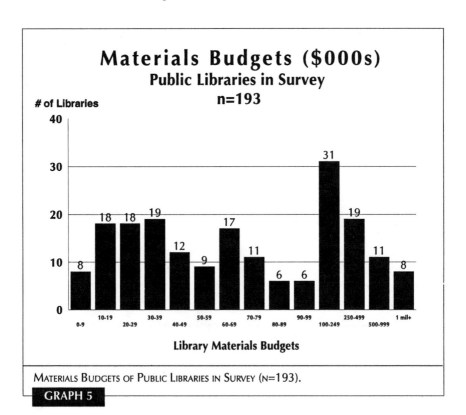

Materials Budgets ($000s)
Public Libraries in Survey
n=193

MATERIALS BUDGETS OF PUBLIC LIBRARIES IN SURVEY (N=193).

GRAPH 5

2. In the past three years (1990, 1991, and 1992), what percentage of its budget has the library spent on monographs, journals/serials, reference, audiovisual materials, electronic sources, and microforms?

	Increase # %	Decrease # %	Constant # %
Monographs (n=153)	46 30%	73 48%	34 22%
Journals (n=159)	59 37%	33 21%	67 42%
Reference (n=159)	41 37%	28 26%	41 37%
Audiovisual (n=147)	66 45%	38 26%	43 29%
Electronic Sources (n=60)	30 50%	8 13%	22 37%
Microforms (n=90)	31 34%	16 18%	43 48%

DIRECTION OF CHANGE IN PUBLIC LIBRARY MATERIALS BUDGETS ALLOCATED TO SPECIFIC FORMATS (CONSOLIDATED RESULTS FOR SURVEY DATA FROM 1990, 1991, AND 1992).

CHART 4

This second question addressed two separate issues: first, what are the various percentages spent by the library on different formats of materials; and second, how has that percentage changed over time.

The object of this question was to see if the ratio of monographs to journals (and other newer types of formats) was changing over time, and if so, was it increasing or decreasing in comparison to the entire materials budget. So much has been written about journal subscription price increases and their effect on academic library budgets. The results of this question could show what was happening to public library materials budgets that might not be as affected by journal price increases, but whose budgets were being strained by the demand for new technologies and new formats, such as audio and visual materials and electronic reference sources.

Monograph budgets of public libraries decreased in 48% and remained level in 22% of the cases (73 and 34 libraries, respectively). Monographic purchases increased for 30% (or 46) of the libraries answering this survey question. See Graph 6 (next page). Again there is a flattening out of the graph as compared to previous survey results. More monograph budgets decreased but many remained level or increased. There doesn't seem to be the same rationale to explain these changes as there is for academic library budgets that showed much more distinct changes in distribution during the same time period. There are clearly fewer monographs being purchased; the question is where are the funds being diverted—to journals, as in academic libraries?

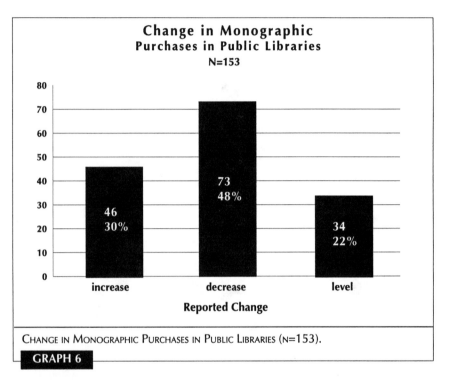

CHANGE IN MONOGRAPHIC PURCHASES IN PUBLIC LIBRARIES (N=153).

GRAPH 6

Journal percentages are different from monographs, although they aren't reversed as monograph purchases were with academic libraries. The majority of journal budgets remained the same over the three years (about 42%), though 37% increased, and 21% decreased. See Graph 7. Since the price of journal subscriptions rose considerably during this period, the number of libraries reporting decreased budgets could be added to the number of libraries reporting level budgets (which might represent a decrease in real dollars for journal spending) for comparison to the budgets that reported increased spending. The "real dollar" decrease in journal spending exceeded the number of libraries indicating an increased journal budget. So, if this "real dollar" scenario is correct, as journals were becoming more expensive, public libraries must have cancelled numerous subscriptions. This means that both monographic expenditures and journal budgets decreased.

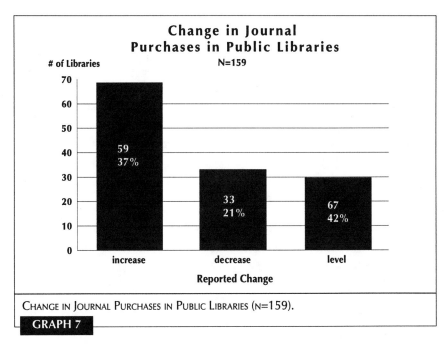

CHANGE IN JOURNAL PURCHASES IN PUBLIC LIBRARIES (N=159).

GRAPH 7

Reference Materials Budgets. For reference materials (which many public libraries did not differentiate from other parts of their materials budgets as electronic or monographic lines), 37% of reference materials budgets increased, 37% remained level, and 26% decreased during this time period. This indicates that reference materials budgets tended to either increase or remain constant and suggests an overall increase. Since prices of reference materials were also going up at this time, an assumption could be made that reference budget spending was at the very least holding its own against other formats and that some of the decreased monograph and journal budgets were being spent in the reference sector.

Audiovisual Materials Budgets. Audiovisual materials budgets increased for 45%, decreased for 26%, and remained constant for 29% of library budgets. In this era of perceived decreases in funding levels, many libraries not only held percentage levels constant for newer formats of materials, but actually increased them. Although both monographic and serial formats were decreasing, the trend for both reference and audiovisual materials was to increase.

Electronic Materials Budgets. In the area of electronic sources, 50% of the public libraries reported increasing their percentage of this format in budgets that were tightening dramatically at this time. Only 13% of the libraries answering this question decreased electronic budgets, though 37% held budgets level over this financially restricting time period. It appears that this new format gained a great deal of influence over materials budgets during this time.

Microform Budgets. For microforms, 34% of the public libraries increased their spending, while 48% remained at the same level; a total of 82% were spending the same or more than they had before on microforms, and only 18% decreased their spending on microforms. An explanation for strong microform budgets could be that as with academic libraries, as journal subscriptions decreased, libraries bought more journals in micro formats, charging them to different budget lines.

3. In the past three years have you experienced decreased, increased, or level funding in your materials budget? (n=186 (1990); 194 (1991); 204(1992))

In 1990, the earliest year of survey data, a little over 60% of libraries indicated that their materials budgets had increased. See Chart 5 (next page). Another 25% of public libraries indicated that their budgets had level funding, while 15% indicated decreased materials budgets for this period. In 1991, the middle year, 54% indicated increased materials budgets, while 22% indicated level funding, and 25% indicated decreased materials budgets. These numbers confirm that the trend in public library materials budget support had definitely been declining, and that the decline was becoming greater. In 1992, the final year of the survey, the budget crunch seems to have been felt in public libraries even more, with the materials budgets increasing in only 47% of the public libraries answering the survey, decreasing for 29% and remaining level for 24%. The percentage of libraries with decreasing budgets increased from 15% in 1990 to 25% in 1991 and to 29% in 1992. The percentage of libraries with increasing budgets went down six percentage points between 1990 and 1991, and seven percentage points between 1991 and 1992. Level funding went down three percentage points between 1990 and 1991, then up two percentage points between 1991 and 1992.

What does this mean? We know for a fact that many library budgets were decreasing during this entire period, that prices of monographs and journals were increasing, and that public libraries were being asked to incorporate many new technologies within tight budget restrictions. While it may be true that academic libraries were possibly protecting their materials budgets by taking larger cuts in services and staff, public libraries seem to be taking more of a cut in materials. Although 47% of public libraries report increased spending on materials, more and more level and decreasing budgets are evident. Since many public libraries, especially those in the small to medium range, do not offer a wide selection of journals and magazines, and therefore have not been as affected by subscription prices rising at enormous rates, it is the newer technologies and formats of materials that public libraries are protecting. Even the public library must succumb to heavy cuts in their budgets of personnel, services, and materials.

	Increase # %	Decrease # %	Constant # %
1990 (n=186)	112 60%	28 15%	46 25%
1991 (n=194)	104 54%	48 25%	42 22%
1992 (n=204)	96 47%	59 29%	49 24%

DIRECTION OF CHANGE IN PUBLIC LIBRARY TOTAL MATERIAL BUDGET FUNDING.

CHART 5

4. What selection aids do you use? (please rank by number; 1=highest)

Although asked to rank selection aids, public as well as academic librarians chose to check off all of the ways in which they select materials, with only some ranking of choices. Although their second favorite source was difficult to analyze, by far their favorite way to select materials was with book reviews. Chart 6 below indicates the number and ranking of aids.

	Ranked # 1	Ranked other than 1
Review media	121	83
Jobbers' catalogs	15	149
Ads	1	162
Publishers' announcements	1	178
Approval plans	1	90
Patrons		49
Other (salespeople, publishers' catalogs, newspapers, local bookstores, bibliographies)		31

PUBLIC LIBRARY SELECTION AIDS (N=204).

CHART 6

The number of libraries using review media first certainly far exceeds any other type of selection aid. Just as in the first two surveys and the same as responded by academic librarians in this survey, both publishers' announcements and ads were also highly favored as selection aids. These choices reflect selection decisions based not on quality of materials, but rather on personal knowledge of the author, publisher, or subject, and do not necessarily denigrate them as purchasing tools. Most reviews come out so late that to wait means either missing the items completely because they are no longer available, or perhaps getting them into the collection too late for patrons demanding them. In either case, especially in public library policies, review media are usually mentioned, but few discuss the process of using ads or announcements.

5. Do you have a collection development policy in force? If so, when was it first written? When was it last reviewed? By whom?

For the first time, the survey asked a question about whether the library had a collection development policy in force (not just written, but approved by some higher authority). I fully expected that almost all of the public libraries would have a written collection development policy, and only one library did not answer this question. Although a large majority answered yes (78%), there were still 22% of public libraries that did not have collection development policies in force as of 1993. A number of the libraries who answered that they did not have such a document responded that they were developing them. One library stated that they didn't expect to ever have one, as they felt it safer not to write things down, and therefore didn't develop any policies unless there was some trouble.

Although many collection development policies were originally written in the 1980s (45%), 17% were written in the 1990s, and 25% were written in the 1970s (the others were written before the 1970s). Since responses cover only 1990 through 1992, the number of policy documents to be written in this decade should surpass the percentage written in the 1970s. Public libraries have more collection development policies and started to write them earlier than academic libraries did.

In public libraries, the policies are reviewed almost exclusively by the board of trustees, and then quite often by the director. After those two main sources of review, a number of libraries rely on collection development librarians, department heads, committees of librarians, etc. The fact that the legal entity of public libraries reviews the policy shows the importance of enforcement as well as writing. Only when the board accepts a policy statement can it truly be considered "in force."

The majority of public libraries queried reviewed their policies some time in the past four years, and a number have reviews ongoing or annual in nature. Still, too many have said it has been many years since they looked at their policies. There is no indication of a formal review policy in most documents, and that surely means that few are reviewed as often or as carefully as they should be.

6. If you are a member of a consortium (network, etc.) please list name:

   a. approximate number of network members:

   b. types of library members:

   c. functions served:

   d. number of years of your membership:

It is surprising to note that 89% of the public libraries answering this survey belong to one or more consortia. Although just 7% belong to more than one network or consortia, only 8% indicated that they belonged to none, while 27% did not answer the question at all.

The size of the various networks of which public libraries are members ranges from two libraries to hundreds, with the largest group of libraries (37) belonging to consortia with memberships of 25 to 49 libraries. See Graph 8 below. Most of the networks were vendors of the larger bibliographic utilities, OCLC and its various geographic vendors distributing its service — SOLINET, WLN, and NELINET. It is customary for a number of smaller public libraries to consolidate in a collective consortia agreement to broker the large networks more efficiently. In addition, for a long time large groups of libraries close to each other have cooperated in union catalogs and shared resources. The next largest group is in the 50 to 99 member range, followed very closely by the 10 to 24, then the 99-plus range, and finally the smallest in the 1 to 9 member league.

In response to the question concerning the basis of network development, libraries responded that networks were grouped by public libraries only (37%), multitype (35%), and geographic proximity (28%), which makes each group close to being equal. More of the geographic-based networks of public libraries tended to be composed of public libraries only than they were on the academic side, where they tended to be multitype.

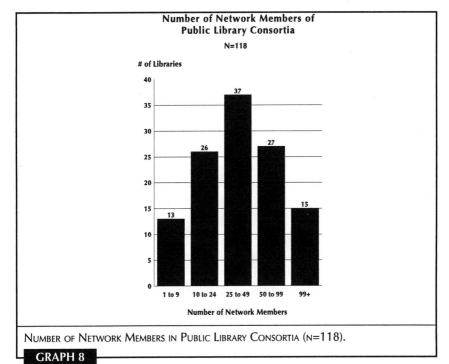

NUMBER OF NETWORK MEMBERS IN PUBLIC LIBRARY CONSORTIA (N=118).

GRAPH 8

The single most popular function performed by these network or consortium agreements revolves around the area of interlibrary loan. The next largest function was reference, followed closely by cataloging. After a wide gap, and close together on the scale of functions satisfied, the next areas were education, acquisitions, and circulation. Following another wide gap, and with 10 or fewer libraries answering in the affirmative, the balance of the categories were: automation, consultation, delivery, and shared resources; and, with just a few mentions were grants, serials, publicity, administration, bookmobiles, legislation, and insurance. It is odd that legislation and shared resources are so far behind the others; also notable is the function of consortia in helping with reference rather than cataloging or circulation.

Many of these consortia are not new, and some public libraries have certainly been members for 20 years or more, with the largest group of libraries belonging from 5 to 9 years. An almost equal number belonged to their networks for over 20 years as belonged to them for 10 to 14 years. A large group had been consortia members from 1 to 4 years, and the fewest number answered that they had belonged from 15 to 19 years. This is considerably different from the academic library responses, but not too surprising. There seems to be a steady rise in the number of libraries joining consortia, and that does match what is happening on the academic side.

7. Is the consortium, network, etc., mentioned in your collection development policy?

Since the collection development policy contains information and policy statements concerning the building and management of the library's collection, mention of consortia membership should be in the document. Network agreements are often written in legalese, but that language does not need to be included in the collection development policy. However, mention that the library does have a network agreement should be included. Of the 121 public libraries answering this question, 87 (72%) said they did not include any mention of their consortium memberships in their policies. There were 34 (28%) who said that they did mention consortia in their policy document. In this regard, at least, public libraries mentioned consortia agreements in their documents far more (almost the reverse) than academic libraries.

8. Does your library have a disaster plan? If so, is it mentioned in your collection development policy?

Although disasters seem to hit public and academic libraries equally, only 25% of public libraries surveyed have written disaster plans. That means that three-fourths of the public libraries answering this survey did not have disaster plans. A few indicated that they were contemplating writing them, but most of them had, I think, no idea that they might some day be useful. After this past winter (of 1994) I should think that a good many of those who weren't concerned in 1992 and 1993 would have changed their minds and be ready to think of these plans. Of those who did have disaster plans, 81% did not have any mention of these plans in their collection development policy. Why not? Most who commented said that they saw no reason to mention it in the policy document. As I have said before, all matters pertaining to the management and building of the collection should come together in one document, and the collection development policy is that document.

TRENDS FOR ACADEMIC AND PUBLIC LIBRARIES

With 357 libraries answering this survey, the results are far from "scientific," and yet they do show us certain trends and allow for some confidence in our "seat of the pants" perceptions. We have a much clearer picture of what is really going on in public and academic libraries concerning their collections, especially where it focuses on what should be, could be, or is in those policies. Perhaps the most interesting point that has been uncovered here is how differently current times are affecting different types of libraries, and con-versely, how similar all libraries are. A comparison of results for academic versus public libraries helps to illuminate the similarities and differences.

The first question in the survey did not yield really interesting results as it is not surprising that there are fewer academic libraries (actually none) that have less than $10,000 for their materials budgets, and fewer public libraries that get more than $1,000,000 to spend on materials. The second question, whether the percentages spent for different formats of materials are changing because of the restrictive budgets, provided some interesting differences.

Monograph purchases are declining in both types of libraries. Fifty-five percent of academic libraries answering the survey reported a decrease in their materials budgets for monographs, while 48% of public libraries reported a decrease in monograph spending. Journal spending is increasing in 52% of the academic libraries, but only in 37% of the public libraries. The rise in prices has hit academic libraries far harder than public libraries, but academic libraries have been unable (or unwilling) to make deep cuts into their journal subscrip-tions. Almost twice as many public libraries maintained the same percentage of journals during these years of budget crunches (42%) than did academic libraries (23%). Given the sharp rise in journal prices, public libraries either made deeper cuts, or the types of journals that public libraries subscribe to did not go up as much as subscriptions for college and university libraries.

The percentage decrease in the audiovisual budgets of both academic and public libraries was virtually the same (27% and 26%, respectively), while those increasing their budgets in these alternative formats was drastically different. Forty-five percent of the public libraries showed increasing budgets, while only 29% of the academic libraries did. These budget differences also show that 44% of academic libraries' budgets remained the same, while only 29% of the public libraries' budgets remained the same in this category.

Microforms and electronic sources figures are comparable, with both public and academic libraries increasing, or at the very least, protecting their electronic source expenditures. Fewer libraries of either type decreased their microform budgets, and academic libraries were far more likely to decrease reference budgets than were public libraries.

A comparison of overall changes in budget funding showed a similar pattern of both academic and public libraries receiving increases in their budgets, but the percentage of the year-to-year budget increases was declining, and the number of libraries receiving a reduced materials budget was increasing each year. Public libraries' budgets reflecting increased funding are declining at a greater rate than academic libraries, which though reflecting a decline in the number of libraries receiving increased materials budgets, still shows over 50% of academic libraries with increasing budgets. The protection of those materials seems exceedingly important to academic libraries, whose research mission would never recuperate from a serious materials cutback in any given year.

Both types of libraries have, for the most part, collection development policies. The percentages are slightly different; over 72% of public libraries and 78% of academic libraries have policies, both close to the three-quarter mark.

In the case of disaster plans, 25% of public libraries and 31% of academic libraries have a plan, and of those that do have written disaster plans, 81% of public libraries and 88% of the academic libraries do not include them in their policies.

So, the trend is to smaller materials budgets, with academic libraries more likely to protect those budgets using some other method of general budget downsizing, protected journal subscriptions in academic libraries, collection development policies for all, and disaster plans for just a few. I think perhaps it might take another generation to alert librarians to the "unnatural" disasters that might hit our collections due to neglect of preservation issues, seeing how long it seems to be taking them to understand the impact of natural disasters on library collections.

Each of the libraries that answered the questionnaire is likely to be more concerned with and more alert to problems about its collections than a library that didn't answer this survey. That makes me feel fully justified in making the statement—we have a long way to go.

PART

2

Full Library Policies

INTRODUCTION

❈ ❈ ❈ ❈ ❈ ❈ ❈ ❈

In this edition, only four full collection development policies have been reprinted. This choice was not made in order to demonstrate there were so few libraries whose policies could have been used in this section, but to show a few specific libraries whose policies are unique in some way, and to discourage the adoption of one library's policy statements by another institution.

The four libraries represented here are from the East, West, Midwest, and South so that there is geographic distribution. They represent large and medium-sized institutions, with representative materials budgets. Each of these policies has a great many strengths, and few (very few) weaknesses. They set a standard that would be advisable for others to meet. There are two public libraries (Santa Cruz and Worcester) and two academic libraries (University of Wisconsin—Stout and Western Kentucky University), and each shows different ways that librarians develop and write policies. By picking one in each category, the reader might be tempted to believe that policy to be a model. There isn't one model meant to be used for any particular type of library or one kind of policy statement. There is, instead, a range of possible interpretations and statements that will fit many different institutions. The policies will give examples and help the smaller library to brainstorm by reading these policies, but in the end, each library is unique and deserves its very own collection development policy, created especially for it by the people most familiar with the community being served.

LIBRARIES WHOSE POLICIES ARE REPRINTED IN WHOLE

University of Wisconsin—Stout, Learning Resources Center, 315 Tenth St., Menomonie, WI 54751-0790

Western Kentucky University Libraries, Bowling Green, KY 42101-3576

Santa Cruz Public Library, 224 Church St., Santa Cruz, CA 95060-3873

Worcester Public Library, Salem Sq., Worcester, MA 01608

University of Wisconsin—Stout Library Learning Center

❀ ❀ ❀ ❀ ❀ ❀ ❀ ❀

Collection Development Policy

CONTENTS

❀ ❀ ❀ ❀ ❀ ❀ ❀ ❀

INTRODUCTION

The Collection Development Policy incorporates guidelines contributed by every academic department in the University, and members of the Library Learning Center faculty/academic staff.

In 1973, the Library Learning Center invited each department to help in preparing a collection development policy statement. Each department prepared a statement of collection need that is analyzed by Collection Develop-

---

*Not reprinted with this policy, but see Appendixes 1, 3, and 6 of this book.
**Not reprinted.

ment Service. To evaluate departmental needs this document has been periodically revised since 1984.

A number indicating the depth of collection is assigned each subject classification. There are four levels. The designator shows the depth of coverage to be maintained for that subject in the library collection.

This policy includes four statements by the American Library Association:

- Library Bill of Rights
- Intellectual Freedom Statement
- Statement of Labeling
- Resolution of Nonremoval of Challenged Library Materials

It is the intention of the Library Learning Center to endorse and implement the above four statements.

I. PHILOSOPHY

Building a University library resource collection is the responsibility of faculty/academic staff, librarians and the LLC collection development staff. The collection can be custom-designed for this University's distinctive needs only if all contributors understand the mission of the University of Wisconsin—Stout and Learning Resources, and the objectives of the Library Learning Center, which are developed from the mission.

II. SELECT MISSION OF THE UNIVERSITY OF WISCONSIN— STOUT

(Approved by Board of Regents, 1992)

UW—Stout, as a special mission institution, serves a unique role in the University of Wisconsin System. Stout is characterized by a distinctive array of programs leading to professional careers focused on the needs of society. Undergraduate and graduate degrees in the study of technology, applied science, art, industrial management, human behavior and home economics are presented through an approach to learning which involves the integration of theory, practice, and experimentation. Extending UW—Stout's mission into the future requires that instruction, research, and public service programs be adapted and modified as the needs of society change.

A. The University offers undergraduate and graduate programs leading to professional careers in industry, commerce, education, and human services through the study of technology, applied science, art, industrial management, human behavior, and home economics.

B. The University integrates the humanities; arts; and natural, physical and social sciences into undergraduate programs. Experiences in these areas provide a foundation for the major field of study, promote continuing personal and professional growth, and prepare the student to deal constructively with issues and opportunities of the future. The University places special emphasis upon student development.

C. The University's programs center on human development and interpersonal relationships, efficient and effective practices in industry, commerce, education and human services, and the relationships of individuals to their environment and to society.

D. The University develops new educational strategies, provides opportunities to learn through involvement and experimentation, and creates a climate of inquiry. The University experiments with new instructional methods in the interest of improving the learning process.

E. The University expects scholarly activity including research, scholarship, development, and creative endeavor that supports its programs at the baccalaureate level, its select graduate programs, and its select mission.

F. The University, through outreach and public service, addresses the needs of society and contributes to the welfare of the state and to its economic and technological development, and cooperates with University of Wisconsin—Extension.

G. The University cooperates with the other University of Wisconsin institutions, the Vocational, Technical and Adult Education System, and other state and national agencies; and participates in statewide, national, and international programs.

III. LIBRARY LEARNING CENTER MISSION
(Approved by the Faculty and Academic Staff of the Library Learning Center, 4/15/92)

The primary mission of the Library Learning Center is to provide the University community with access to information.

A. The LLC will preserve, maintain and improve the collections and services now provided to library users.

B. The LLC will evaluate existing resources and will develop new collections and services to meet the needs of a changing society.

C. The LLC will teach students information literacy and critical thinking skills to prepare them for potential roles in society including professional careers.

D. The LLC will develop staff members' skills and will recruit new staff members with skills to address the changing needs of the library.

E. The LLC will use appropriate technology to foster access to information in support of our primary focus on service to people.

F. The LLC will support University programs in instruction, public service and research.

G. The LLC will provide a physical environment which is functional, accessible and aesthetically satisfying.

H. The LLC will provide means of coordinating and sharing universal library resources to improve user access to information.

I. The LLC will seek extramural support to enhance its programs and resources.

IV. SELECTION GUIDELINES

A. INTRODUCTION

The importance of judicious selection has increased proportionately with the increased production of books, periodicals, audiovisual media and computer software. Rising costs of collecting, organizing, housing and servicing resource collections also demand a definitive selection policy.

A collection development policy must be reviewed regularly. A too-detailed policy is almost immediately obsolete, as is a policy that is too broad in scope and unclear in definition. This selection statement will avoid both extremes.

The first step in building a collection development policy is to define obligations and limitations of the collection. These parameters, along with a preview policy to insure the usefulness of expensive selections, are guidelines to protect the interests of each subject specialization in a balanced collection.

B. GUIDELINES

Course Work

The library must provide resources to facilitate and enrich classroom instruction for each department of the University.

Diversity

All library collections (with the exception of the Archives collection) will provide information which represents the diverse and varied background of the university community. The collections will also provide an opportunity for members of this community to acquaint themselves with people of different race, creed, color, or sexual orientation.

Research

Collections must include more specialized materials needed by students and faculty for independent research.

General Information

Balanced learning requires general information resources in subject areas not covered by classroom instruction and research programs.

Recreational Reading

The Library will provide a recreational reading collection for the university community. Funds for this collection will be limited.

Language

Material will be collected primarily in the English language.

New Curricula

The Library Learning Center must maintain fiscal flexibility to develop collections in new programs and to expand existing subject collections to meet curriculum changes.

University of Wisconsin—Stout History

The Library Learning Center has the responsibility to preserve printed and audiovisual materials concerning the history and development of this university, and to collect and preserve publications of its departments and schools. This material is housed in the University Archives (see Archives Policies).

Intellectual Freedom

Collection policies should agree with the American Library Association's "Interpretation of the Library Bill of Rights," "The Intellectual Freedom Statement," "Statement of Labeling," and the "Resolution on Non-Removal of Challenged Library Materials" approved by the Intellectual Freedom Committee, July 1, 1981. (See Appendices)

Single Copies

To prevent serious dilution of library fiscal resources, the usual procedure will be to purchase only one copy of a title. The LLC will purchase more than one copy only if heavy and continued use can be shown. *Instructional Resources Service* provides additional copies.

Shared Resources

Holdings of other libraries in Wisconsin and getting items through Interlibrary Loan will be a factor in purchase decisions. Interlibrary loan transactions will be analyzed by collection development staff.

Out-of-Print

The purchase of current materials will have priority over out-of-print publications.

Alternate Formats

If an original edition is not available or cost is prohibitive the materials may be purchased in suitable reproductions that will often include microformats.

Textbooks

Resources used as textbooks for specific UW—Stout courses will normally not be acquired for permanent holdings. Exceptions are stated in section XIII.

Research Projects

Collection Development Service will not purchase in depth for short term faculty, academic staff and graduate research unless the policy stipulates appropriate coverage. Interlibrary Loan is encouraged.

Format Balance

Learning occurs most effectively when all types of media—audio and video cassettes, films, computer software, filmstrips, transparencies, slides, microforms, periodicals, newspapers, electronic data bases, documents, pamphlets—are available and used. All of the forms are considered potential resource materials for the library collection, to be acquired, organized and maintained in a balanced structure.

V. PREVIEW POLICY—BOOKS AND OTHER MEDIA

Because of the high costs of materials and their range of quality, materials costing more than $350 may be ordered either "on approval," "for examination," or "for preview." If a vendor does not have an arrangement, materials from this source will be acquired only if the item in question has been examined by the requestor, and/or if the item has received favorable professional reviews.

Reviews may be located and evaluated. A decision to purchase expensive materials may be made based on reviews only in exceptional cases.

If a preview is requested, one or more faculty/staff in the subject area, will preview the material and report results of the examination.

Using the following criteria, the Collection Development Officer will make the final decision regarding purchase:

A. Quality—content and technical.

B. Cost of unit.

C. Consistency with the Collection Development Policy.

D. Maintaining subject balance in the collection as indicated by selection level.

E. Availability and cost of lease or Interlibrary Loan.

VI. GIFTS

Gift materials may be a valuable source of information for a library collection. Because the giving and receiving of gift materials involves public relations, adherence to a clearly stated gift policy is very important.

The Collection Development Officer or in his absence the Director shall make a definite commitment to accept gifts for L.L.C. Acceptance of these gifts shall include a clear statement that the library is free to keep or to give away materials according to the judgment of the Collection Development Officer.

Gifts that have significant monetary value, primarily rare books, manuscripts and films, will require a transfer of legal title by gift in a properly executed form. This form must be:

A. Signed and dated by the donor, and;

B. Witnessed and dated by another party who is neither related to the donor nor employed by the institution receiving the gift.

There are to be no restrictions on disposal of unwanted items. The Library Learning Center will not accept any temporary deposits. The Executive Director of the Stout University Foundation, Inc. and the Director of Research Promotion Services should be notified when significant gifts are presented so that appropriate publicity and appreciation may be arranged.

By order of the Board of Regents, the University of Wisconsin—Stout and the Library Learning Center cannot provide a statement of the value of gift items for income tax deductions or other purposes. Donors will be referred to appropriate catalogs, book dealers and indices if they wish to determine the value themselves.

VII. SERIALS

The selection of serials requires a more specific selection process than other media. When a serial is selected there is a continuing commitment to the base cost of the title, including subscription maintenance, shelf integrity and storage. The rapidly expanding serials market demands that care must be exercised in reviewing serial titles before it is purchased for the collection. The increasing number of electronic indexes will be a factor in serial selection.

A. DEFINITIONS

Serials- Publications issued in successive parts bearing numeric or chronological designations and intended to be continued indefinitely. Included in this definition are: periodicals, newspapers and annuals.

Periodicals- Publications issued and received on a regular basis and are placed into the Periodical Collection. These are journals, magazines and newspapers.

Annuals- Continuations/Serials that are received on a regular basis that are classified, and are placed in collections other than the Periodical Collection.

Indexes- Regularly published lists of periodical article citations.

B. SELECTION

The need for serial publications to support scientific and technical academic programs becomes more and more important as information is increasing exponentially. Access to current and timely information can best be accomplished through serial formats.

The Library Learning Center has a limited Serials budget. Serial inflation averages 10–12% annually. Therefore the selection decisions for serials must be made with great care.

1. Priorities

    a. Curriculum support for students

    b. General education and news coverage

    c. Faculty research

2. Recommendations

    Recommendations for the selection and review of the serial collection may be made by:

    a. Faculty and Academic staff

    b. Students

    c. University staff

    d. Collection Development Committee

3. General Selection Criteria

    Serials will be selected to support the continuing information needs of the university community. The selection levels as listed in Section XIX of the Collection Development Policy will be carefully considered as well. General factors to be considered are:

    a. Academic programs

    b. Majors

    c. Minors

    d.   Enrollments in programs or departments

    e.   Mission relevance

    f.   Undergraduate/graduate research level needs

    g.   General education needs

    h.   Specific collection needs

    i.   Recreational needs

Collections within the library may have more specific criteria which are listed in the Collection Development Policy of that collection. The final decision will be made by the Collection Development Officer.

4.   Specific Criteria Periodicals, Continuations and Annuals.

Selection of specific titles will include a careful evaluation of the following:

    a.   Indexing- What indexes provide access to the contents of the title? Does the library own any of these titles?

    b.   Abstracts- Does the library own any of the abstracts that provide access?

    c.   Electronic access- What's available either in the library or by remote access to provide electronic indexing and/or abstracting to the contents of the periodical?

    d.   Interlibrary loan- Is this a title that has been requested frequently on ILL? Would it be more cost effective to provide ILL access rather than own the title?

    e.   Projected use- For unindexed titles, can use be assured by specific class assignments or research topics?

    f.   Reviews in the literature- What do they say about the title?

    g.   Cost- What is the specific cost of subscription? What is the cost per issue?

    h.   Frequency?

    i.   Does it meet stated research needs of students or faculty?

    j.   Format- Newsletter? Newspaper? Electronic journal?

    k.   Subject content of the journal.

    l.   Subject coverage- How in-depth, scholarly, technical, etc. are the articles?

    m. Audience- For what audience is this journal intended?

5. General Newspapers

   The Library will acquire general newspapers on a current basis to meet the teaching and general information needs of the university community. In selecting new subscriptions, the relevance of the newspaper to specific courses, current coverage of major geographical areas, and representation of diverse political and social viewpoints will be considered.

6. Indexes

   1. For paper & fiche indexes

      a. Subject coverage in relation to our programs and collections.

      b. Currency—How quickly does the index include current articles?

      c. Frequency of publication.

      d. UW—Stout Library Learning Center collection needs to provide access to periodicals owned.

      e. Current journals owned by UW—Stout that are uniquely indexed.

      f. Number of journals in indexes presently owned by LLC and affect on ILL.

      g. Ease of use.

      h. Potential load on Interlibrary Loan for titles included in the index now owned by UW—Stout.

      i. Document delivery availability for those titles not owned. To be delivered in:

         (1) Electronic format

         (2) Paper format

         (3) Microformat

   2. Electronic Indexes
      In addition to the criteria for paper copy the following should be considered for the CD-ROM and mainframe electronic indexes:

      a. Cost of hardware to support the index service.

      b. Index compatibility with existing hardware.

      c. Reputation of software vendor.

      d. Service support of the vendor.

      e. Possible access of mainframe online database.

      f.   Cost per search for "online" database searching vs. actual purchase lease.

      g.   Estimated patron use in the LLC or campus wide.

      h.   Duplication with paper copy.

7. Serial Review

The continuing change in the serial marketplace and the constant demand for "up to date" information by the library patron presents the UW—Stout Library Learning Center with a constant challenge to *review* and *select* in both the serial "continuation" collection as well as the periodical collection. Reviewing must occur continuously in a five year sequence.

1. Serials Review Criteria

The additional criteria for title review are:

a. Use of serial

b. Currently an actively published title

c. Last title held in state of Wisconsin

These criteria should provide for a comprehensive decision process for the selection and review of the journal collection.

VIII. VIDEOCASSETTES, VIDEO DISCS AND FILMS (16mm)

Selection judgment of any 16mm film and videotapes or discs will consider these points:

A. Technical quality of the film/video format.

B. Cost.

C. Projected use.

D. Relevancy of the title to the UW—Stout curriculum.

E. Anticipated life of the film/video either content or physical condition of the medium.

F. Lease availability. (Stout no longer offers a rental service.)

G. Videocassettes will be the preferred medium.

IX. MICROCOMPUTER SOFTWARE ACQUISITIONS POLICY (11/24/84)

A. Definition

There are two types of software which are appropriate to the collections 1) Utility programs and 2) Discipline programs.

The definition of each are:

1. Utility Software—general purpose programs with no specific course related content, which is used to manipulate information entered by users, e.g., Word Star, Bank Street Writer, spread sheets, etc.

2. Discipline Software—subject specialty, educational content, associated with Stout's curriculum, e.g., nutrition, power mechanics, welding, etc.

B. Policy

1. Utility programs as defined in 1. will not be selected as these programs will be made available through the Campus Computing Laboratories.

2. Discipline programs . . . which fit the mission statement and the Collection Development Policy will be selected for the main collection using Library Learning Center media acquisitions funds.

3. Computer software format will be selected for the library collection using the following criteria:

   a. The software is compatible to the microcomputers available in the Library Learning Center.

   b. The content of the software contributes to the mission and curriculum. Games will not be purchased.

   c. Software will be shelved in the appropriate collection as determined by content.

   d. A master of each disc will be archived when permitted by copyright provision.

   e. The university reserves the right as part of selection to duplicate all discs for archival purposes when permissible.

X. TEXTBOOKS

Textbooks may be selected in areas where research material is limited. Multiple copies of texts will not be purchased unless a specific justification is approved by the Collection Development Officer.

XI. REPRINTS—MONOGRAPHS

Collection Development Service selects monographs in reprint or microformat if the original cannot be located in the out-of-print market at a reasonable price. Decisions regarding purchase of monographs in reprint or microformat will be based upon cost and projected use.

XII. THESES AND DISSERTATIONS

A microform copy of each Plan A, B, Masters and Ed.S. papers is added to the collection.

XIII. PAPERBACKS

The Library will purchase paperbacks to supplement the Browsing Collection.

If the original hard-bound edition is out of print, the paperback edition is considered for selection. When possible, paperback editions also are purchased as additional copies for "Reserve" use.

XIV. SPECIAL COLLECTION

The Special Collection consists of:

A. Books, manuscripts, or portfolios of unusual format or significant value in strong subject fields.

B. Unusual limited editions.

XV. SELECTION RESPONSIBILITY

A. Collection Development Committee.

1. The Collection Development Committee is a standing committee advisory to the Director. The Collection Development Officer will serve as chairperson. Three additional librarians will be appointed by the Director. Functional collections will be represented.

2. The committee recommends policy, reviews collection development issues of concern to the committee and the professional staff of the library.

3. Provides input for various collection development processes.

4. Provides information and oversight to the collection review process.

5. Will also receive charges from itself, and the Director.

B. Role of the Collection Development Officer.

1. Library selection is a responsibility of the university faculty/staff and the Collection Development office. Faculty and staff recommendations are solicited. While it is the prerogative of professional librarians to provide recommendations for materials for the collections, the final responsibility for the development of all library collections—including adequacy and quality of selection—rests with the Collection Development Officer

2. Collection Development Service also will evaluate all collec-
    tions with a view to locating and selecting retrospective and
    current titles from the reviewing mediums.

3. The Collection Development Officer will initiate the annual
    review of the collection development policy. The Collection
    Development Officer will work with the Collection Develop-
    ment Committee and submit a final copy to the Director for
    approval, The Director will forward the policy to the Associate
    Vice Chancellor and to the Vice Chancellor for Academic
    Affairs.

XVI. SUBJECT SELECTION LEVEL*

Accounting 3

Adult education 1

Advertising 3

Aesthetics 2

Anthropology
    Archeological 3
    Cultural 2
    Human ethnology 2
    Physical 2

Appliance and equipment maintenance 2
    Household and commercial food service equipment 1

Art
    Art therapy 3
    Ceramics 2
    Design 2
    Drawing 2
    Glass 2
    Metal 2
    Painting 2
    Sculpture 2
    Wood, plastics 2

Art history
    Art (including past to present) 2
    Architecture 2

Aviation
    Mechanics and technology 3
    Pilot training 4

---

*Note: This policy contains 11 pages of additional subject selection levels, most of
which have not been reproduced here. To indicate the set-up of this section, all
levels are included at least once in the 27 areas shown above.

XVII. EQUIPMENT CATALOG FILE

PURPOSE

To provide current specifications, and where possible, prices for specified equipment categories in response to recurring assignments.

SCOPE

A. The file may include equipment and supply catalogs characterized by one or both of the following:

   1. Must be related to a major Stout program; e.g., Technology Education and Hospitality and Tourism.

   2. Must be recommended and used by a specific instructor or department.

B. Catalogs in this file will be kept no longer than three years.

XVIII. EDUCATIONAL MATERIALS CENTER (EMC)

A. Objectives of the EMC Selection Policy.

   1. To establish the subject scope of the EMC collection.

   2. To set criteria for the acquisition of EMC materials.

   3. To set criteria for the de-selection of EMC materials.

B. Scope and purpose of the EMC.

   1. The EMC collection provides samples of preschool–12 instructional resources that support UW—Stout's teacher education programs. The Teacher Education programs are:

      Art Education
      Early Childhood Education
      Guidance and Counseling
      Home Economics Education
      Marketing Education
      School Psychology
      Special Education (Secondary)
      Technology Education

   2. EMC collections serve as a curriculum laboratory by providing examples of preschool–12 curricular materials for teacher education students. The materials within these collections are used for planning or implementing curricula within UW—Stout's mission areas.

   3. Materials in the EMC may be of use to students in other programs although materials will not be selected specifically for those programs.

4. All types of media are considered for purchase; however certain collections, by their nature, will dictate media type. For example, curriculum guides will usually be in printed copy.

C. Subject scope of the individual collections.

1. Text Collection.

a. According to Good in the DICTIONARY OF EDUCATION texts are books "dealing with a definite subject of study, systematically arranged, intended for use at a specified level of instruction, and used as a principle source of study material for a given course." The EMC includes these "traditional" textbooks used in a formal classroom setting as well as other instructional materials such as activity books, AV material and computer software.

2. Curriculum Guide Collection.

a. This collection contains curriculum guides, courses of study, competency checklists, unit plans and other similar materials used to plan educational experiences for students.

3. The Juvenile Collection.

a. This collection contains two types of materials:

(1) children's literature to provide a sample collection for Early Childhood Education students.

(2) supplementary materials for UW—Stout's other teacher education programs. Examples include nonfiction books and media presentations on subjects like robotics or family life on a preschool–12 level.

4. Student Created Units.

a. Teaching units by UW—Stout students, obtained from instructors and made available to students.

5. Catalogs.

a. Samples of catalogs from suppliers of textbooks media, supplies and equipment to enable students to perform realistic budget exercises.

6. Juvenile Periodicals.

a. A small sample collection of magazines designed for preschool–12 students.

D. Selection of EMC materials.

1. The EMC Librarian has the primary responsibility for collection development of the EMC.

2. The EMC Librarian will actively encourage faculty and academic staff in the departments served by the EMC to select materials for the collection.

3. The EMC budget is developed by the Collection Development Committee of which the EMC Librarian is a member and is recommended to the Director.

4. The following principles, not in priority order, will serve as guidelines for the selection of materials for the EMC:

   a. The importance of the material to UW—Stout's teacher education programs.

   b. Faculty and academic staff recommendations.

   c. Favorable reviews in professional literature.

   d. Price of the material.

   e. Date of publication.

   f. Reputation of the author or publisher.

   g. Circulation of other materials on topic.

E. Evaluation and de-selection of the collections.

   1. Periodic evaluation of materials in the EMC is considered of equal importance to the acquisition of new materials.

   2. Weeding of material designated as no longer useful to the EMC collection shall be done on a regular basis in a systematic fashion.

   3. Guidelines in addition to those mentioned above which may be used as principles to be followed are:

      a. Physical condition of the material.

      b. Availability of later editions.

      c. Availability of materials which reflects current trends.

   4. Removal of older editions of text and curriculum material is done automatically as new or revised editions are added.

XIX. REFERENCE COLLECTION DEVELOPMENT POLICY

A. Objectives of the Reference Collection Policy.

   1. To establish guidelines, as concrete and definite as possible, for both the subject scope of the reference collection and the materials included in it.

   2. To set procedures for acquiring new materials and for weeding the collection which will ensure the development and maintenance of a complete, current, and convenient reference collection.

B. Subject Scope of the Collection.

1. The Reference Collection provides basic and in depth information sources in the mission areas of this university. The collection also provides selective coverage of subjects of current interest not directly within these academic disciplines.

2. In addition, the collection also provides reference information not directly related to mission areas but which is basic to general knowledge. Examples of this group of information sources may be found in The Enoch Pratt Free Library's *Reference Books: A Brief Guide*, Katz, *Introduction to Reference Work*, ALA, *Reference Sources for Small and Medium Sized Libraries*, Cheney, *Fundamental Reference Sources*.

C. Size of the Reference Collection.

The Reference Collection has no absolute limit on size. However, prevailing demand, fiscal restraint, changes in the curriculum, and student enrollment in various disciplines serve as guidelines to the relative size of subject areas within the collection.

D. Types of Materials Included in the Collection.

A reference book is often defined as "a book designed by the arrangement and treatment of its subject matter to be consulted for definite items of information rather than to be read consecutively," and a reference collection as a "collection of reference books and other materials in a library, useful for supplying authoritative information or identifying sources, kept together for convenience in providing information service, and generally not allowed to circulate." (*ALA Glossary* . . . 1988)

1. Almanacs and yearbooks. Reference collects current editions of major publications for the United States and Canada and for select individual countries as determined from curricular emphases.

2. Annual Reviews. The collection includes those for major mission disciplines. Most annual reviews are housed in the main collection.

3. Bibliographies. Those with narrow subject scope, such as single author bibliographies, are normally kept in the Main collection. More general bibliographies on broad topics are included in the reference collection. Exceptions are made for topics in great demand or of considerable current interest. National bibliographies are no longer housed in the reference collection. The policy is as follows for trade bibliographies:

a. The entire collections of *Cumulative Book Index* and the *American Book Publishing Record* are kept in the reference collection.

b. The current year of *Books in Print* and other *PTLA* components are considered reference materials.

4. Biographies. Comprehensive national and international biographies, including both retrospective and current biography is/ are shelved in the reference collection.

5. Concordances. Only concordances for very important authors and works are included in the reference collection; others are housed in the stacks. (Examples of works collected are concordances for Shakespeare and the Bible.)

6. Corporate Annual Reports. A file of corporate annual reports is maintained containing the latest two years available and solicited from corporations noted in the Reference log, companies interviewing on campus and appearing in the *Corporate Fact Book* and *Dun's*.

7. Dictionaries. The reference collection provides unilingual, bilingual, and polyglot dictionaries in major languages. The section also provides specialized dictionaries (for example, covering slang, idiomatic expressions, and historical aspects of language) for English. Dictionaries with very limited use are not retained in reference.

8. Directories. The reference collection includes the current edition of major directories in all fields within the mission statement and may contain certain retrospective editions of directories based on demonstrated use. Directories of limited scope or low use will be replaced occasionally rather than regularly.

9. Encyclopedias. The reference collection includes major general encyclopedias, both single and multi-volume. The reference section will attempt to acquire revised editions of *World Book, Encyclopedia Britannica, Encyclopedia Americana,* and *Collier's Encyclopedia,* one per year, on a rotating basis, as funds permit. In addition to the general encyclopedias, Reference collects authoritative encyclopedias in specialized subject areas to support research in mission-related programs.

10. Geographical Sources. The reference collection provides authoritative atlases, maps, and gazetteers covering all areas of the world. Current editions of relevant world-wide yearbooks are also maintained; e.g., *Europa, Statesman's*.

Topographic maps for the immediate regional vicinity are acquired. Travel brochures are in the Vertical File. Major city street and highway maps are kept in the Vertical Map Files.

11. Handbooks. The reference collection attempts to collect current and authoritative handbooks in all mission-related fields.

12. Indexes and Abstracts. Because of fiscal commitments necessary for the purchase of an index and/or an abstract and because of the commitment to provide the materials to be indexed or abstracted, the acquisition of an index or abstract should be closely related to existing periodical holdings and the selection levels of the "Media Selection Policy." The reference collection will also provide basic indexes to satisfy the general information-seeking needs of the university community.

    Indexes in alternative formats such as microforms and electronic databases (e.g., CD-ROM indexes, hard disk indexes) are equally open to consideration and must be evaluated in the context of their function in the collection. Evaluation factors to consider in addition to those commonly applied are:

    a. Estimated frequency of use. Will the format stand up to heavy use? Does format require extensive manipulation (handling, wear) in performance?

    b. Subject coverage. Is the index coverage appropriate to UW—Stout's existing or future mission areas?

    c. Level of sophistication. What level of training or education does the index require for the average user?

    d. Require support. Power? Equipment? Space? Peripherals? Maintenance?

    e. Cost. How does cost compare with counterparts in other formats? What is gained or lost for the difference? Is any format noticeably more cost effective than another?

    f. Function. How does the function of the index compare with the counterpart formats? How will users be affected by the difference?

    g. Duplication. Will the print based index subscription have to be maintained along with the alternative format? Costly duplication should be undertaken only for unusually compelling reasons and should be avoided whenever possible.

h. Indexes tied to text (e.g., full-text databases). The contents of the text will need to be evaluated along with the index.

i. Index support. How well is the index supported by the periodical collection? Is there a financial commitment for providing additional periodical titles?

j. Interlibrary Loan. If indexed periodicals aren't available in our periodical collection, what time, cost and workload considerations are implied for ILL?

k. Mainframe database. Is the index best suited for access via a mainframe database or an electronic index station?

l. Vendor. Is the vendor reputable? Is support service prompt and adequate?

Online index searching ability will be maintained through contracts with vendors. On-line searching will be used in lieu of other formations under appropriate conditions, such as:

a. The topic is occasionally, but seldom, requested and there-fore is rarely supported in the index collection.

b. A counterpart index's focus is peripheral to UW—Stout's mission areas.

c. A counterpart index is likely to have much appeal to but a few individuals such as faculty members engaged in special-ized research.

d. The on-line base has no counterpart formats.

e. An available index is not suitable for complex or extensive searches.

13. Legal Materials. Reference materials—legal encyclopedias, dic-tionaries, digests, citators, etc.—are kept in Reference.

14. Library Catalogs. The reference collection holds catalogs for important collections of major libraries, emphasizing subject fields not well controlled by indexes and bibliographies.

15. Plot Summaries. The collection provides major, comprehensive collections of plot summaries, e.g., Magills but not Cliffs.

16. Sacred Books. The reference collection maintains a small col-lection of major translations of the Bible in English, as well as English translations of sacred works significant to major world religions if compelling reasons are present. Ordinarily, such works are housed in the Main collection.

17. Standards. Because of the technical nature of the University mission, certain standards are a part of the Reference collection. These standards must closely relate to the current fields of study, preferably in those areas offering a graduate degree, or having a (1) assigned in the "Collection Development Policy." The frequency for updating each will be determined at the time of purchase. Generally, standards purchased individually with no intention of completing a set will be cataloged individually and placed in the Main collection.

18. Statistics. Basic ongoing statistical summary information in both general and mission-related fields will be provided by Reference. Works available in Reference through such services as ASI (American Statistics Index) should generally not be duplicated as unique purchases.

19. Style Manuals. The reference collection includes major mission-related style manuals.

20. Telephone Books. Reference has current telephone directories for 50 of the largest U.S. cities and many Wisconsin cities and towns.

21. Theses. The collection provides bibliographic information and indexing about academic theses and dissertations through *Dissertation Abstracts International* and other sources, including some in specific mission-related areas.

E. Selection of New Reference Materials.

1. The Information Access Librarians have the primary responsibility for pursuing a systematic and continuous collection development program for Reference, coordinated by the IAS Reference Emphasis librarian. All other members of the library professional staff are encouraged to provide input as their interest and time permit. All requests for Reference acquisitions shall be forwarded by the IAS Reference Emphasis librarian to the Collection Development Officer.

2. The following principles, not in order of importance, serve as guidelines for selection:

   a. Judged usefulness of the publication, considering the existing collection.

   b. Strengths and weaknesses of the existing collection related to current demonstrable needs of the university.

      c. Favorable reviews or inclusion in basic reference collection guides.

      d. Reputation of the author.

      e. Currency of the topic.

      f. Date of publication.

      g. Price of the publication.

      h. Language of the publication.

      i. Standing order obligations.

  3. Procedures. See Selection Procedures, page 64.

  4. The budget year extends from July 1 to June 30. Material is ordered and encumbered accordingly.

F. Reference Collection Review Evaluation and Weeding.

  1. *Regular Evaluation.* Periodic evaluation of the works already in the collection is as important as selection of new materials, since it is a working collection of important, frequently consulted publications. Careful, regular, and systematic weeding removes older, less desirable works from the collection.

  2. *Principles and Guidelines.* Information Access Librarians follow the same principles and guidelines in evaluation as in selection of new materials. Since each discipline covered by the Reference Collection requires different types of materials, it is impossible to establish absolute standards to be followed in evaluation. For some disciplines the Reference Collection should provide current material only; for others it must also provide retrospective and historical works. However, some general criteria which should be considered are:

      a. Significance of publication.

      b. Age and currency of the publication.

      c. Availability of later editions.

      d. Availability of this edition; e.g., is it still in print?

      e. Physical condition of the publication.

      f. Duplication of the contents in more recent works.

      g. Language of the publication.

      h. Use.

      i. Appropriateness to the demonstrated needs of the University community; e.g., mission, curricula, reference queries.

      j. Standing order obligations, if applicable.

3. *Method.* The reference collection is evaluated in two important ways: automatic weeding of older editions of a work and periodic evaluation by IAS librarians.

    a. Older volumes of many publications, particularly standing orders such as directories and yearbooks, are automatically removed from the Reference collection according to decisions made at the time of purchase. Standing order titles are also reviewed along with all other reference titles during the continuous Reference review.

    b. In conjunction with the review of older volumes, the remainder of the reference collection is also evaluated through the continuous reference review.

4. Procedures. See Appendix II-Reference Review.

G. Reference Collection Inventory.

Inventory of the reference collection is accomplished during the continuous triennial reference review. Searches are initiated for titles not on the shelf; the IAS Reference Emphasis librarian is responsible for determining the necessary replacements/withdrawal of missing items.

H. Appendix I: REFERENCE ACQUISITION CRITERIA

1. What are the strengths and weaknesses of the existing reference collection in the subject area in question?

2. Is this topic an important one in the university curriculum?

3. Is this topic a current or popular one? Is it likely to be a passing fad or to be of continued interest?

4. Is this topic likely to be important in the future?

5. Has the work received favorable reviews?

6. Is the work included in one or more basic reference collection guides?

7. What are the author's qualifications and reputation?

8. What is the date of publication? (In general, order works with recent publication dates if possible. Exceptions are made if the publication is a standard reference work in its subject or if the older materials is of current value to the collection.)

9. How much does the publication cost? (Titles costing more than $100 are screened carefully. When a very expensive title is under consideration, the IAS Librarians may consult other libraries to determine whether or not they intend to purchase the title.)

10. Does the work duplicate material in titles already in the collection?

11. What is the language of the publication? (Works in English will be purchased in preference to those in other languages.)

12. Is the work a serial? If so, what commitment is required—all editions (standing order), alternate editions, or only occasional editions? A retention decision will be specified for each new standing order.

PROCEDURES

1. Information Access Service librarians search relevant professional literature to ensure that important reference works within the University mission and the demonstrated needs of reference are in the collection. This literature searching consists primarily of:

   a. Scanning review sections of these journals regularly:

      Booklist

      Choice

      College & Research Libraries

      Journal of Academic Librarianship

      Library Journal

      RQ

      RSR: Reference Services Review

      Wilson Library Bulletin

   b. Examining publishers leaflets and catalogs.

   c. Review annual lists of reference books, such as *American Reference Books Annual.*

   d. Comparing *Sheehy's Guide to Reference Books, Walford's Guide to Reference Material,* and other authoritative reference bibliographies with the library's holdings. The reference librarians will review holdings to evaluate the need in the reference collection for titles not owned.

2. IAS Librarians are responsible for checking reviews of titles to be ordered for the reference collection.

3. The IAS Reference Emphasis Librarian maintains a desiderata file of order cards and brochures on newly published material received from university and library staff members.

4. The Information Access Services librarians meet as necessary to review the file and identify materials to order.

5. Ordering information for recommended publications is sent through the IAS Emphasis librarian to the Collection Development Officer; for processing: titles rejected by the IAS librarians are returned to the recommending party with reasons for the rejection noted. Suggestions that appear desirable for the library but not appropriate for Reference shall be forwarded to the Collection Development Officer for decision and disposition.

I. Appendix II: REFERENCE REVIEW CRITERIA

1. How important is this publication?
   a. Is it included in a general guide to reference works, such as Enoch Pratt or Sheehy?
   b. Is it listed in a subject bibliography?
   c. How is it rated by faculty members and/or subject specialists?

2. How comprehensive is this publication? Are its scope and depth such that it belongs in the reference collection?

3. Is the discipline one which requires a large group of reference works? If not, is this work truly essential, or is it a marginal one which could be sent to the general collection or be discarded?

4. What is the language of the publication? If it is not English, will its use be very light?

5. How frequently is this publication likely to be used in the future? How frequently has it been used?

6. Is there a later edition which supersedes this publication? If so, what is the appropriate disposition for this and older editions?

7. How old is the publication? If it is an older work, is the subject matter such that current information is required by the vast majority of patrons?

8. Is the work on continuation? If so, should some or all of the older volumes be sent to the stacks?

9. Is the material in this work largely or entirely duplicated in other reference works? If so, does demand justify the duplication?

10. Are there multiple copies of this title in the reference area? If so, are they justified by heavy demand on the publication?

11. Is the book badly worn, defaced, or otherwise in poor condition? If so, can it (or should it) be replaced?

12. Is the work principally a bibliography? If so, is its scope so narrow that it should go into the main collection? (e.g., single-author bibliographies; highly specialized, technical or scientific lists) Is it inappropriate for any collection?

13. Is the work (entry) complete? If not, should (can) the gaps be filled?

14. Do existing reference works cover current reference needs? Are there gaps in the information available that should be filled if possible?

15. Is the edition still in print?

PROCEDURES

1. A continuous review will be maintained, such that the entire Reference collection, call numbers A–Z, is reviewed no less often than triennially.

2. The IAS Reference Emphasis librarian is responsible for assigning subject areas for review to Information Access Services librarians and shall revise the assignments when necessary.

3. Collection evaluation activity is staggered throughout the year to minimize workflow problems for the staff involved in the collection evaluation process.

4. The librarian responsible for the initial evaluation of an assigned subject area shall note recommendations—keep, replace, withdraw, etc.—on an inventory list of titles. The list is circulated among Information Access Services librarians for comment.

5. The Information Access Services librarians will meet as a group to discuss and decide upon each title for which some changes have been recommended.

6. The IAS Reference Emphasis librarian will summarize those decisions, provide a copy to the Collection Development Officer and initiate such action requests as are necessary.

XX. VERTICAL FILE GUIDELINES

A. Guidelines for Inclusion.

1. Format considerations:

a. Pamphlets or short booklets providing general information, suitable for the lay person, related to travel and tourism.

Examples:

Promotional material containing facts and information.

Tourist brochures for states, regions, cities, specific sites and events.

"How to" information related to tourism.

Consumer information for travelers.

2. Subject matter, level consideration—Must be travel, tourism or place related. At adult reading level.
3. Currency—Date less important than usefulness of information.
4. File will be reviewed yearly, by Collection Development Committee or its designee. Catalogers can routinely discard previous editions of brochures.

B. Guidelines for Exclusion.

1. Format considerations:
   a. Periodical issues and reprints (unless specifically requested and original is not owned)
   b. Catalogs
      Examples: Equipment, Supply, College, Technical School, Publisher, AV
   c. Law reprints
   d. Maps
2. Subjects outside the scope of travel and tourism.
3. Level—Juvenile, pre-college material.
4. Travel and tourism statistical material.

XXI. AN EVALUATION WEEDING AND REPLACEMENT PROGRAM

A. Preliminary Statement.

An institution that serves a specialized research program must keep in mind that weeding to whatever extent may be both expensive and controversial.

The permanent library collection shall be defined as that part of the total library holdings which remains in the central research collection as active and serviceable.

B. Philosophy of Program.

Weeding and replacement shall be based on the University of Wisconsin-Stout's mission and overall objectives of the Library Learning Center. Both weeding and replacement shall be deemed as part of the same process; that of keeping the collection alive. If a document is dead, but the subject alive, new material must be found to meet current needs. This is replacement. Weeding shall be termed as quality control of the collection's usefulness, consisting of both withdrawal and storage as policy dictates.

C. Administration of Program.

The Collection Development Officer is responsible for the implementation of this function. Other staff as is necessary may assist whenever possible. Advice will be drawn from faculty and academic staff subject specialists.

D. Principles of Program.

Three factors are considered in evaluating a title: content, past and projected use, and physical/technical condition. The principles outlined in the next pages should be regarded as being flexible guidelines to be used with perceptive judgment.

1. Books and Audiovisual Software

   (To be Removed from the Collection)

   a. Any book or media item over 10 years old that shows little evidence of use, especially those in areas of remote institutional interest.

   b. Early printing of classics dated by print, binding, illustration, etc., not of "rare" value.

   c. Out-of-date materials which no longer conform to prevailing ideas of presentation, i.e., courses of study, travel books, films, audiotapes, etc.

   d. Any general works of science which are not of classic rank and have been effectively superseded.

   e. All textbooks of economics, education, sciences, and useful arts, except mathematics and occult sciences which are ten years old. Obsolescent anthologies, ephemeral fiction, and outmoded translations not of determined research interest.

   f. Personal narratives and biography of an obscure person.

   g. Non-Stout dissertations and theses with little evidence of use, especially outside institutional research areas.

   h. Reprints of titles where original is a part of collection and in good condition.

   i. Worn or frail titles that serve no unique purpose, in too poor a condition to remain in collection.

   j. Books that are in unusual languages that are available in libraries having particular responsibilities, i.e., Farmington Plan and P.L. 480 area assignments.

   k. Copies of media that have been transformed into other formats.

2. Serials

    (Candidates for Discard)

    a. Serial runs that are duplicated in microfiche.

    b. Volumes of statistical series that contain essentially the same information (keep only latest edition).

3. Replacement

    a. Worn out copies with heavy and recent circulation statistics that still serve a unique purpose.

    b. AV prints that are damaged or have missing segments and that have shown use.

    c. Titles that have been superseded, in subject areas such as economics, child care, pure sciences, etc.

    d. Books with obsolete format, old standards of bookmaking which contain out-of-date illustrations, graphs, charts, etc.

4. Summary

    a. The mechanics of weeding and replacement depend on two main factors:

        (1) Identification of items to be considered.

        (2) Securing the best judgment as to disposal.

    b. Automated procedures and statistical data from circulation can assist in the first, that of identification. The second factor, judgment, remains for the most part subjective. In this program, automated data will be utilized to the extent that the public catalog can provide. Some examples of the system's facility are:

        (1) Duplicates and materials that have definite and frequent use will be systematically considered for weeding and replacement by using publication data as a sorting factor.

        (2) Provision for material considered a permanent part of the collection will be done by assigning a specified code.

        (3) Lists of incomplete serials can be produced periodically for consideration of storage.

5. Process for Reviewing Main Library Collections

    a. The Collection Development Committee will determine the area to be reviewed.

b. A profile unique to this area will be developed by the Collection Development Committee. The following criteria will be included in the profile:

   (1) Use

   (2) Subject matter

   (3) Age of titles

   (4) Curriculum needs

   (5) Titles being published

   (6) Does the collection reflect the current literature of the discipline?

   (7) Special consideration, such as uniqueness and/or historical commitment on the part of the University

   (8) A close review of the LLC Collection Development Policy.

   (9) Input from classroom faculty and staff.

   (10) Appropriate media balance.

c. This profile statement will provide criteria for the review of this area by the Collection Development Officer.

d. Titles will be reviewed by the Collection Development Officer and decisions made using the following decisions:

   (1) Withdraw

   (2) Reclass

   (3) Retain

   (4) Replace

e. On a title by title basis.

   (1) Increase the collection coverage in a specifically defined area.

f. The department faculty and staff as well as the professional library staff will be given the opportunity to review the list of decisions.

g. The review decisions will be forwarded to the Collection Development Committee for final comment. The final decision for each title will be made by the Collection Development Officer.

h. These decisions will be implemented by sending the list of actions to the Coordinator of Bibliographic Services for action.

i. Collection building decisions will be implemented by the Collection Development Officer. Funding priorities will be established for these areas on an annual basis.

XXV. AREA RESEARCH CENTER (ARC) COLLECTION DEVELOPMENT POLICY

The UW—Stout Area Research Center is the result of a contractual agreement of the University of Wisconsin—Stout and the State Historical Society of Wisconsin. The ARC has a threefold purpose to collect, preserve, and encourage use of historical materials. The ARC Collection Development Policy is meant to articulate specific criteria and the scope of this special collection. The ARC Collection Development Policy will be reviewed biennially.

A. Priorities for collecting records.

(July 14, 1992)

1. While all archives' manuscripts and records are important, the collecting and storage of materials relating to UW—Stout will take first priority for the ARC. This priority is due to fiscal and storage constraints.

2. The second priority for collecting and storage will be for materials originating in Dunn County.

3. The third priority will be for materials originating in Barron and Pepin Counties.

4. Future obligations will include the conservation of electronic and digital records. This process will be jointly pursued with Computing and Telecommunications.

B. Objectives of the ARC Collection Development Policy.

1. To establish the subject scope of the Area Research Center collection.

2. To establish collection guidelines for the types of materials housed in the Area Research Center.

C. Subject Scope of the Area Research Center Collection.

1. A primary goal of the ARC is to acquire strong collections which document regional life and development for the three counties assigned; Dunn, Barron and Pepin Counties by the State Historical Society of Wisconsin and to sustain significant research projects based upon this documentation.

2. A primary goal of the ARC is the continued collection and retention of historical evidence of the University of Wisconsin—Stout as a provider of higher education since its founding.

3. A secondary goal of the ARC is to collect supportive material to provide sources of information in the areas of genealogy, local history, Wisconsin history, historic sites, and the University of Wisconsin System as it relates to UW—Stout.

4. A secondary goal of the ARC is to collect archival, historical, scarce, or other materials in need of special handling which relate to Stout's primary curricular emphasis.

D. Area Research Center (ARC) Materials.

1. A variety of materials are housed in the Area Research Center. These materials are organized into several collections consisting of: 1) ARC Manuscripts; 2) ARC County Archives; 3) ARC University Archives; 4) ARC Photos; 5) ARC Maps; 6) ARC Serials; 7) ARC Oral History; and 8) ARC Collection.

2. University materials that require more than ordinary security because of archival or historical value; preservation of copies; or basic locator or aid tools which provide direct access to materials already in the ARC or in other historical collections; will become part of the ARC collection.

E. Acquisition of ARC Materials.

1. The Archivist has the primary responsibility for ARC collection development.

2. The archivist encourages involvement of the State Historical Society of Wisconsin, Library Learning Center staff, the Stout community, the regional community, and ARC patrons in ARC collection development.

3. ARC materials are normally acquired in the following manner:

a. Donation - Donation of materials is both an active process of soliciting for particular materials and a passive process of accepting materials which are brought into the Area Research Center. It is the ARC's policy to encourage donation of materials which are brought into the Area Research Center. It is the ARC's policy to encourage donation of materials so long as the materials are useful to the university and community within the ordinary purposes of the Area Research Center. Gifts of materials with mixed historical values may be accepted as long as the Archivist has the right to discard or otherwise remove unwanted items. Further, the Archivist must retain the right to "break up" a donated collection into appropriate categories, in accordance with established library and archival procedures.

Donations which carry stringent donor restrictions should not be accepted. The Archivist will determine that the donor has, in fact, the right to make the donation, and that the donation is not encumbered by ethical and legal problems. The Executive Director of the Stout Foundation should be notified when significant gifts are presented so that appropriate publicity may be arranged. All donations must be represented on a legal donor form which includes a description of the materials, the name, address, and signature of the donor, the date of donation, a description of any restrictions attached to the donation, and the signature of the ARC representative accepting the donation.

b. Transfer of Custody - Custodial transfer is the means by which most university and county records are acquired by the Area Research Center. Custodial transfer applies only to public records and means that legal custody is transferred from one agency or office to another. Wisconsin Statutes 16.61, 19.21, 19.23, and 44.09 cover custodial transfer of local governmental records to the State Historical Society for permanent deposit in the appropriate Area Research Center and of university records to the official university archival depository.

c. Deposit - Materials on deposit in the Area Research Center must be covered in a contractual agreement between the University or the ARC and the depositing agency. The State Historical Society of Wisconsin has permanently deposited ARC Manuscripts and ARC County Archives collections in the Area Research Center. Other collections may also be deposited in the Area Research Center if a contractual agreement had been established and approved by the archivist and/or Director of the Library Learning Center. Any such collection must be useful to the university and community within the ARC collection guidelines. The Area Research Center will not accept contractual deposit of historical manuscript materials relating to Barron, Pepin, and Dunn Counties if these materials do not become the property of the State Historical Society of Wisconsin.

d. Purchase - Purchase of manuscript and archival materials is discouraged. If a significant collection becomes available only through purchase, such acquisition must be considered on its own merits. It must be noted that purchase of such materials tends to discourage donations by other potential donors. If more than one institution is involved in bidding for materials, the needs of patrons may be subverted. For these reasons, purchase of materials is generally limited to commercially published materials.

F. Emphasis and Direction in Collection.

1. The Area Research Center collects materials both in response to patron demonstrated need and the Archivist's determination of collection emphasis. There should be attention given to the needs of patrons as can be demonstrated in daily activities. Weaknesses in the collection can be addressed through purchase and donation, in many cases. The changes in the university's academic mission influence the ARC less than other departments, but a special archival collection category can be useful to many academic areas.

2. In the area of local and regional history, the Area Research Center seeks to acquire and preserve suitable materials before need is evident. This is justified on the basis of unique information in certain categories of records. Further, the ARC consistently acquires current records so that future research may be served. The contemporary scene becomes historical. Research, donation, and goodwill are all served by a facility that encourages and appreciates its patrons. A community that comes to the ARC for assistance will also know where to deposit its records. So long as this facility is seen as a community resource, its usage and acquisitions will be self-sustaining.

G. Historic Appraisal of Manuscripts and Archives.

1. Historic appraisal is the basis for selecting records and papers which are to be retained in the Area Research Center. The Society of American Archivists Committee on Terminology has defined historic appraisal as "the process of determining the value and thus the disposition of records based upon their current administrative, legal, and fiscal use; their evidential and informational or research value; their arrangement; and their relationship to other records."

2. Historic appraisal depends largely upon the professional skill and knowledge of the Archivist and is a process of weighing the factors described in *Factors in Historic Appraisal* (see page 84) in relation to each other to arrive at a disposition decision.

H. Duplication of Materials.

1. Under extenuating circumstances, materials may be housed in more than one library collection and the ARC collection. Any duplication may be continuously monitored and may occur only under the following circumstances:

   a. The item serves as a preservation copy due to its scarcity and/or physical condition;

   b. Or the item is part of a limited number of resources serving a "ready reference" function in the ARC.

2. The decision to duplicate an item in the Library and ARC collections will be made jointly by the Collection Development Officer and the Archivist.

I. Growth of the Collection.

The Area Research Center exists to collect, preserve, and encourage use of historical materials as outlined in the ARC Collection Development Policy. Due to the priority given to collection and preservation of historical materials, most action regarding limiting collection growth occurs at the time material is offered and/or acquired by the ARC.

Careful historic appraisal of materials is of primary importance in eliminating unwanted materials and unnecessary growth. Materials which are accepted into the ARC will undergo careful historic appraisal as a group.

Preliminary and subsequent weeding of a record or manuscript group occurs as the materials are being processed. Processing involves arrangement, weeding, foldering, labelling, boxing, and providing cursory and in depth finding aids to individual record or manuscript groups. Record or manuscript groups which are being processed will undergo careful historic appraisal item by item.

If historic appraisal has been carefully undertaken initially, the occurrence of fully processed materials being permanently removed or weeded from the ARC collection should be rare. However, the factors which make up a historic appraisal decision are not fixed in time and subsequent historic appraisal may be necessary.

Limits to growth of fully processed materials may also be accomplished through other means including compact or remote storage and/or miniaturization.

J. Area Research Center Collections.
  1. ARC Manuscript Collection
    a. Scope

      By contractual agreement with the State Historical Society
      of Wisconsin, the Area Research Center will collect manu-
      script materials relating to the three-county area of Dunn,
      Barron, Pepin Counties. Manuscript material may be
      defined as recorded information which has been created in
      the day-to-day activities of individuals, businesses, organi-
      zations, and groups.

    b. Types of ARC Manuscripts (this list serves as an example of
      possible items)

      (1) Church Records
      (2) Cemetery Records
      (3) Genealogies
      (4) Business Records
      (5) Reminiscences
      (6) Scrapbooks
      (7) Speeches
      (8) Correspondence
      (9) Financial Records
      (10) Diaries
      (11) Minutes of Meetings
      (12) Histories and Papers
      (13) Farm Records
      (14) Organization's Records
      (15) Family Records
      (16) Memoirs

    c. Ownership

      The State Historical Society of Wisconsin holds title to the
      ARC Manuscript collection and by contractual agreement
      deposits the material permanently in the Area Research
      Center. These materials are cataloged, processed, and boxed
      at the State Historical Society and then sent for permanent
      deposit in the Area Research Center. The catalog data is
      sent to the ARC and this information is also kept at the
      Society in Madison for a union catalog of statewide

resources. The agreement with the State Historical Society also provides for the loan of these materials to other ARC's and to the Society in Madison upon the request of a patron.

2. ARC County Archives

    a. Scope

        By contractual agreement with the State Historical Society of Wisconsin, the Area Research Center serves as the regional depository of local governmental records of Barron, Pepin, and Dunn Counties. Non-current local public records of historical value may be transferred to the State Historical Society, for permanent deposit in the ARC, according to the provisions of Wisconsin Statutes 16.61, 19.21, 19.23, and 44.09. Records created or received during the conduct of business of any county office, township, city or village, and school district in Barron, Pepin, and Dunn Counties constitute public records and as such would fall under the scope of this collection.

    b. Types of ARC County Archives (This list serves as an example of possible items.)

        (1) School Attendance Records

        (2) Minutes and Financial Records of School District

        (3) Court Case Files

        (4) Naturalization Records

        (5) Court Records

        (6) Proceedings of the County Board of Supervisors and of City Councils

        (7) Tax Records

        (8) Minutes and Financial Records of Townships

        (9) Township Assessors Field Books

        (10) Probate Records

    c. Ownership

        The State Historical Society holds title to the Dunn, Barron, and Pepin County Archives and by contractual agreement, deposits the material for permanent preservation in the Area Research Center. These materials are cataloged, processed, and boxed at the Society in Madison and then returned to be permanently housed in the ARC. Catalog data is provided to the ARC by the Society and the

Society also keeps this information in Madison for a union catalog of statewide resources. The agreement with the State Historical Society also provides for temporary transfer of this material to other ARC's and to the Society in Madison upon the request of a patron.

3. ARC University Archives

    a. Scope

    In accordance with Wisconsin Statute 16.61, the UW—Stout Area Research Center serves as the official repository for the non-current original records and reproductions of historical value for the University of Wisconsin—Stout.

    b. Types of University Archival Materials

    (1) Records of the office of the chief administrator, including correspondence, administrative subject files, and reports.

    (2) Correspondence, subject files, and reports of the chief academic affairs officer.

    (3) Correspondence, subject files, and reports of the chief administrative officer.

    (4) Correspondence, subject files, and reports of the chief officers of units of the university operating with a high degree of independence such as schools and unit offering services.

    (5) Correspondence, subject files, and reports of the office of the chief student affairs officer.

    (6) Minutes, memoranda, and reports of all major academic and administrative committees, including the Faculty Senate, the Academic Staff Senate and the Student Senate and their official committees.

    (7) Accreditation reports and supporting documentation.

    (8) Annual budget and audit reports.

    (9) A select number of departmental records including minutes, reports, syllabi, and sample test questions.

    (10) A select number of personnel records of retired, resigned, or deceased faculty and academic staff.

    (11) Records of the registrar including timetables and class schedules, non-current student transcripts, enroll-

ment reports, graduation rosters, and other reports issued on a regular basis.

(12) Alumni records including the minutes, correspondence, and reports of the alumni association.

(13) Reports of the admissions office, the office of institutional research, the office of campus development.

(14) Records of student organizations.

(15) All publications, newsletters, or booklets distributed in the name of the university; including yearbooks, catalogs, special bulletins, student newspapers, university directories and faculty/staff rosters, faculty and university newsletters, alumni magazines, and ephemeral materials.

(16) Audiovisual materials documenting the development of the institution such as video cassettes and motion picture films.

(17) Maps, plot plans, and blueprints documenting physical growth and development.

(18) Reports of research projects, including grant records.

(19) A select number of personal papers of faculty and alumni.

(20) Records of national professional associations relating to the university's primary mission areas.

c. Ownership

The University of Wisconsin—Stout shall hold title to its non-current records of historical value. These records will be acquired through custodial transfer from various offices and units to the Area Research Center. Records of the UW—Stout Alumni Association, and individual faculty and alumni will be acquired through donation. Records of national professional associations may be acquired through depository agreement. These materials are cataloged, processed, and boxed at the Area Research Center. An agreement with the University of Wisconsin System Archives Council and the State Historical Society of Wisconsin provides for temporary transfer of these materials to any member of the University of Wisconsin System Archives Council upon the request of a patron and the permission of the UW—Stout Archivist.

4. ARC Photos

    a. Scope

       Still photographs, negatives, and prints relating to UW—Stout, Dunn, Pepin, and Barron Counties, and of general subject nature comprise the photograph collection.

    b. Ownership

       Materials in the photograph collection may be acquired through custodial transfer, deposit, purchase, or donation. In general, the Area Research Center, UW—Stout will hold title to the material, but this varies with the legal agreement and whether the donor has title to the material. The photograph collection is described and processed at the Area Research Center. This material is not subject to transfer and must be either used in the Center or a copy print requested at the requestor's expense.

5. ARC Maps

    a. Scope

       Maps relating to UW—Stout, and maps and plat books relating to Barron, Pepin, and Dunn Counties and Wisconsin comprise the map and plat book collection. Both current and non-current materials will be acquired for this collection since current materials quickly become historical and collection and acquisition is easier when materials are readily available.

    b. Ownership

       Materials in the ARC Maps collection are the property of the Area Research Center, UW—Stout. Requests for temporary transfer of this material will be handled on a case-by-case basis and will generally be limited to the State Historical Society and other ARC's.

6. ARC Serials

    a. Scope

       The periodical and newspaper collection will be limited to the areas of genealogy; Dunn, Barron, Pepin County and Wisconsin organizations dealing with genealogy; Wisconsin history; and serials specifically within the Dunn, Barron and Pepin County area both currently and retrospectively.

    b. Types of ARC Serials (This list serves as an example of possible items.)

(1) *Colfax Messenger*

(2) *Barron County News-Shield*

(3) Newsletter of the National Register of Historic Places in Wisconsin

(4) *Rice Lake Chronotype*

(5) *Exchange* (Wisconsin Council for Local History)

(6) *Newsletter of the Wisconsin State Genealogical Society*

(7) *Inscriptions* (Wisconsin State Old Cemetery Society)

(8) *History News* (American Association for State and Local History

(9) *Boyceville Press-Reporter*

(10) *Columns* (Newsletter of the State Historical Society of Wisconsin)

(11) *Wisconsin Mapping Bulletin*

(12) *Cumberland Advocate*

(13) *Turtle Lake Times*

(14) *Chetek Alert*

(15) *Dunn County News*

c. Ownership

Materials in the ARC Serial collection are the property of the Area Research Center, UW—Stout. These materials are not available for transfer normally, but photocopies of articles may be requested by another library from the Library Learning Center Interlibrary Loan Service.

7. ARC Oral History Collection

a. Scope

Oral histories collected under the auspices of the Stout Oral History Program, oral histories of residents of Dunn, Barron, and Pepin Counties, oral histories collected relating to Stout's primary subject missions, and recordings of speakers or events occurring at UW—Stout, Dunn, Barron and Pepin Counties, are part of the ARC Oral History collection.

b. Ownership

Materials in the oral history collection may be acquired through custodial transfer, deposit, or donation. In general, the Area Research Center, UW—Stout will hold title to the materials, but this varies with the legal agreement and whether the donor actually has title to the material.

The oral history collection is described and processed at the Area Research Center. User copies of the oral history collection are subject to ARC network transfer upon the request of a researcher.

8. ARC Collection

    a. Scope

This collection consists of books, pamphlets, and microform materials which require more than ordinary security because of historical value, which serve as preservation copies, or basic locator or aid tools which provide access to materials already in the ARC collections or other historical collections. Both current and retrospective materials will be acquired for this collection.

The collection includes but is not limited to the following subject areas:

(1) Genealogy

(2) Wisconsin in general

(3) Parts of Wisconsin (especially Dunn, Barron and Pepin Counties)

(4) University of Wisconsin—Stout

(5) History and Historical Methods

(6) Historic Sites and Museums

(7) Archival and Manuscript Repositories

(8) Stout's Primary Mission Areas

    b. Types of ARC Collection Materials (This list serves as an example of possible items.)

(1) Historical city and county telephone directories of cities and localities in Dunn, Barron, and Pepin Counties.

(2) Microfilmed original manuscripts of the U.S. and Wisconsin State Census individual-by-individual list of people by locality.

(3) Regional, county, and local histories and biographies.

(4) Genealogies of families prevalent in the Dunn, Barron and Pepin County area.

(5) Historical Wisconsin Blue Books. (Cooperatively held between ARC and Library Learning Center.) An appropriate cut-off date establishes what books will be in the Library Learning Center collections before transfer to the ARC. The cut-off date will be mutually agreed upon by the Archivist and the Collection Development Officer.

(6) Historical Wisconsin Statutes and Laws of Wisconsin. (Cooperatively held between ARC and Library Learning Center). An appropriate cut-off date establishes what books will be in the Library collection before transfer to the ARC. The cut-off date will be mutually agreed upon by the Archivist and the Collection Development Officer.

(7) Historical Wisconsin Legislature Bulletins.

c. Ownership

Materials in the ARC collection are the property of the Area Research Center, UW—Stout. Normally, the materials are not available for transfer, but requests for transfer will be handled on a case-by-case basis.

9. Relevant Policies and Statements

The following list of materials make further statements about the Area Research Center and may be consulted for further reference. This document supersedes all statements in the following documents relating to collection development in the Area Research Center, however.

a. University of Wisconsin—Stout. Area Research Center. *Archives and Records Management Manual, 1980.*

b. University of Wisconsin—Stout. Area Research Center. "Program Statement, UW—Stout Oral History Program," 1980.

c. (Area Research Center Agreement between the University and State Historical Society), 1971.

d. Addendum to Area Research Center Agreement, 1980.

e. University of Wisconsin System. Archives Council. *Core Mission and Minimum Standards for University Archives in the University of Wisconsin System, 1977.*

K. Factors in Historic Appraisal.

1. Characteristics of Records

a. Age. The older the record the more likely it will have historical value regardless of other factors. This is largely due to increasing scarcity of older records and that more historically valuable records have been destroyed necessitating preservation of available records covering the same period.

b. Volume. Volume of the material must be balanced against other factors. Extensive bulk necessitates careful examination of the records in relation to other factors.

c. Physical Form. The physical form of records establishes basic patterns for their historic appraisal. For example, in appraising photographs and sound recordings, the Archivist must also consider the technical quality of the records.

d. Functional Characteristics. The Archivist must consider the procedural significance and character of the records. Each record has a function, which is usually reflected in its title. Basic functions are not mutually exclusive. The function of a record provides an initial indication of its significance. Functions may be either substantive or facilitative in nature. Generally, records documenting facilitative functions are not of historical value.

e. Evidential Value. Evidential value is the evidence the record contains of the functioning, organization, policies, decisions, procedures, operations or other activities of the agency that produced them. The Archivist must know three significant facts in determining evidential value: 1) the office position in the agency's administrative hierarchy; 2) The substantive and facilitative functions performed by the office; and 3) the activities carried on under a given function by an office in the administrative hierarchy.

f. Informational Characteristics. Most records contain factual data about the persons, corporate bodies, events, problems, and conditions with which the office dealt. Informational characteristics re-evaluated on the basis of the uniqueness and form of the record, the information it contains, and the importance of the content.

2. Administrative Values

    a. Administrative Uses. The Archivist must consider the importance of the administrative office that produced the records, the extent of agency authority, and the research importance of the functions recorded. Administrative uses may include planning, organizing, staffing, directing, coordinating, reporting, and budgeting functions. High-level administrative, policy, and substantive files are preferred over housekeeping and facilitative records of subordinate offices.

    b. Financial Values. Fiscal responsibility requires that records documenting financial authorizations, obligations, and transactions shall be retained to support financial statements and to provide an audit trail for subsequent verification. Much of this material has no historical value, but some financial records do have continuing administrative value.

    c. Legal Values. A major administrative value of archives is their use to prove the legal or civil rights of individuals to citizenship, property, and employment benefits. Legal values are an important factor in the evaluation of records.

3. Research Values

    a. Uniqueness. Uniqueness is an important attribute of records having research value. Uniqueness involves determination of the extent to which the information in a record is physically or substantively duplicated elsewhere.

    b. Credibility. Credibility is a basic research value. The Archivist must consider authenticity and understand the context in which a document was created.

    c. Understandability. Understandability is a prerequisite for future usefulness. Records may have meaning and value to the author alone, to a few specialized researchers, or to many users in the future.

    d. Time Span. There must be enough examples of records covering a span of time to permit investigations of sufficient scope for drawing valid conclusions. Otherwise, the records are isolated curiosities. Researchers prefer records that offer information over a long time period and comparable data enhances the validity of research based on archival sources. The regularity and uniformity of information in selected records increases their value.

e. Accessibility. The research value of records depends on their accessibility. A researcher must be able to consult the records within a reasonable time after their donation or transfer to the Area Research Center. Perpetual, indefinite, or long-term restrictions on access significantly reduce the value of a collection. As well, concentrated information increases the accessibility of the source material. While a record collection may be physically accessible to users, its informational content may be buried in a mass of other materials or obscured by an arrangement that precludes use.

f. Frequency of Use. Research values are good criteria for potential use. Past, present, and future demand must justify retention. The Archivist must balance the fact that research interests of scholars change and new directions in research methodology emerge with the actual research use a series of records is likely to receive.

g. Type of Quality of Use. The Area Research Center is used for both scholarly and popular research. The Archivist has a responsibility to guide and improve the quality of amateur historical research; however, records which support extended, in-depth scholarly research must not be slighted due to lack of frequent use. Frequency of use, type, and quality of use must be balanced in relation to each other.

4. Archival Values

a. Relationship to Other Records. Collection evaluation and description characterize the archival approach to documentation. The Archivist works with aggregates, batches, or collections and thus acquires skill and achieves consistency in dealing with documents in relation to each other, in relation to the content of other documents, and in relation to the selection policies of the ARC. Record series selected for their archival value should document significant policies and operations and contain information that makes them complement other record series of archival value and represent the many record series that cannot be retained. Gaps in existing archival documentation are a major consideration in historic appraisal.

b. Processing Costs. Every record taken into the Area Research Center has a price tag that includes the staff time required for its processing and description. These costs are weighed against the usefulness of the records. Well-organized files save time in processing. Although processing costs vary for different materials, it is a constant factor in archival appraisal.

c.   Preservation Costs. The cost of staff, equipment, and supplies for preserving or restoring documents must be considered in determining archival value.

d.   Storage Costs. The Archivist must weigh available financial resources against the prospective usefulness of the records.

Western Kentucky University Libraries

❀ ❀ ❀ ❀ ❀ ❀ ❀ ❀

Collection Development Statement

CONTENTS

VI. *Special Policies*
   Gifts   Community College Materials
   Interlibrary Loan   Leisure Reading Collections
   Withdrawal and Replacement Preservation

VII. *Narrative Profiles of Academic Programs in the Colleges*

*Appendices**
   A. *Western XXI* Priorities for Academic Programs
   B. Narrative Profile Sheet for Departmental Programs
   C. ALA/RLG Collection Intensity Codes and Definitions
   D. WKU Libraries Non-Print Materials Policy
   E. U.S. College Book Prices, 1991 (*Choice* Table)

                    ❋ ❋ ❋ ❋ ❋ ❋ ❋ ❋

I. INTRODUCTION

The mission of the Western Kentucky University Libraries is to provide essential services in support of the University's three principal endeavors: instruction, research, and public service. The Libraries assume a pivotal role in Western Kentucky University's commitment to excellence through the efficient and effective selection, acquisition, and dissemination of scholarly information. The selection of materials to meet current and future needs of Western's faculty, staff, students, and the local citizenry is a critical service element in the Libraries' mission and is the very core of collection development.

The purpose of this Collection Development Statement is to specify curricular and disciplinary priorities to guide the selecting and acquiring of informational materials up to the twenty-first century. A formal statement of the priorities which will energize and focus our efforts will be a valuable blueprint for rational collection development.

Effective collection development will require sufficient funding to meet the needs of an expanding student population, new courses and programs, and changing faculty research interests. In addition, it will require coping with escalating inflation rates for books, serials and resources in newer formats such as compact-disc technology. Accelerating developments in information technology exert a special challenge to conventional library collection needs. The range of information format options is expanding just at a time when funding stability (not to mention

---

*Not reprinted.

growth) is ever more uncertain. All of these developments highlight the necessity for efficient planning in developing the resources of Western Kentucky University's Libraries.

This statement is prepared in accord with *Western Kentucky University's Spirit of Excellence: Values and Directions for the Twenty-First Century*, a document approved by the University's Board of Regents in late 1990 (hereafter referred to as *Western XXI*). It is also compatible with *University Libraries: A Five Year Plan, 1990/91–1994/95*, also adopted in 1990 by WKU Libraries (hereafter, *Strategic Plan*). The outline of the Statement relies upon a *Guide for Written Collection Policy Statements* endorsed by the American Library Association in 1989 (hereafter, *ALA Guidelines*), especially pp. 4–6. Collection standards expressed in ALA's *Standards for College Libraries* in 1986 (hereafter, *ALA Standards*) are taken into account as well. Lastly, conformance with the 8th edition of SACS (Southern Association of Colleges and Schools) *Criteria*, section 5.2 is also adhered to. Familiarity with these materials, as well as with the Libraries' prior collection development statement (adopted in early 1984), would enhance a reader's understanding of this Statement.

While evaluation of the strength of existing collections is a major concern of academic libraries (see *Strategic Plan*, p. 6 and *ALA Standards*, pp. 191–192), it will not be emphasized here. Instead, selection criteria for future development, i.e. *what* will be selected and *why*, will be highlighted. As stated in the *ALA Standards*, "the best way to improve quality in a library collection is to adhere to rigorous standards of discrimination in the selection of materials to be added." Assessment of quality in existing collections is not to be ignored, merely delayed until this forward-looking statement is adopted and implemented. (In passing, it should be noted that this statement is *not* meant to delineate policies for development of Special Collections resources in the Kentucky Library or University Archives.)

This policy statement departs from the Libraries' earlier statement (and from many other university library collection development policy statements) in two ways. First, as will be explained, a conspectus approach is not directly applied to Library of Congress classifications. The *ALA Guidelines* do not insist upon that application but allow application of the approach instead to academic departments (and departmental programs) as it will be deployed here. Second, this statement will explicate some factors to actually be considered in distributing materials budget funds. The goal in this statement is to underpin the need for a more systematic process embodied in a formula, which once in place, would "drive" the materials allocation process. In most collection development policies, the only criterion which purports to affect *distribution* of the materials budget is "collection intensity level." While "collection intensity levels" by curricular program will be profiled in this document and may correlate highly with allocation differences between departments, these intensity levels for programs will not be the determining factor in allocation decisions.

Collection development is a planning function which involves the overall molding of library collections to meet users' needs. It is implemented at Western Kentucky University Libraries by a Coordinator of Collection Development and several subject librarians (bibliographers) in the Department of Library Public Services who are specifically charged with the responsibility. In keeping with *ALA Standards* and SACS guidelines, however, the involvement of teaching faculty in college departments is encouraged; they are the best judges of their needs for professional materials. A faculty member in each department is named by the Head of that department as its library representative. This individual serves as liaison with the subject librarian assigned primary responsibility for a host of collection development duties for the programs and discipline(s) centered in that department. This liaison channels book and serial requests from the department's faculty to the appropriate subject librarian. The selection of materials deemed useful for academic purposes in accord with precepts of academic freedom (primarily with that of freedom of unrestrained pursuit of knowledge) is a major duty of these librarians.

The Libraries contract with various book jobbers to receive prompt notification of newly published academically-oriented publications (for books and non-print items). One primary serials vendor (Faxon) serves as a broker to sustain serials control over thousands of subscriptions to periodicals and ongoing series. The Acquisitions and Serials units of the Department of Library Automation and Technical Services process requests for books and serials which are cataloged or registered upon receipt by the Catalog and Serials units, respectively, to maintain an expeditious flow of desired materials into the hands of users.

II. INSTITUTIONAL ENVIRONMENT

The current WKU undergraduate and graduate catalogs (1991–1993) and *Western XXI* set forth the context in which the Libraries of Western Kentucky University create this statement. The historical background of the Libraries is drawn from the former source and from its own *Strategic Plan*.

Western Kentucky State Normal School, Bowling Green, was established by an act of the 1906 Kentucky General Assembly. Prior to 1906, there had existed in Bowling Green the Southern Normal School and

Bowling Green Business University, whose president was Henry Hardin Cherry. In 1907, the Southern Normal School was transferred to state control and Dr. Cherry was named as first President. in 1930, the school's name was changed to Western Kentucky State Teacher's College and in 1948 to Western Kentucky State College. In 1966, the Kentucky General Assembly designated Western as a University and changed its name to Western Kentucky University. The granting of university status gave the Graduate School (renamed the Graduate College in 1969) the power to strengthen existing programs and to offer a wider spectrum of programs. Currently, thirty-three degree-awarding departments are distributed in four Colleges: the (Potter) College of Arts, Humanities, and Social Sciences: the College of Business Administration; the College of Education and Behavioral Sciences; and the (Ogden) College of Science, Technology and Health. In addition, Area Study Programs, a Community College and Extended Campus teaching programs were developed in the 1980's to further enhance educational opportunities for residents of the Commonwealth.

Library collections date back to 1909 when a small collection was started in Potter Hall. Gordon Wilson Hall housed library holdings for over thirty years, beginning in 1931. In 1963, the facility moved to the former gymnasium, renamed the Helm Library; in 1971 the Cravens Graduate Center and Library was completed as a nine-story stacks tower. Margie M. Helm headed the College Library from 1923 to 1965. Ms. Helm's successors were Ms. Sara Tyler (1965–1969), Dr. Earl Wassom (1969–1985), and since 1985, Dr. Michael Binder. At present, four library/resource centers serve the Bowling Green campus. They are (1) the Helm-Cravens Library, (2) the Kentucky Library and Museum, (3) the Science Library housed in Kelly-Thompson Central Complex, and (4) the Educational Resources Center. Western's Libraries hold more than one-half million books, over 1.2 million microform items, approximately 100,000 bound periodical volumes and over one-quarter million government documents. The Helm-Cravens Library, located near the center of campus, houses the major circulating book collection (in Cravens) and the main reference, government documents, periodicals and microforms, and law collections (in Helm). The main circulation and reserve desks, the technical services units, and the extended campus services office are located in Cravens. The two buildings are connected via two walkways. Four decks in Gordon Wilson Hall serve as a storage facility for older, rarely used print materials.

The Educational Resources Center (ERC) primarily supports the needs of faculty and students in the Department of Teacher Education and enriches its instructional programs through provision of both print and non-print materials. Textbooks, manuals, activity books, curriculum guides, and tests, all keyed to application in grades K–12 are typical print materials as are college-level methodology books and a few journal subscriptions. Non-print materials include audio-visual software such as multi-media kits, filmstrips, slides, audio and video recordings, pictures, realia, and microcomputer programs. Appropriate electronic indexes (such as ERIC and PsycLit on CD-ROM) are housed here as well.

The Science Library provides books, periodicals, compact disc workstations, and reference/circulation services vital for instruction and research in the sciences and technology. Severe overcrowding there has necessitated cataloging of all such books acquired since 1990 for the Cravens stacks.

A reference library housed in the Glasgow Campus managed by a full-time librarian emphasizes CD-ROM reference assistance and TOPCAT access to collections on the main campus rather than developing an independent circulating collection. An endowment fund supports purchase of many of its reference materials. FAX service of journal articles and frequent courier service of books to this campus (and to the Owensboro center) are a boon to students at these sites. Access to the collections for other off-campus students is coordinated by an Extended Campus Librarian stationed in Cravens. The increase in the extended campus population has served as a challenge for the Libraries to make collection access as equal as possible for all WKU students.

A multitude of technological networks tie these operations together. The system software for acquisitions, cataloging, circulation and the online catalog are from NOTIS Systems, Inc. (Northwestern Online Total Integrated Systems). The online catalog for the entire cataloged collection, known as TOPCAT here at Western, became fully operational in January, 1992.

While the Special Collections housed in the Kentucky Library and Museum and the University Archives are not focused upon in this document, a brief mission statement of these units is in order. The Kentucky Library collects print and non-print materials pertaining to the state's history in all genres. The Folklife Archives and Manuscripts sections contain unpublished primary source materials with special emphasis upon Kentucky, while the University Archives (housed in Helm) collects the records and correspondence of administrative officials and faculty of the University. Both primary research and instruction are facilitated in these special collections.

III. BUDGET ALLOCATION CRITERIA IN COLLECTION DEVELOPMENT

The major unit of collection analysis is and will continue to be academic program within academic departments. Allocating the Libraries' materials budget to departments has evolved by what is called "The Historical Method" in *Guide to Budget Allocation for Information Resources*, p. 9 (produced by the Association for Library Collections and Technical Services of ALA in 1991). It is remarkable that this method has thus far produced allocations which fit as closely as they do the relative costs of available academic books discipline by discipline. A table in the Appendix attests to this. If one compares the cost breakdown of books reviewed in *Choice* in 1991 with departmental allocations for the 1990–91 fiscal year, one will see a close, albeit coincidental, correspondence. Nevertheless, a more systematic approach to allocations is worthy of consideration and a serious review of formula-based allocations is in process. Some criteria of potential importance in a formula developed to apportion book and/or serials funds department by department are:

1. the status of degree programs at baccalaureate and graduate degree levels as enunciated in *Western XXI*. See the Appendix for a listing of these priorities.

2. the number of students instructed in lower-division, upper-division, and graduate-level courses as measured by student credit hours at those levels.

3. the number of majors enrolled or degrees granted.

4. the number of full-time equivalent faculty.

5. the estimated cost of current publications available by discipline which are appropriate to Western curricula and research foci.

6. the collecting intensity emphasis as stipulated in the collecting level codes reported for programs in the departmental profiles. See *Collecting Level* in the next section for explanation of these codes.

7. some measure of use of the collection, e.g., the circulation of books by Library of Congress Class of book circulated.

It should be observed that just as difficult as selecting the most appropriate criteria for an allocation formula is deciding the proper weighting of the selected factors in an equation. There is no magic formula awaiting our discovery. No extensive justification of any of the potential components listed above is given here, except for *Western XXI* priority (all of the others are mentioned in the *Guide to Budget Allocation for Information Resources* for academic libraries cited earlier.) The assignment of Prominent, Essential, Desirable, or Nonessential classifications to academic programs in the *Western XXI* document was the end-result of protracted deliberation across campus and is the official framework for future university-wide decisions, particularly the strengthening, enhancing, maintaining, or deletion of programs. Thus, *Western XXI* will be incorporated as an element in budgeting decisions as soon as is practicable.

IV. THE COLLECTING PARAMETERS TO PROFILE DEPARTMENTS

The purposes and collecting needs of departmental degree programs are profiled in this document. (A copy of the form employed to profile them is shown in the Appendices). These profiles were prepared by appropriate subject librarians in conjunction with departmental liaison faculty in late 1991. In these narratives, *Western XXI* status and level of collecting intensity are coded for each degree program above the associate degree level. The parameters are described below.

Subject:
Library materials are selected in all areas of inquiry taught within university departments, including interdisciplinary area programs and the Community College. Degree programs (majors/minors at undergraduate and graduate levels) essentially set these boundaries in their "Purpose of Degree program" statements.

General (Non-Subject) Parameters:
Language - English Language materials will predominate in nearly all program areas. The phrase "English predominates" will be specified in each profile with exceptions noted in a few departments.

Date of Publication - refers to emphasis upon current or retrospective year of publication. Here again, current (i.e., still in print or recent) years may predominate in most departments but great variance between departments is to be expected.

Chronological Coverage - refers to the historical time periods of greatest interest in a department. Here, too, variance between departments is to be expected.

Geographic Coverage - the scope of interest (local, regional, national, or international) will be specified in a department's profile; departments will vary widely.

Formats Preferred - refers to the medium in which information is encoded; paper versus various electronic media is a major decision-point. Print-on-paper sources are still predominant in most programs. Also specified here will be the relative emphasis upon monographs, journals, edited works, etc. preferred by a department. In some departments, emphasis upon government documents (in whatever format) will bear specification.

Formats/Excluded - Generally, introductory level textbooks (aimed at 100–200 level courses) will be excluded as will be master's theses and doctoral dissertations (unless published by a recognized press). Copies of Master's theses completed for degree requirements at Western are cataloged in the circulating collection, however. Instructor's manuals and student study guides keyed to particular textbooks (at any level) will generally not be collected. Added copies of works will also not typically be acquired. Each department may indicate its unique mix of exclusions desired but the typical pattern just described will be reported as the "Standard Exclusions."

Collecting Level - refers to the level of intensity with which materials in an area of scholarly study at Western Kentucky University are sought for the collections. As already implied, Western XXI priority and presence of graduate degree programs will determine this level. For programs leading only to undergraduate degree majors or minors, this level will typically be what *ALA Guidelines* term the "Study or Instructional Support Level (Introductory)"; for programs offered at both baccalaureate and master's degree levels (or at master's level only), the typical level will be the "Study or Instructional Support Level (Advanced)". In the profiles, the former level is coded as 3a and the latter is coded as 3b. Level 4 (the "Research" level) will be accorded only a few programs offering post-Master's level degree programs if the programs are identified as Prominent or Essential in *Western XXI* and have a research component. See the Appendix for more detailed definitions of these ALA/RLG Conspectus definitions.

V. TREATMENT OF SPECIAL FORMATS

Before turning to the profiles for academic departments, guidelines for acquiring particular genres of publication and special policies appertaining thereto are in order.

Newspapers: The WKU Libraries maintains a representative collection of international, national (U.S.A.), and local (regional and county) newspapers in hard copy. The most current two months of leading foreign newspapers as well as of several major American dailies (including all eight indexed in *Newspaper Abstracts on Disc*) are held. Microfilm backfiles of the latter are obtained. Daily and weekly papers representing as many regions of the state as possible are acquired for patron enjoyment. The Glasgow Campus Library has acquired the *New York Times* and *Washington Post* in full-text CD-ROM versions.

Microforms: An extensive and diverse collection in this space-saving format is held. Many retrospective sources of inestimable research value are now available only in this form. The early backfile of many periodicals is held only in microfilm. The Periodicals Librarian is consulted prior to the purchase of costly microform sets. It should be noted that federal documents (see Government Documents) are increasingly issued only in this format.

Maps/Atlases: The WKU Libraries collects contemporary, historical and thematic atlases, predominantly in English-language editions. Housed in the Helm Reference Room, atlases support a range of instructional and research needs, particularly for area studies, study abroad programs, and for the Department of Geography and Geology. The reference map collection highlights topographic and geologic maps of the Commonwealth (received as U.S. depository items) and maps of surrounding states but also holds several other types for the United States, the world, and selected regions. The ERC also holds a collection of maps which circulate for use in elementary or secondary classrooms.

Non-Print: The Libraries adopted an audio-visual collecting policy in 1991 which for the first time legitimized the acquiring of non-print materials to be cataloged for the collection (text is in the Appendices). Videotapes, audio-tapes and sound recordings in a range of formats (e.g., compact disc) and microcomputer software programs are judged in terms of their support of the Libraries' mission and purchased in the same manner and from the same budget lines as are books. The profiles of the Art and Music departments set forth their priorities in obtaining such materials. The ERC collects the widest array of non-print items. The ERC, Science Library, and the Circulation Unit in Cravens will oversee shelving and circulation of these materials in their respective buildings.

Electronic Formats(CD-ROM databases, etc): Sources in this fast-evolving format already have had an impact upon the reference collection (and service). An ongoing expense of this new technology is the investment in and maintenance of new hardware (not acquired via materials funds). In the 1980's, electronic sources could be divided into *two* categories: (1) online database searching of offsite computerized files mainly to create specialized bibliographies. Performed by librarians free of charge to faculty, the demand for this service dwindled as the popularity of another technology, (2) the searching of CD-ROM indexes by patrons, arose. The popularity of CD-ROM indexes among retrievers of information and the Libraries' fixed costs for subscriptions to them insure that the Libraries will increasingly prefer them as alternatives to both their print and online counterparts. If the quality, ease of access, and currency of CD-ROM indexes surpass print versions of the same or similar tools, the Libraries will in many cases *replace* the print versions if cost-effectiveness can be demonstrated. In the 1990's, full-text systems of periodicals on disc and electronic delivery services for articles identified online will compel our attention. Such systems are developing rapidly. Also, many journals will increasingly be issued in electronic format only.

Reference Materials: The main reference collection in Helm-Cravens Library supports the academic needs of the university community. The definitions of collecting intensity as applied to departmental programs also apply to the reference tools supporting those programs. Thus, support ranges from "Basic or Minimal" for subjects tangential to the curricula here all the way to "Research" level for those programs whose level of collecting intensity warrant. The research, general and recreational needs of patrons will also be addressed at appropriate levels. The language of the materials will be primarily in English (even foreign language dictionaries will emphasize those with English-language definitions). The Science library will house the major reference apparatus for Agriculture, Biology, Chemistry, Computer Science, Engineering Technology, Industrial Technology, Mathematics, and Physics/Astronomy. Only ready-reference tools for those disciplines will be kept in Helm Reference. The major reference collection for all other Ogden College departments will be held in Helm-Cravens because the entire circulating collections (and periodicals) for those disciplines are held there. Medical reference tools will continue to be split between the two locations to facilitate the needs of Biology and the Allied Health disciplines, respectively. The ERC houses most of the reference works used by Library Media Education faculty and students in the study of school media librarianship.

Government Documents: The University has been the site of a federal selective depository library since 1934. The depository collection received a rating of Good in an early 1992 federal inspection. Items are selected if they are anticipated to fulfill the curricular and informational needs of students, faculty and staff of the university and residents of South Central Kentucky (2nd Cong. District). Currently, the library selects about 48% of the Federal item numbers offered. Over 20,000 paper and microfiche items are added each year. More and more, items are made available to us only in microform or electronic format. If items are available in multiple formats, selection will be dictated by space considerations. Recommendations for selection from the academic and local community are encouraged. Access to the materials is facilitated by a CD-ROM index of the *Monthly Catalog* and other specialized indexes. No documents are at present cataloged into TOPCAT. Kentucky state and local documents are collected and displayed as are statistical series from adjoining states. United Nations documents are not collected. Some commercially produced titles to supplement Federal and state-level collections will be acquired, as funds permit. Documents are housed in Helm Ground Floor.

Law Collection: This collection has been a joint venture of the Warren County Law Library and Western Kentucky University since 1965 and serves both constituencies. The primary focus of the collection is the statutory, administrative, and case law of Kentucky and the United States (case law of other states may be found in the regional reporters, however). The American Digest System provides access to case law and Shepard's citators give subsequent judicial and legislative histories. As funds permit, secondary source material (e.g., law reviews) is collected along with topical materials and treatises in order to support curricular needs or as recommended by the Warren County Bar Association Library Committee. These latter materials are placed in "Law Reference" and are accessible via TOPCAT. The collection is supplemented by WESTLAW and made available to WKU faculty and students for educational use only. Other finding tools may be obtained but not textbooks or international law materials.

Juvenile Collection: The ERC maintains a large Juvenile Collection of books collected over a long number of years. Selections for this circulating collection will give even representation to all categories of books for pre-College readers (from books for the young to young adult) as recommended by ALA's *Booklist* and other sources. The collection is accessible on TOPCAT.

VI. SPECIAL POLICIES

Gift Materials: The University libraries will accept donated books and other materials from individuals or organizations. If these materials match areas of research and instruction within the University, they will be considered for cataloging into the collections. If already held or not deemed suitable for the Libraries' collections, donated works will be surplused. One valued source of collection support is the Friends of WKU Libraries. Membership monies may be designated by a Friend of the Libraries for a work in a specific collection and in so doing underwrite the Libraries' costs. A bookplate is inserted in a book or periodical volume in honor of the donor, or as the donor stipulates, as a symbol of this gift.

Interlibrary Loan: Because no one facility can hope in this age to house the text of all desired materials, the exchange of publications with other libraries will increase (at least until electronic means eliminate the need for hard copy transfer). The OCLC Interlibrary Loan system serves to rapidly identify the most expeditious loan sources for materials needed by WKU faculty, staff and students at no charge. Interlibrary loan policy is based on state, regional, national, and international codes which govern our procedures. Participation in SOLINET, the Center for Research Libraries, the British Lending Library and other consortia open up the entire world of information to serve the research needs of an active academic community. Commercial delivery of articles via electronic means (e.g., via fax) is being explored as a service to quicken access to needed materials.

Community College Materials: Materials are currently obtained in support of Associate Degree programs *only* via allocations to the departments most closely affiliated with the programs. This practice will undergo review in the near future to determine if a separate account line is needed.

Leisure Reading Collection: The University Libraries participates in a McNaughton Leisure Reading Plan with Brodart, Inc. in which we now receive approximately 40 popular new fiction and nonfiction books per month for an annual subscription fee. These books serve the recreational reading interests of our patrons; circulation periods are for two weeks. After one year, the Libraries can decide to add some of the books to the regular collection at a minimal cost; the remainder are returned to Brodart. Approximately 600 titles may be held at any one time. A leisure magazine collection in Helm-Cravens is starting in 1992–93 to augment a similar collection maintained in the Science Library.

Withdrawal and Replacement Policies: Just as evaluation of the present collection is not addressed in this statement, neither is the review of the condition of the existing collections. Weeding of "obsolete" or of brittle, unusable materials is acknowledged as important and a policy statement addressing this concern is currently under review. WKU Libraries will be guided by the *Guide to Review of Library Collections: Preservation, Storage and Withdrawal,* adopted by the American Library Association in 1991. Currently, funds are budgeted by the Libraries to replace copies of lost, missing, and damaged books.

Preservation: Serious consideration of preservation of the collections must similarly be given soon so as to retard natural processes of deterioration, especially in print-on-paper materials. Currently, funds for repair are allotted in the Libraries' budget, but preservation is a broader concern. Preservation of the materials in Special Collections and in the Kentucky Museum is of obvious importance.

VII. NARRATIVE PROFILES OF PROGRAMS IN ACADEMIC DEPARTMENTS

The listing of collection development profiles here will be alphabetical by department within the four Colleges. No broad mission statements of the Colleges will be delineated; the interested reader is referred to WKU Catalogs and College-level statements. A part of the materials budget is allocated to a general account in each of the four Colleges, usually overseen by the Dean of that College or a representative selected thereby. Many important general and interdisciplinary materials might never be selected unless monitored at the College level in coordination with a subject librarian. For those materials transcending more than one College's interest, subject librarians make selections with input from faculty invited.

Four area study programs are profiled within the profiles for Potter College even though their budget allocations might never be formula-funded (they are not assessed in *Western XXI*). They receive small budget allocations overseen by a faculty liaison and a designated librarian. The degree programs assessed by *Western XXI* are the preponderant focus here. Thus, the collecting intensity level for the M.A. in Education degree programs in the departments outside of the College of Education and Behavioral Sciences (e.g., the M.A. in Education - History Major or Minor) will not be coded.

COLLEGES
Business Administration
Education and Behavioral Sciences
Arts, Humanities, and Social Sciences (Potter),
     including Area Studies
Sciences, Technology, and Health (Ogden)

ACCOUNTING

Purpose of Degree Programs
To support instruction and research in accounting leading to a major in accounting and the B.S. degree. A newly approved Professional Accountancy master's degree program will enable students to take C.P.A. examinations under new guidelines now being established. The Council on Higher Education approved the program in April, 1992.

Collecting Parameters
Language: Code level E (English predominates).
Date of Publication: emphasis on current publications and historical development of both theory and pronouncements.
Chronological Coverage: primarily current; also historical development of theory and pronouncements.
Geographic Coverage: primarily United States; also some other industrialized nations and regions. Increased emphasis on international areas (A.A.C.S.B.).
Formats Preferred: monographs and journals. Loose-leaf AICPA and FASB pronouncements and tax services are important resources. Course proposal bibliographies have been developed for Master of Professional Accountancy program.
Standard Exclusions.

Western XXI Status of Programs
Accounting, B.S.:   Prominent
Master of Professional Accountancy: Prominent (tentative)

Collecting Levels for Programs Emphasized: all 3b except as noted
Accounting
    History and General Works
    Auditing
    Public Accounting (treat as 4 for federal and Kentucky information sources)
    Taxation
    Systems and Computers
    Cost and Managerial Accounting
    Governmental Pronouncements

ECONOMICS

Purpose of Degree Programs
To support instruction and research in Economics leading to a major in business economics and the B.S. or a major in Economics and the A.B. The M.A. with a major in Economics and the M.A. with a major in Education are also offered.

Collecting Parameters
Language: Code level E (English predominates).
Date of Publication: emphasis on current publications.
Chronological Coverage: items relevant to economic history and theory, up to and including current topics in economics are needed, but primary emphasis upon contemporary analyses.
Geographic Coverage: primarily United States; also European and Latin American materials. United Nations level data also needed.
Formats Preferred: monographs and journals. Government documents are vital as well.
Standard Exclusions.

Western XXI Status of Programs
Economics, A.B.:   Prominent
Business Economics, B.S.:   Prominent
Economics, M.A.:   Essential

Collecting Levels for Programs Emphasized: all 3b
Economics
General Economics: Principles and Theory
Economic History and Thought
Statistics and Quantitative Economics
Monetary and Fiscal Theory and Policy
Economics of Industry and Labor
Economics Development and Fluctuations
International Economics
Aging/Geriatrics
Law and Economics
Nonprofit Transfer Pricing
Sports Economics

FINANCE AND MANAGEMENT INFORMATION SYSTEMS

Purpose of Degree Programs
To support undergraduate instruction and research in Finance and Management Information Systems leading to a major in finance-financial management, a major in finance-financial planning, or a major in Computer Information Systems. (Minors offered in latter two areas.) Also to support the A.A. in Banking, the A.A. in Information Systems, and the A.A. in Real Estate.

Collecting Parameters
Language: Code level E (English predominates).
Date of Publication: emphasis on current publications, specifically on financial planning, financial management, and computer information systems.
Chronological Coverage: primarily current and last ten years' historical coverage, especially financial management.
Geographic Coverage: primarily United States, but some general international scope.
Formats Preferred: monographs and journals.
Standard Exclusions.

Western XXI Status of Programs
Finance-Financial Management, B.S.:   Essential
Finance-Financial Planning, B.S.:   Essential
Computer Information Systems, B.S.:   Essential
Finance, B.S.:   Essential

Collecting Levels for Programs Emphasized
Finance
Financial Management	3a
Financial Planning	3a
Computer Information Systems	3a
Real Estate	2b
Banking	2b

NOTE: The name of this department was changed in 1992 to Computer Information Systems.

MANAGEMENT

Purpose of Degree Programs
To support instruction and research in Management leading to a major in management, a major in general management, a major in human resources/personnel management, or a major in production/operations management and the B.S. degree. Also to support the A.A. degree in Small Business Management and the A.A. degree in Office Systems/Technologies.

Collecting Parameters
Language: Code level E (English predominates).
Date of Publication: emphasis on current publications, specifically in human resources/ personnel management/law.
Chronological Coverage: primarily current; also business history, such as the development of the labor movement and corporate managerial theories.
Geographic Coverage: primarily United States; also some other industrialized nations and regions and less developed countries.
Formats Preferred: monographs and journals. Publications from professional societies and Commerce Clearing House personnel administration/law loose-leaf publications. Bureau of National Affairs publications also valued.
Standard Exclusions.

Western XXI Status of Programs
Management, B.S.:   Essential
General Management, B.S.:   Essential
Human Resources/Personnel Management, B.S.:   Essential
Production/Operations Management, B.S.:   Nonessential

Collecting Levels for Programs Emphasized
Management

General Management	3a
Human Resources/Personnel Management	3a
Production/Operations Management	2b
International Business	3a
Legal Environment of Business	3a
Small Business Management	2b
Office Systems/Technologies	2b

MARKETING

Purpose of Degree Programs
To support instruction and research in Marketing leading to a major in Marketing or a minor in Marketing and the B.S. degree. Also to support the A.A. degree in Retailing. See W.K.U. catalogs.

Collecting Parameters
Language: Code level E (English predominates).
Date of Publication: emphasis on current publications, specifically international marketing, retail management, service industries, consumer behavior, sales and sales management.

Chronological Coverage: primarily current.
Geographic Coverage: primarily United States; also Europe and other United Nations regions for materials relating to statistics, policies, historical information, trade, etc.
Formats Preferred: monographs and journals. Relevant Government Documents needed.
Standard Exclusions.

Western XXI Status of Programs
Marketing, B.S.: Essential

Collecting Levels for Programs Emphasized
Marketing

Marketing	3a
Retailing	2b
International Marketing	3a
Services Industries	3a
Consumer Behavior	3a
Sales and Sales Management	3a

EDUCATIONAL LEADERSHIP

Purpose of Degree Programs
To offer graduate programs to prepare school personnel for effective leadership in the elementary and secondary schools and in student personnel services in Higher Education. Offers two programs in counseling and in schools administration and one in student personnel services. All lead towards appropriate certification (M.A. in Education and Specialist Degrees).

Collecting Parameters
Language: Code level E (English predominates).
Date of Publication: current in-print publications; selective retrospective.
Chronological Coverage: current developments are of primary concern.
Geographic Coverage: international. Particularly U.S.A., Great Britain, Canada, Australia, however.
Formats Preferred: monographs and journals; audiovisuals, microforms and software where appropriate.
Standard Exclusions; also, no 16 mm films.

Western XXI Status of Programs
Graduate
Prominent for School Administration (M.A. in Education and Specialist Degrees)
Essential for School Counseling (M.A. in Education and Specialist Degrees)
Desirable for Student Affairs in Higher Education (M.A. in Education)
Desirable for Mental Health Counseling (M.A. in Education)

NOTE: Non-degree programs are not rated as such (e.g., Rank I and certification). Library resources for students enrolled in a joint Doctoral program with the University of Kentucky would expect to draw primarily upon the resources of its libraries.

Collecting Levels for Programs Emphasized: all 3b except
(School) Counseling Education   4
School Administration   4

HOME ECONOMICS AND FAMILY LIVING

Purpose of Degree Programs
To support instruction and research in Home Economics and Family Living leading to
B.S. degrees with majors in: Interior Design; Textiles and Clothing; Institutional
Administration; Dietetics; Home Economics Education; Comprehensive Interior
Design; and Comprehensive Textiles and Clothing. Minors are also offered in these
areas: Interior Design, Textiles and Clothing, General Home Economics, and in Child
Development and Family Living. Also, the M.A. in Education (Home Economics
Education major and minor).

Collecting Parameters
Language: Code level E (English predominates).
Date of Publication: emphasis on current publications in all subdisciplines; occa-
    sional purchase of retrospective works not now held or needing replacement.
Chronological Coverage: institutional administration: most recent applications; Inte-
    rior Design and Textiles and Clothing: ancient times to the present; Dietetics and
    Home Economics Education: most recent developments and applications.
Geographic Coverage: worldwide.
Formats Preferred: monographs, serials. All types of treatments (theory, history,
    surveys, popular applications) desired.
Standard Exclusions.

Western XXI Status of Programs
Interior Design (B.S.):   Desirable
Textiles & Clothing (B.S.):   Desirable
Institutional Administration (B.S.):   Desirable
Dietetics (B.S.):   Desirable
Home Economics Education (B.S., M.A. in Education):   Desirable

Collecting Levels for Programs Emphasized: all 3a except:
Home Economics Education   3b

MILITARY SCIENCE

Purpose of Degree Programs
To prepare well-educated students with leadership potential to serve as officers in the
Army of the U.S., the Army Reserve and the Army National Guard. Selected enlisted
personnel of the ANG and AR may enroll in the advanced ROTC program. A minor
in Military Science is offered.

Collecting Parameters
Language: Code level E (English predominates).
Date of Publication: current in-print publications; selective retrospective.
Chronological Coverage: current developments.
Geographic Coverage: U.S. primarily, but worldwide in deployment.

Formats Preferred: monographs and journals. Also, Department of Defense publications.
Standard Exclusions.

Western XXI Status of Programs
Not applicable: primarily funded by U.S. Government.

Collecting Levels for Programs Emphasized: all 2b except
Military Leadership (advanced phase)   3a

PHYSICAL EDUCATION

Purpose of Degree Programs
To provide opportunities for technical study in athletic coaching, training and management of PE and recreational programs leading to B.S. degrees. At the Graduate level - to provide students of PE the opportunity to qualify for continuing certification (M.S. and M.A. in Education degree). Recreation - prepares professional recreational practitioners in a wide range of recreational and leisure services which lead to the M.S. degree and to doctoral study.

Collecting Parameters
Language: Code level E (English predominates).
Date of Publication: current and in-print publications.
Chronological Coverage: currency important.
Geographic Coverage: international, but particularly the United States, Great Britain, and Canada.
Formats Preferred: primarily monographs and journals; audiovisuals and software where appropriate.
Standard Exclusions; no 16 mm films; occasional purchase of physical education theses and dissertations in microfiche.

Western XXI Status of Programs
Undergraduate
    Physical Education (B.S.):   Essential
    Recreation (B.S.):   Desirable
Graduate
    Physical Education (M.S., M.A. in Education):   Desirable
    Recreation (M.S.):   Desirable

Collecting Levels for Programs Emphasized: all 3b

PSYCHOLOGY

Purpose of Degree Programs
To offer courses, programs and research opportunities which contribute to the professional and pre-professional training of psychology students, offering the A.B. degree in psychology as well as minors in gerontology and psychology. Graduate degree programs leading to a master of arts degree are offered in general psychology, industrial, experimental, clinical, and school psychology.

Collecting Parameters
Language: Code level E (English predominates).
Date of Publication: current in-print materials; retrospective works occasionally.
Chronological Coverage: current developments and historical treatments.
Geographic Coverage: United States a primary research site. Selected cross-cultural
   interests need representation too.
Formats Preferred: monographs; serials; proceedings; audiovisuals, microforms and
   software where appropriate. Historical, biographical, critical, and analytical
   materials.
Standard Exclusions.

Western XXI Status of Programs
Baccalaureate Degree (A.B.):   Prominent
Master of Arts Degree (M.A.):   Prominent

Collecting Levels for Programs Emphasized
Psychology, General   4
Clinical Psychology   4
Industrial-Organizational Psychology   4
School Psychology   4
Experimental Psychology   4
Gerontology   3b
Developmental Psychology   3b
Abnormal/Personality Psychology   3b

TEACHER EDUCATION

Purpose of Degree Programs
Undergraduate programs lead toward B.S. degrees certification in a variety of subject
majors and minors. All programs meet the standards of the Kentucky Department of
Education, SACS and NCATE. Graduate programs lead to Standard Elementary,
Middle School, Secondary, and Exceptional Child Teacher Certification; also to Rank
I and/or the Specialist degree. Rank II leads to Rank I.

Collecting Parameters
Language: Code level E (English predominates).
Date of Publication: current and in-print publications.
Chronological Coverage: current developments and historical treatments.
Geographic Coverage: international. Primarily U.S.A., Great Britain, Canada,
   Australia, however.
Formats Preferred: monographs and journals; audiovisuals, microforms and micro-
   computer software where appropriate. Research Studies, Proceedings, and a wide
   array of nonprint and other materials appropriate in a Resources Center for
   Teacher Education.
Standard Exclusions; also exclude 16mm film.

Western XXI Status of Programs
Undergraduate
Elementary Education, Middle Grades Education, Secondary Education programs
(B.S.):   Prominent
Exceptional Child Education (B.S.):   Essential
Communication Disorders (B.S.), Library Media Education (A.B.), Business Education (B.S.), and Vocational/Tech. Education: Desirable
Graduate
Elementary Education (M.A. in Education and Specialist):   Prominent
Exceptional Child Education (M.A. in Education) and Secondary Education (M.A. in Education and Specialist):   Essential
Communication Disorders (M.S.) and Library Science (M.S.):   Desirable

Collecting Levels for Programs Emphasized: all 4 except
Exceptional Child Education	3b
Communication Disorders	3b
Library Media Education	3b
Middle Schools Education	3b
Business Education	3a
Vocational/Tech. Education	3a

ART

Purpose of Degree Programs
Major undergraduate programs prepare students for careers in art and art-related professions with an emphasis on studio art. Art education programs at the bachelor's and master's levels prepare art teachers for public school systems.

Collecting Parameters
Language: Code level E (English predominates).
Date of Publication: current and in-print publications as well as retrospective materials (when available), are essential.
Chronological Coverage: prehistory to the present.
Geographic Coverage: major emphasis on Western art; minor emphasis on world art.
Formats Preferred: primarily monographs and journals; occasional audio-visuals as appropriate.
Standard Exclusions; exhibition catalogs are collected; realia is not collected. Architecture materials sought only minimally.

Western XXI Status of Programs
All baccalaureate programs (B.F.A.; B.F.A. in Graphic Design; A.B. in Studio Art; Minor in Art; Minor in Art History) are Essential. The Art major or minor offered in conjunction with the Master of Arts in Education degree is not assessed.

Collecting Levels for Programs Emphasized
History and criticism	3a
Graphic design	3a
Studio Art	3a

COMMUNICATION AND BROADCASTING

Purpose of Degree Programs
Undergraduate programs prepare students for various careers: secondary education, employment in various mass media fields, and in communication units within organizations. Graduate programs are concentrated in several areas, including communication theory and research, organizational communication, rhetoric and public address, and speech education.

Collecting Parameters
Language: Code level E (English predominates).
Date of Publication: primarily current, in-print materials.
Chronological Coverage: major emphasis on current materials, while including some historical materials.
Geographic Coverage: major emphasis on North America.
Formats Preferred: monographs and journals; audio and video materials as appropriate.
Standard Exclusions.

Western XXI Status of Programs
All programs (A.B. in Corporate and Organizational Communication; A.B. in Mass Communication; A.B. in Broadcasting; A.B. in Speech; A.B. in Speech and Theatre; M.A. in Communication) are Essential.

Collecting Levels for Programs Emphasized
Corporate and organizational communication	3b
Mass communication and broadcasting	3b
Speech	3b
Rhetoric and public address	3b
Communication theory	3b
Film studies	3a

ENGLISH

Purpose of Degree Programs
In addition to the study of American, English, and world literature, English programs emphasize analysis, close reading, research, and writing, thus preparing students for graduate study and/or employment in a variety of fields. The graduate programs prepare students for school and junior college teaching or doctoral study in English.

Collecting Parameters
Language: Code level E (English predominates).
Date of Publication: current and in-print materials as well as retrospective material, when available.
Chronological Coverage: approximately 500 B.C. to the present.
Geographic Coverage: while the primary emphasis is on English language literature, world literature is also treated in theory courses.

Formats Preferred: monographs and journals; audio and video when appropriate. Individual texts, some anthologies, biographical and critical materials relating to literature as well as materials relating to the study of writing and linguistics are collected.
Standard Exclusions; textbook-style anthologies are not collected. Rare editions of works not collected.

Western XXI Status of Programs
All programs (A.B. in English, Literature Option; A.B. in English, Writing Option; Major in English and Allied Language Arts; Minor in English; Minor in Writing; M.A. in English) are Essential. The English major or minor and the English and Allied Language Arts major offered with the Master of Arts in Education are not assessed.

Collecting Levels for Programs Emphasized
Literature (including historical, biographical, and critical material)	3b
Linguistics	3b
Writing	3b
TESL	3b
Kentucky Fiction and Poetry	4

GOVERNMENT

Purpose of Degree Programs
To further awareness and understanding of political concepts and processes, and to foster the development of critical and analytical abilities and the creation of a knowledgeable citizen. The Master of Public Administration is designed to provide knowledge and skills appropriate for professional career development in governmental or related organizations.

Collecting Parameters
Language: Code level E (English predominates).
Date of Publication: emphasis on current imprints.
Chronological Coverage: unrestricted.
Geographic Coverage: while primary emphasis is on the United States, the collection should support advanced courses on European, Canadian, British, Asian and Middle Eastern governments and political systems.
Formats Preferred: books, serials, microforms.
Standard Exclusions.

Western XXI Status of Programs
A.B. in Government: Essential
Master of Public Administration: Essential

Collecting Levels for Programs Emphasized
Kentucky Government	4
American Government and Politics	3b
Public Administration and Public Law	3b
Africa	2b

Latin America	3a
Great Britain	3a
Europe	3a
Canada	3a
Asia	3a
Middle East	3a

HISTORY

Purpose of Degree Programs
The undergraduate degree in history is aimed at providing the student with a strong liberal arts background advantageous for any number of career choices. The graduate program is designed to prepare students for the teaching of history on the junior or senior college level; to provide the initial graduate work for those who intend to pursue a doctoral degree; or to enhance the preparation of secondary teachers of history who desire to meet certification requirements. Library materials must support instruction and research in History leading to the A.B., B.S. in Education (History or Social Studies Program), M.A., and M.A. in Education.

Collecting Parameters
Language: Code level E (English predominates). Some foreign language works are acquired.
Date of Publication: current, in-print publications; considerable retrospective purchasing; completing runs of journals; and acquiring backfiles.
Chronological Coverage: ancient times to the present.
Geographic Coverage: major emphasis on Kentucky, Colonial U.S., and Southern U.S. Emphasis on North America, Europe (including Great Britain and Russia), Asia, Far East, Middle East, and Latin America.
Formats Preferred: specialized monographs, journals, selected microforms, and newspapers. Appropriate bibliographic tools, memoirs, government documents, society and association publications are needed.
Standard Exclusions; very selective collecting of undergraduate textbooks, original sources, and manuscript collections, only as finances permit.

Western XXI Status of Programs
History A.B.:   Prominent
History M.A.:   Essential

NOTE: A joint doctorate in History with the University of Kentucky is in place, but is not assessed.

Collecting Levels for Programs Emphasized
United States	3b
Colonial	4
Kentucky	4
Southern	4
North America, except U.S.	3b
Europe	3b
Asia	3a

Far East   3a
Middle East   3a
Latin America   3a

JOURNALISM

Purpose of Degree Programs
The basic commitment of the department's faculty is to educate students in the responsibilities and skills of the professional journalist. The A.B. degree is offered with majors in advertising, print journalism, photojournalism, and public relations. Writing and editing skills are at the heart of the various curricula and each major involves students in the practice of the medium chosen.

Collecting Parameters
Language: Code level E (English predominates).
Date of Publication: current publications of higher priority.
Chronological Coverage: some historical emphasis in journalism and press law, less so in public relations and advertising. Biographies of journalists and photographers have a built-in historical dimension.
Geographic Coverage: primary emphasis upon Anglo-American countries.
Formats Preferred: in photojournalism, volumes of photographer's works are important (minimal text). Limited use of audio- and videocassettes.
Standard Exclusions.

Western XXI Status of Programs
All programs are undergraduate degree programs
Photojournalism: Prominent
Advertising: Essential
Print Journalism: Prominent
Public Relations: Essential

Collecting Levels for Programs Emphasized
Photojournalism   3b
Journalism (print)   3b
Advertising   3a
Public Relations   3a

NOTE: The Journalism Resources Center was established as a reading room for the Department of Journalism. The Center contains newspapers, magazines, books and periodicals of interest to journalism students and faculty. The JRC was moved in 1992 from Helm Library to Gordon Wilson Hall to be more accessible to Departmental operations.

MODERN LANGUAGES AND INTERCULTURAL STUDIES

Purpose of Degree Programs
Degree programs are related by and interest in understanding different cultures through the study of languages and traditional forms of expression in non-English speaking nature and the United States. Degrees offered: Master of Arts in Education: Spanish,

French and German; Master of Arts in Folk Studies, with an option in Historic Preservation. At the A.B. degree level, majors and minors in French, German, and Spanish and minors in Folk Studies and African-American Studies are all offered.

Collecting Parameters

Language: Code level W (Wide selection in applicable languages). Primary material collected should be in the language of origin. Secondary works should be in English, or in the language of the primary work which it discusses. Translations desired only after the primary work has been acquired, with the exception of major internationally known works which are popular in translation. For language teaching, English language texts are preferred.

Date of Publication: materials currently in print regardless of publication date.

Chronological Coverage: all major time periods of literature, including critical works, biographies and literary histories.

Geographic Coverage: all countries in which the various languages taught are spoken.

Formats Preferred: books; serials; some videocassettes and audiocassettes, if appropriate.

Standard Exclusions.

Western XXI Status of Programs

Folk Studies (Master of Arts Degree):   Prominent
Modern Languages (A.B.):   Essential

Collecting Levels for Programs Emphasized

Folk Studies	4
Modern Languages	3a*
Afro-American Studies	3a
*Languages other than those in which we offer minors and majors:	2b

MUSIC

Purpose of Degree Programs

Music programs are intended to prepare professionals and music teachers; the Liberal Arts major is intended for those students who do not choose to emphasize performance. The graduate programs provide instruction for performance and private/college teaching as well as training public school music teachers.

Collecting Parameters

Language: Code level E (English predominates); vocal scores are collected in their original language.

Date of Publication: current and in-print materials; retrospective collecting as materials are available and appropriate.

Chronological Coverage: ancient Greece to the present, although primary emphasis is on 1500 to the present.

Geographic Coverage: Western art music and its history.

Formats Preferred: historical, biographical, critical, and analytical monographs are collected; scores and score/parts sets (i.e. chamber music) for study purposes are collected; compact discs are the preferred format for sound recordings; sound recordings primarily will support classroom instruction.

Standard Exclusions; popular recordings and those for "leisure" listening will be collected only if the budget permits; parts for large ensembles and scores/parts intended only for public performance will not be collected.

Western XXI Status of Programs
All undergraduate programs (A.B. in Performance; A.B. in Music Education; Double Major in Elementary Education and Elementary Music; A.B. in Music (Liberal Arts); B.F.A. in Performing Arts; Minor in Music) are Essential. The two Master of Music programs are Desirable.

Collecting Levels for Programs Emphasized: all 3b
Applied (scores)
Theory, Literature, and History
Music education

PHILOSOPHY AND RELIGION

Purpose of Degree Programs
Through careful reading, critical and constructive thinking, undergraduate students develop skills essential in many areas. The graduate program in Humanities expands students' understanding of the intellectual and cultural developments of world civilization through a synthesis of several humanities disciplines.

Collecting Parameters
Language: Code level E (English predominates), although some French, German, and Greek materials are required for the master's program.
Date of Publication: current and in-print materials; retrospective collecting when appropriate.
Chronological Coverage: beginning of recorded thought to the present.
Geographic Coverage: world-wide coverage.
Formats Preferred: primarily monographs and journals. Primary materials as well as critical, biographical, and historical sources are collected.
Standard Exclusions.

Western XXI Status of Programs
All undergraduate programs (A.B. in Philosophy; A.B. in Religious Studies; A.B. in Philosophy and Religion; Minor in Philosophy; Minor in Religious Studies) are Essential. The Master of Arts in Humanities program administered by the Department is Desirable.

Collecting Levels for Programs Emphasized: all 3b
Logic
History of Philosophy
Ethics
Theory of knowledge
Metaphysics
Religious tradition/history
Religious texts
Religious structures
Religion and modernity

SOCIAL WORK

Purpose of Degree Programs
The B.S. in Social Work is offered (major and minor). The program's purpose is preparation for entry-level professional practice in social work. Special emphases are placed upon diversity and social justice, public sector practice, rural practice, and feminist approaches to social work practice.

Collecting Parameters
Language: Code level E (English predominates).
Date of Publication: current (i.e., in print) publications.
Chronological Coverage: social welfare history is a necessary focus.
Geographic Coverage: primarily United States and Canada. Secondarily, international foci.
Formats Preferred: all formats considered, even computer software.
Standard Exclusions.

Western XXI Status of Programs
B.S. in Social Work: Essential

Collecting Levels for Programs Emphasized: all 3a
Social welfare history, policy, philosophy
Feminist approaches
Public welfare services, especially services for children and the aged
Research in social work practice (especially qualitative methods)
Radical/Marxist/progressive social work
Rural social work
Newer technology applied to human services

SOCIOLOGY AND ANTHROPOLOGY

Purpose of Degree Programs
To support instruction and research in Sociology and in Anthropology leading to minors and the A.B. degrees in Anthropology and in Sociology, respectively; also, the M.A. degree in Sociology and the M.A. in Education (Sociology minor). Preparation for occupations and for further graduate study in the two disciplines are goals of the program.

Collecting parameters
Language: Code level E (English predominates).
Date of Publication: emphasis on current publications in both disciplines; occasional purchase of retrospective works not now held or needing replacement.
Chronological Coverage: in Sociology, emphasis upon developments since World War II. Some analysis of worldwide phenomena in a broader time-frame desirable, especially as affecting current society. In Anthropology, the proper range of treatment is from Prehistory to the present.
Geographic Coverage: in Sociology, worldwide, but with emphasis upon the United States. In Anthropology, worldwide, but with emphasis upon North American Indians and North American Archaeology.

Formats Preferred: monographs, journals. Some increased emphasis upon video-cassettes, slide sets, and films for undergraduate instruction. Standard Exclusions.

Western XXI Status of Programs
Sociology A.B.:   Essential
Sociology M.A.:   Desirable
Anthropology A.B.:   Desirable

Collecting Levels for Programs Emphasized
Sociology
Statistics	3b
Research methods	3b
Theory	3b
Criminology	3b
All other areas	3a

Anthropology
Physical Anthropology	2b
Kentucky Archaeology and Native Americans	3b
All other areas	3a

THEATRE AND DANCE

Purpose of Degree Programs
The undergraduate programs prepare students for professional careers in the entertainment industry, to teach, or to pursue advanced degrees. Master of Arts in Education students may complete a minor in Theatre.

Collecting Parameters
Language: Code level E (English predominates).
Date of Publication: current and in-print materials; retrospective collecting as appropriate.
Chronological Coverage: ancient Greece (ca. 500 B.C.) to the present.
Geographic Coverage: primarily Western, with major emphasis on American and English traditions.
Formats Preferred: monographs and journals; video and audio as appropriate. Plays are collected both singly and in anthologies.
Standard Exclusions.

Western XXI Status of Programs
All undergraduate programs (B.F.A. in Theatre; A.B. in Theatre; B.F.A. in Performing Arts; A.B. in Speech and Theatre; Minor in Dance; Minor in Theatre Drama) are Essential.

Collecting Levels for Programs Emphasized
Theatre (including historical, biographical and critical materials)	3a
Acting	3a

Production   3a
Dance   2b

ASIAN STUDIES

Purpose of Degree Programs
The goals of this program are to introduce the history and cultures of Asian societies; to widen students' perspectives on international issues, particularly the perspective of developing areas. At present, an undergraduate minor is offered.

Collecting Parameters
Language: Code level E (English predominates).
Date of Publication: current, but with retrospective purchases as deemed necessary to obtain "classics" not acquired prior to program's inception.
Chronological Coverage: all historical periods, particularly for China.
Geographic Coverage: area ranges from "Middle East" through South Asia to East Asia. Approximately one-half of the world's residents reside therein.
Formats Preferred: primarily print: monographs and journals.
Standard Exclusions.

Western XXI Status of Programs
Not applicable for minors.

Collecting Levels for Programs Emphasized: 3a

CANADIAN STUDIES

Purpose of Degree Programs
To foster increased knowledge about Canada emphasizing its regions, peoples and cultures. A certificate is offered upon completion of specified courses which must include Canadian history.

Collecting Parameters
Language: Code level F (English and French language publications ordered).
Date of Publication: current in-prints with some retrospective coverage in the area of French Canadian Literature.
Chronological Coverage: 1500 to present.
Geographic Coverage: Canada.
Formats Preferred: books, serials, videocassettes.
Standard Exclusions.

Western XXI Status of Programs
Not listed for minors.

Collecting Levels for Programs Emphasized: 3a

LATIN AMERICAN STUDIES

Purpose of Degree Programs
To foster increased knowledge about Latin America, emphasizing its regions, peoples and cultures. The undergraduate minor includes courses in Anthropology, Economics, Geography, Government, History and Spanish.

Collecting Parameters
Language: Code level F (English and Spanish works obtained).
Date of Publication: emphasis on current imprints.
Chronological Coverage: from 3000 B.C. to present, but with primary concern given to events since 1492 A.D.
Geographic Coverage: all countries of Latin America, Spain and Portugal and Spanish speaking populations in the United States with special emphasis on Ecuador and Belize.
Formats Preferred: books, serials, videocassettes.
Standard Exclusions: no textbooks.

Western XXI Status of Programs
Not listed for minors.

Collecting Levels for Programs Emphasized: 3a

WOMEN'S STUDIES

Purpose of Degree Programs
Women's Studies is an interdisciplinary program that offers courses which examine scholarship about women, their roles in society, and their creative endeavors. This program leads to a minor in Women's Studies.

Collecting Parameters
Language: Code level E (English predominates).
Date of Publication: emphasis on current publications and retrospective works to fill gaps.
Chronological Coverage: all time periods.
Geographic Coverage: worldwide, with emphasis on North America.
Formats Preferred: books and serials primarily.
Standard Exclusions.

Western XXI Status of Programs
Not applicable for minors.

Collecting Levels for Programs Emphasized: 3a

AGRICULTURE

Purpose of Degree Programs
To fill the needs of the student who requires general technical knowledge to engage in farming as well as those who need specific training to pursue agriculturally-oriented careers. The department offers a WIDE variety of programs including agronomy, animal science, agricultural economics, agricultural mechanization, agricultural education, and horticulture.

Collecting Parameters
Language: Code level E (English predominates).
Date of Publication: current with some attention to retrospective imprints if critical omissions are identified, or if new programs are initiated which have not received attention in the past.
Chronological Coverage: current 20th century applications stressed.
Geographic Coverage: domestic with some attention to Latin American and Eastern countries as influenced by graduate student enrollment and needs.
Formats Preferred: mostly hardback books with attention to emerging technology in CD-ROM materials for reference and research. Serials important.
Standard Exclusions.

Western XXI Status of Programs
B.S. in Agriculture: Essential
M.S. in Agriculture: Essential

Collecting Levels for Programs Emphasized

Agronomy	3b
Animal Science/Nutrition	3b
Genetic Improvement of Livestock	3b
Horticulture	3a

ALLIED HEALTH

Purpose of Degree Programs: Dental Hygiene
To prepare dental hygienists for careers in teaching, research, organization and management, and clinical practice in a variety of settings. Curriculum is structured to meet the requirements for accreditation by the Council of Dental Education of the American Dental Association.

Collecting Parameters
Language: Code level E (English predominates).
Date of Publication: current information is emphasized. Most materials added will be more than five years old.
Chronological Coverage: current practice is emphasized.
Geographic Coverage: U.S. materials are emphasized. Canadian, European and other materials may be ordered as needed by faculty members.
Formats Preferred: primarily print format.
Standard exclusions except selected dissertations/theses acquired.

Western XXI Status of Programs
B.S. Degree program: Desirable

Collecting Levels for Programs Emphasized: 3a
Associate of Science in Dental Hygiene
Bachelor of Science in Dental Hygiene

NOTE: The Associate Degree program in Medical Information Systems is not
          assessed here, even though the program receives funds for collection
          development, because it is not assessed in *Western XXI*.

BIOLOGY

Purpose of Degree Programs
To present to the student an organized program that will provide a liberal arts
background in Biology and also serve to direct students toward vocational interests.

Collecting Parameters
Language: Code level E (English predominates).
Date of Publication: current with attention to retrospective acquisition of critical
     resources in emerging fields if added to the curriculum or needed by new faculty
     with diverse research interests.
Chronological Coverage: not applicable.
Geographic Coverage: predominant interest in U.S.
Formats Preferred: hardback books with some computer materials advised; high
     priority on serials and proceedings.
Standard Exclusions.

Western XXI Status of Programs
B.S. in Recombinant Genetics: Prominent
B.S. in Biology: Essential
M.S. in Biology: Essential

Collecting Levels for Programs Emphasized
3b in all areas except a "4" to recombinant genetics (even though it is listed as only a
baccalaureate degree program, students are also getting Masters' with an emphasis in the
cellular/molecular area.) The other major area at the graduate level is "organism/
ecology."

CHEMISTRY

Purpose of Degree Programs
To prepare students for positions in governmental and industrial laboratories as well as
for teaching.

Collecting Parameters
Language: Code level E (English predominates).

Date of Publication: current with attention to addition of older critical materials needed for new course offerings utilizing newer technology.
Chronological Coverage: not applicable.
Geographic Coverage: domestic with some attention to journals from important research centers—Germany, Japan, etc.
Formats Preferred: mostly hardback books with some computer materials; a high percentage of materials needed are serials.
Standard Exclusions.

Western XXI Status of Programs
B.S. in Chemistry: Essential
M.S. in Chemistry (Coal Science program):   Prominent
M.S. in Chemistry: Essential

Collecting Levels for Programs Emphasized
All 3b, except special attention given to coal science option ("4"). Thermodynamics and polymers also deserve special consideration in collection development for Chemistry.

COMPUTER SCIENCE

Purpose of Degree Programs
To present theory and application and to enunciate the role of Computer Science in other scientific fields. The graduate level program is designed to prepare students for careers in computer science.

Collecting Parameters
Language: Code level E (English predominates).
Date of Publication: current.
Chronological Coverage: current applications only.
Geographic Coverage: not applicable.
Formats Preferred: many manuals and other types of documentation required. New software products as well as video tapes considered.
Standard Exclusions.

Western XXI Status of Programs
B.S. in Computer Science: Essential
M.S. in Computer Science: Essential

Collecting Levels for Programs Emphasized: 3b
While some materials on theory must necessarily be collected, the major emphasis is on "nuts and bolts" (how-to) documentation. Information systems, systems programming and algorithms are areas of emphasis in the programs.

ENGINEERING TECHNOLOGY

Purpose of Degree Programs
To prepare students for the application of scientific and technical knowledge and methods as well as skills to perform engineering activities.

Collecting Parameters
Language: Code level E (English predominates).
Date of Publication: current.
Chronological Coverage: current only.
Geographic Coverage: domestic.
Formats Preferred: books; many standards and specifications manuals needed.
Standard Exclusions.

Western XXI Status of Programs
B.S.:   Essential

Collecting Levels for Programs Emphasized: 3a

GEOGRAPHY AND GEOLOGY

Purpose of Degree Programs
To support instruction and research in Geography and Geology leading to minors and B.S. degrees in Geography, Earth Science, and Geology, respectively; to minors in City and Regional Planning, and Environmental Studies; to M.S. degrees in Geography, and City and Regional Planning, and to the M.A. degree in Education with a major or minor in geography. See below for respective program emphases.

Collecting Parameters
Language: Code level E (English predominates).
Date of Publication: emphasis on current publication in both disciplines with occasional retrospective acquisition of works determined to be lacking in the collection or in need of replacement.
Chronological Coverage: no time limitations.
Geographic Coverage: worldwide.
Formats Preferred: journals, monographs, maps, atlases, electronic and non-print.
Standard Exclusions.

Western XXI Status of Programs
City and Regional Planning M.S.:   Desirable
Geography M.S.:   Essential
Geography B.S.:   Essential
Geology B.S.:   Essential
Earth Science B.S.:   Essential

Collecting Levels for Programs Emphasized
Geography
City and Regional Planning	3b
Conservation of Natural Resources	3a
Economic Geography	3a
Education	3b
General Geography	3a
Geography	3b
Geography for Teachers	3a
Geomorphology	3a
Human Geography	3a
Mapping and Cartography	3a
Meteorology and Climatology	3a
Physical Geography	3a

Geology
Geophysics	3a
Hydrology	3a
Earth Science	3a

INDUSTRIAL TECHNOLOGY

Purpose of Degree Programs
To provide graduates with information and skills which will enable them to solve technical, managerial, and production problems in industry.

Collecting Parameters
Language: Code level E (English predominates).
Date of Publication: current.
Chronological Coverage: current only.
Geographic Coverage: domestic.
Formats Preferred: hardback books; some machine readable items to assist CAD-CAM offerings; many how-to (documentation) materials as well as technical manuals.
Standard Exclusions.

Western XXI Status of programs
B.S.:   Essential

Collecting Levels for Programs Emphasized: 3a
An option in occupational safety/health was reinstituted in 1992.

MATHEMATICS

Purpose of Degree Programs
To prepare students to pursue careers as teachers in elementary and secondary education as well as other careers in business and industry. At the master's level, the program is designed to give a thorough understanding of the main areas of pure and applied mathematics.

Collecting Parameters
Language: Code level E (English predominates).
Date of Publication: current.
Chronological Coverage: minimal historical treatment of development of mathematics and of mathematicians.
Geographic Coverage: not applicable.
Formats Preferred: books and serials.
Standard Exclusions.

Western XXI Status of Programs
B.S. in Mathematics: Essential
M.S. in Mathematics: Essential

Collecting Levels for Programs Emphasized: 3b

NURSING

Purpose of Degree Programs
Associate degree: to prepare students for nursing in a structured setting, guided by a professional nurse. Bachelor of science degree: to prepare students to be professional nurses having the knowledge base for graduate study in nursing. Both programs are accredited by the National League for Nursing and prepare students for the examination leading to licensure as a registered nurse.

Collecting Parameters
Language: Code level E (English predominates).
Date of Publication: current information is emphasized; most materials added to the collection will be no more than five years old.
Chronological Coverage: materials relating to famous nurses and nursing history are needed as well as those on current nursing practice.
Geographic Coverage: U.S. materials emphasized. Materials relating to other countries may be acquired as recommended by faculty for comparative and historic purposes.
Formats Preferred: primarily print format
Standard Exclusions.

Western XXI Status of Programs
B.S. in Nursing: Essential

Collecting Levels for Programs Emphasized: 3a

PHYSICS AND ASTRONOMY

Purpose of Degree Programs
To provide scientific framework to support professional interests and goals of graduates.

Collecting Parameters
Language: Code level E (English predominates).
Date of Publication: current.
Chronological Coverage: considerations given to important works interpreting historical development of physical sciences and physicists.
Geographic Coverage: not applicable.
Formats Preferred: books with some attention to star atlases and globes.
Standard Exclusions.

Western XXI Status of Programs
B.S. in Physics: Essential
Graduate
    M.S. degree suspended several years ago. Western XXI suggests (page 23) consideration of reinstatement of M.S.

Collecting Levels for Programs Emphasized: 3a
Astronomy less emphasized than physics.

PUBLIC HEALTH

Purpose of Degree Programs
The Department offers programs of instruction geared to preparing students for careers in community health, health education, and health care administration. Undergraduate majors are offered in these three areas as well as in Allied Health Education. The M.A. in Health Education and the M.S. in Public Health are graduate degree programs designed to meet the needs of a wide range of health professionals.

Collecting Parameters
Language: Code level E (English predominates).
Date of Publication: in-print materials are emphasized. Older materials may be ordered as advised by faculty.
Chronological Coverage: current materials are emphasized, but materials covering earlier time periods may be collected if needed to support faculty and student interests.
Geographic Coverage: emphasis upon United States but with some attention to global issues.
Formats Preferred: primarily print format.
Standard Exclusions.

Western XXI Status of Programs
Bachelor's
    Health Care Administration: Essential
    Community Health: Desirable
    Health Education: Desirable
Graduate
    Health: Essential

Collecting Levels for Programs Emphasized

Health and Health Care Administration	3b
Community Health	3b
Health Education	3a
[Occupational Safety and Health	3a]

[NOTE: Occupational Safety and Health options are described in Industrial Technology.]

Santa Cruz Public Libraries

❀ ❀ ❀ ❀ ❀ ❀ ❀ ❀

Collection
Development Plan 1990–1995

AUGUST, 1990

This collection Development Plan was developed by the management staff of the Santa Cruz City County Library System during 1989 and 1990. Fred Ulrich, and his predecessor as Adult Services Coordinator, Mary Franich Bignell, had principle leadership responsibility for research, drafting, and coordination of the discussion process at all staff levels.

Library Management Staff, 1990

Anne M. Turner, Director of Libraries
Susan Elgin, Public Services Librarian

Gary Decker, Reference Services Coordinator
Janis Schechter, Children's Services Coordinator
Fred Ulrich, Adult Services Coordinator
Margaret Souza, Head, Technical Services

CONTENTS

❊ ❊ ❊ ❊ ❊ ❊ ❊ ❊

1.0 PURPOSE

This document is intended as a framework for collection development throughout the Santa Cruz City-County Library System for the period from 1990 to 1995. It is based on the document A PLAN FOR THE DECADE OF THE 1990's and like that document is expected to be a "living" piece, periodically reviewed and revised as the design of library service in Santa Cruz County evolves.

1.1 The Santa Cruz City-County Library System is governed according to provisions of California law, and on the basis of a Joint Exercise of Powers Agreement between the City of Santa Cruz, a charter city, and the County of Santa Cruz, a political subdivision of the State of California.

The Library System is obligated by California and local law to provide free access to information to all people in the County. It also endeavors to provide equal access to information, without regard to residence or economic status.

Collection development is ultimately a responsibility of the Director of Libraries, within the context of policies adopted by the Library Oversight Committee. The actual day-to-day work of evaluation, selection, and deselection is delegated to the staff of professional librarians.

---

*Editor's Note: Included in Appendix 1 of this book

1.2 The mission of the Santa Cruz City-County Library System is to provide materials and services which help community residents meet their personal, educational, cultural and professional information needs. Special emphasis is placed on meeting the needs of county residents for information about local resources, on stimulating young children's interests in and appreciation for reading and learning, on providing popular reading and other materials, and on providing educational enrichment for elementary and secondary school-aged youngsters.

2.0 SERVICE ROLES: FIVE COMPONENTS OF SERVICE

The Santa Cruz City-County Library System has identified five service roles as appropriate to our library system. Not every role can be filled by every branch facility. Some roles overlap and some library activities apply to more than one role. The roles are a *guide* for determining which services each branch can reasonably deliver. These roles are not presented in priority order.

2.1 Reference and Community Information Library

The library provides timely, accurate, and useful information for community residents to aid in their pursuit of personal and professional interests. The library promotes on-site and telephone reference and information services to assist users in locating information on subjects ranging from practical questions to specialized business-related research. It also supports people pursuing independent programs of learning. The collections emphasize informational materials, and the staff are particularly skilled in using reference tools—both print and electronic. The library maintains a high profile as a source of information about community programs and services.

2.2 Early Childhood Education Services Library

The library encourages an interest in reading and learning in young children through services for children and their families. Parents and other adult caregivers can locate materials on child care, child development, reading readiness, and parenting. The library's collection has a variety of materials and formats for preschoolers and for adults working with young children. The staff are knowledgeable about early childhood development and children's literature.

2.3 Popular Materials Library

The library features current, high-interest materials, both fiction and non-fiction, in a variety of formats for people of all ages. The library actively encourages the use of its collection. A substantial percentage of the collection has been published within the past five years. The staff are knowledgeable about current popular interests and anticipate publishing trends.

2.4. Educational Enrichment for Elementary and Secondary School-Aged Youngsters

Although public libraries cannot duplicate the services for which school media centers are designed, the library does provide supplemental support to students at the elementary and secondary levels. The library offers tours for classes, instructs students on using library tools and assists students in locating information for assignments. The collection contains materials in a variety of formats to support the educational levels specified. The staff are knowledgeable about educational programs in the community and work closely with local educators. The library's goal in providing these services is to enrich the educational resources available to young people and to promote lifelong use of public libraries.

2.5 Community Activities Center

The branch is a central focus point for community activities and services. It works closely with other community organizations to provide a coordinated program of social, cultural and recreational services. The appropriateness of this role for a branch of the Santa Cruz-County Library System depends on its geographic location and the specific needs of its service population.

3.0 LIBRARY SYSTEM STRUCTURE: THE TIER SYSTEM
The Santa Cruz City-County Library System has adopted a Tier System of Library Services which allocates different collection sizes and envisions different service roles according to size and location of branch. The Tier System plan depends on the functioning of an integrated, online automation system for management of, and access to, its collections and other databases.

3.1 TIER I BRANCHES—These branches are smaller neighborhood libraries which have neither the space nor resources to provide complete information service to their communities. Instead, each Tier I Branch fills appropriate service roles from among the choices below. The roles selected for the branch depend on the particular needs of its service population and resources available. Below are listed the Tier 1 branches and their service roles.

Boulder Creek Branch	LaSelva Beach Branch
Felton Branch	Live Oak Branch
Freedom Branch	Scotts Valley
Garfield Park Branch	

Popular Materials Libraries (except Live Oak)

Early Childhood Education Services Libraries

Educational Enrichment Center for Elementary School Youngsters

Community Activities Center (Boulder Creek only)

3.2 TIER II BRANCHES—These are larger facilities with service roles both for the local populations and for an adjacent "regional" population. They have larger materials collections and provide more reference and information services. In addition, they fill the role of Educational Enrichment Centers for *Secondary* School-Aged Youngsters. In 1990, there are two Tier II branches: the **Aptos** and **Branciforte** Branches.

Service roles for Tier IIs

Popular Materials Library

Early Childhood Education Services Library

Educational Enrichment Center for Elementary and Secondary School-Aged Youngsters

Reference and Community Information Library

The PLAN FOR THE DECADE OF THE NINETIES anticipates construction of two more Tier II facilities by 1996:

MidCounty Branch

Scotts Valley Branch (replacing existing Scotts Valley Tier I Branch)

3.3 TIER III BRANCH—The Central Branch is the single Tier III Branch in the library system at this time. In addition to providing all five components of service, it serves as System headquarters for administration, technical services and special projects. It houses additional special collections and reference resources, and provides the most comprehensive reference and information services in the System.

3.4 OUTREACH—The Santa Cruz City-County Library System delivers library materials and services at several sites to people unable to reach one of the branch facilities. These include migrant farm camps and correctional facilities. For purposes of collection development, guidelines for Outreach will be the same as those for Tier I branches.

4.0 RELATIONSHIP TO OTHER LIBRARIES

While its immediate objectives are to fulfill the service roles outlined above, the Santa Cruz City-County Library System also seeks to foster cooperative relationships with other libraries.

4.1 Monterey Bay Area Cooperative Library System (MOBAC)

The Santa Cruz City-County Library System will continue to participate as an active member in MOBAC and relative to the objectives of this document, encourage and support collection development among its members. The Library System will also continue to participate in Interlibrary Loan via MOBAC both as a lender and to acquire, on behalf of our patrons, items which fall outside the collection parameters set forth in this document.

4.2 University and College Libraries

Three institutions of higher learning operate in Santa Cruz County: 1)The University of California at Santa Cruz (UCSC), 2) Cabrillo College (a junior college) and 3) Bethany Bible College. The Santa Cruz City-County Library System does not support the curricula of these local colleges. However, in our attempt to serve the Santa Cruz community, we acquire materials which may prove supplemental to the educational resources available at local colleges. Local college students, as members of the community, are welcome to use the public libraries for educational enrichment as well as for their personal and recreational needs. In addition, public library patrons have access via MOBAC (see 4.1) to the collections of Cabrillo College and UCSC.

4.3 Special Libraries

Santa Cruz County Law Library and various private business libraries serve specialized needs within the community. The Santa Cruz City-County Library System does not duplicate the resources and services offered by special libraries. However, referrals from one library to another are mutually beneficial and are regularly done.

4.4. School Libraries

As mentioned above in the section on Service Roles (2.0) the Santa Cruz City-County Library System offers materials to facilitate educational enrichment for elementary and secondary school students but does not duplicate the materials available through school library/media centers.

5.0 SELECTION OF LIBRARY MATERIALS

Under the authority of the Director of Libraries, the three System Coordinators (Adult, Children's and Reference) have overall responsibility for the selection of library materials. Direct responsibility for selection and deselection are delegated to individual professional librarians. Specific criteria of selection (and deselection) of materials are enumerated below (5.3).

5.1 Staff select materials from general and specialized review media, trade publications, publishers' and booksellers' catalogs and flyers, in response to library users' requests, and from inspection of the material itself when possible.

5.2 Materials are selected and retained on the basis of their content, not their authors' origins, background or views. The Santa Cruz City-County Library System tries to represent all points of view. The System's selection principles follow the American Library Association's "Library Bill of Rights."

5.3 Criteria for Selection of Library Materials

- Level of materials funding
- Library's mission and service roles
- Informational and recreational needs of users, including patron requests which fall within the parameters of the Collection Development Plan.
- Collections in special, academic and school libraries to which patrons have access
- Community needs surveys and assessments
- The authority, accuracy, and accessibility of presentation
- The currency of the information in rapidly changing fields
- Reputation of author, publisher or issuing body
- Importance of item to provide diversity in the collection
- Physical quality of material
- Suitability of format for subject and user's needs
- Inclusion of the work in bibliographies and indexes

5.4 Gifts

Gifts that will enrich the Library's collections are actively sought. Gifts are added to the collection according to the same criteria for selection of purchased materials (5.3). Donations are final and become the property of the Santa Cruz City-County Library System. The Library reserves the right to dispose of unneeded materials and to refuse gifts of materials. Most materials the library is unable to use are given to the Friends of the Santa Cruz Libraries, Inc. for sale or disposal.

In the case of a large collection of material which is to be integrated into the collection:

—The appropriate System Coordinator will work with the donor group.

—Materials which are considered outside the scope of the collection as outlined in this Collection Development Plan may be returned to the donor or given to the Friends of the Santa Cruz Libraries, Inc. per the donor's wishes.

—The Library will consider the request of the donor regarding location or branch of the gift but reserves the right to make the final decision based on the parameters established in this Collection Development Plan.

For more information on policies and procedures relating to gifts and donations, see Donations section in the *Public Services Manual*.

6.0 SCOPE OF ADULT COLLECTION

In the following pages the depth of coverage appropriate for various subjects is established and broken down by branch according to Tier Level. "Depth" is here defined in terms of both quantity of titles acquired (and held) and quality of presentation (introductory or advanced). The format of the material (book, periodical, audio-visual) collected is based on the appropriateness of that format to the subject (within financial constraints).

6.1 A system of 4 levels of depth is employed and each of those levels is defined below.

I. POPULAR LEVEL

    A. PURPOSE—The popular collection is intended to provide an *introductory overview* of a subject.

    B. DEPTH—A popular collection will embrace only a few *general works* on a subject and those will be nonscholarly or popular discussions.

II. BASIC LEVEL

    A. PURPOSE—The basic collection is intended to provide *general coverage and instruction* in a subject with some attention given to recent developments. Only a few titles per subject will be devoted to advanced coverage.

    B. DEPTH—A basic collection will embrace a *representation of the major titles* available on a subject.

III. STUDY LEVEL

    A. PURPOSE—The study collection is intended to meet an *extensive range* of use by public library patrons including general introductions and some advanced works with recency of coverage given a high priority.

    B. DEPTH—A study collection will embrace the more *important and substantive works* available as well as a wide selection of general treatments of the subject (within financial constraints).

IV. COMPREHENSIVE LEVEL

A. PURPOSE—A comprehensive collection is intended to meet the *full range* of use for public library patrons from general introduction to original research; from complete historical coverage to latest developments.

B. DEPTH—A comprehensive collection embraces all works on a subject. An effort will be made to locate and acquire published works currently and retrospectively without regard to cost, format, quality of material, or level of presentation.

Collecting levels apply to subjects as a whole. Categories within more general subjects may be targeted for different levels. For example, technology materials are collected at the basic level but materials on seismic design of buildings are collected at the study level.

6.2 Adult Collection Scope Levels by Subject*

DESCRIPTION	TIER 1 BRANCH	TIER 2 BRANCH	TIER3 BRANCH
Adult Fiction			
Fiction, general	Popular	Basic	Study
Fiction, genre (Mystery, Western, Science Fiction)	Popular	Basic	Study
Adult Nonfiction			
Agriculture/Gardening	Popular	Basic	Study
Anthropology/ Archeology	Popular	Popular	Basic
Computers	Popular	Popular	Basic
Consumer	Popular	Basic	Study
Earth Sciences	Popular	Basic	Study
Ecology/Environment	Popular	Basic	Study
History	Popular	Basic	Study
History, Local	Popular	Basic	Comprehensive

---

*Editor's Note: The Santa Cruz Public Libraries' policy contains complete listings of all subject levels in each of the three tiers. Those given in the box above are selected examples only.

6.3 Special Format Materials

To meet the informational and recreational needs of the general public, the Santa Cruz City/County Library System collects materials in a variety of formats including books, periodicals, newspapers, microform, audiotapes, videotapes, compact discs, pamphlets, and others. The formats are chosen for durability, ease of use, and appropriateness of format to subject area. The library collection includes specialized formats for special clientele (e.g. books on tape for the visually impaired).

The Santa Cruz City-County Library System collects materials in the following formats, some for specialized collections only.

MONOGRAPHS are hard-cover, except for titles published only in soft-cover or copies added for short-term demand. Paperbacks are purchased for browsing collections and to duplicate popular titles, especially in the children's collection. Special bindings are purchased where appropriate (e.g., board books for young children.)

PERIODICALS are purchased for all branches. These cover a wide range of subject areas and interests from current events and consumer publications to specialized journals in the arts, sciences, and business. A large collection of backfiles of periodicals is maintained in system storage at the Central Branch to meet the present and future information needs of the county-wide community. Smaller backfiles are kept in the other branches (depending on size of the branch and regional need). Backfiles are acquired in or converted to microform when they meet the criteria for microform (below).

NEWSPAPERS are collected from Central Coast areas at most branches. In addition, the Central Branch collects newspapers from major cities on the West Coast and several national papers such as the *New York Times* and *Wall Street Journal* for national news and business coverage. Backfiles are acquired in or converted to microform for several newspapers and housed at the Central Branch and selected other branches (depending on size of branch and regional need).

MICROFORM materials are added when one or more of the following apply:

The material is published only in microformat.

Microform costs appreciably less than hard copy.

Microform saves substantial shelving space.

The originals are deteriorating.

VIDEOCASSETTES are collected in ½" VHS format. The selection criteria for purchasing video cassettes derives from the "appropriateness of format to subject" rule articulated at the beginning of the Format statement (6.3). For example, subjects such as sign language, home repair, and gardening are especially collected in video format. Also collected on video are classic and significant feature films and documentaries and other works of literary or local interest.

AUDIOCASSETTES are collected for the Listening Library Collection (books, plays, poems, language tapes, sound effects, etc. on tape) for the adult collection and songs and stories for the children's collection.

COMPACT DISCS are collected as part of the music collection at the Central Branch. Presently, the CD collection encompasses Opera, Blues, Classical, Jazz, Folk Music and Show Tunes.

OTHER NONBOOK FORMATS (pamphlets, sheet music, musical scores, government documents, college catalogs, and telephone books) are collected by specialized sections.

Materials in NEW TECHNOLOGIES are added when they provide additional information or substantial ease of access.

6.4 Subject fields and formats that are excluded are those provided by other libraries or organizations with appropriate missions and roles or via interlibrary loan. Exceptions to the list of excluded items (below) may be made by specialized departments within the library such as Local History/Californiana.

Items excluded are:

Highly technical and specialized research materials.

Rare books.

Text books (except when they provide the best or only treatment of a needed subject).

Any format that will not withstand repeated public use.

Slides, 16mm films, filmstrips, phonodisc.

Art prints, sculpture.

Music on audiocassette for adults.

6.5 Adult Collection Scope Levels by Format

Adult Large Print	Popular	Basic	Basic
Audiocassette	Popular	Basic	Basic
(Listening Library)			
Adult Paperbacks	Basic	Basic	Basic
(browsing collection)			
Adult Periodicals	Popular	Basic	Study
Adult Reference	Popular	Basic	Study
Californiana Video	——	——	Popular
Compact Disc	——	——	Basic
Federal/State	——	——	Basic
Local Documents	Popular	Popular	Study
Periodicals/			
Microfilm, Local	——	——	Comprehensive
Videocassettes	——	——	Basic

Pamphlets—All branches of the Santa Cruz City-County Library System acquire and make available pamphlets on a wide variety of subjects. The purpose of pamphlet files is to supplement the information in books, periodicals, and other media. Therefore, the pattern of collection development for pamphlets in a given subject will, at the Central Branch, follow that for books. However, at the other branches, depth of coverage in high demand subjects (e.g., controversial social issues, country studies, etc.) will take precedence over breadth of subject coverage.

7.0 SCOPE OF CHILDREN'S COLLECTION

Children's materials are collected to serve the needs of young people from infancy through eighth grade. In practice, the upper range of materials purchased from the children's materials budget has been fuzzy because there have been no young adult selection categories. Selection librarians in children's categories for Fiction, Nonfiction, Spanish Language, Reference, and Paperbacks have included Young Adult materials whenever possible.

Four children's librarian positions are responsible for selection of children's materials. As a result, selection categories in children's materials are very broad. Currently, they are:

Picture Books, Readers, Fairy Tales/Folklore
Fiction (grades 3 and up)
Nonfiction

Spanish Language
Reference
Periodicals
Media (includes audiocassettes, cassette/book sets,
    videocassettes)
Paperbacks (includes children's and young adult)

A new category, Young Adult Fiction, will be added in FY'90. The Young Adult Fiction category will include books in both hardback and paperback formats and will address the needs of young people in grades nine through twelve.

7.1 Selection Team—Organization and Procedures

While each individual selection librarian for children's materials is challenged to match available materials with system needs and budget in a particular category, selection choices are made with the support of all children's librarians. Distinct from adult selection procedure, the children's librarians form a selection team which continually refines the framework for selection choices.

Children's librarians meet every other month, exchange order cards, make recommendations, and discuss current demands on the collection. Annual visits to the branches are made—sometimes as a group and sometimes individually. All order cards are submitted to the Children's Coordinator. The team then creates a supportive environment for each selection librarian.

For example, nonfiction is developed according to a rotating plan. A focus for nonfiction is chosen for each fiscal year—this year, for instance, the focus will be science. Approximately 60% of the nonfiction budget is spent on updates, new titles, replacements in the focus area. The remaining 40% of the budget is spent on new titles and updates in the remaining areas of nonfiction. The children's librarians, as a team, select the focus area based on recommendations from the selection librarian for nonfiction materials. Announcement of the focus is made before a children's services staff meeting so that all branch staff responsible for children's services are made aware of the plan.

Each of the other selection categories has a similar plan for each fiscal year. The plan is developed by the selection librarian and presented to the other children's librarians. Once the children's librarians have reached agreement, the plans are outlined at a children's services staff meeting.

7.2 Service Roles in Children's Collection Development

The Santa Cruz Library System has adopted two service roles which are critical to children's service throughout the system. All branches will be an:

1. Early Childhood Library Services Center and an

2. Educational Enrichment Center for Elementary School-Aged Youngsters

Tier II branches will also be Educational Enrichment Centers for *Secondary* School-Aged Youngsters. That being the case, all branches (within space and staff constraints) need strong solid collections appropriate for children from their parents' first request for a counting boardbook to their own eighth-grade need for something explaining the Pythagorean theorem.

7.3 Reading, Age, and Interest Levels

The need to cover a variety of age, interest, and reading levels within subject areas makes the definitions of collection scope levels for children's materials different from those for adult materials. While in adult selection categories, definitions imply certain NUMBERS OF TITLES, in children's selection categories, definitions imply a RANGE of titles within READING, AGE, AND INTEREST LEVELS. What defines whether a range is BASIC for a given subject depends on need. Therefore a Tier I Branch and a Tier II Branch can both have basic collections of picturebooks, even though the Tier II Branch may have more titles—it is the RANGE of titles that is significant.

7.4 Definitions of Children's Collection Scope Levels

POPULAR LEVEL-Quality overview materials on frequently requested subjects. Collection should reflect at least two different reading, age, and interest levels.

BASIC LEVEL-Quality materials providing general coverage and instruction in a subject and as current as possible. Collection should reflect a representation of titles and at least three different reading, age, and interest levels.

STUDY LEVEL-Materials should meet an extensive array of needs for as many reading, interest, and age levels as possible. Materials should be as current as possible and of the highest quality available within each reading, interest, and age level range.

As children soon learn in their own lives, treatment can be fair but not equal. We can easily say we buy everything there is on missions (for the fourth graders) for each branch, but most subjects need to be covered in a variety of age ranges. The dinosaur book that is perfect for the 4-year-old's love affair with triceratops will be of little help to the 6th grader writing a research report. So when we say we want a basic collection on dinosaurs, we mean we want the best there is on dinosaurs for at least three different reading, age, and interest levels. When we say we want a basic collection on the missions or the gold rush, we mean we want a range but most of the materials should be appropriate for fourth graders because those are the materials most in demand.

The permutations of this formula are endless, so this plan, like any other good collection development plan, asks for a leap of faith from its interpreters and the good graces of thoughtful, creative children's librarians.

7.5. Children's Collection Scope Levels by Subject

DESCRIPTION	TIER 1	TIER 2	TIER3
Picturebooks	Basic	Basic	Basic
Readers	Basic	Basic	Basic
Fairytales/Folklore	Popular	Basic	Basic
Fiction (Grades 3 up)	Popular	Basic	Basic
Spanish	Popular (in GP, Free, LO only)	Basic	Basic
General Nonfiction	Basic	Basic	Study
Young Adult Fiction	Popular	Popular	Basic
Children's Californiana	Basic	Basic	Basic

7.6 Children's Special Format Materials

To meet the recreational and informational needs of young people, materials are collected in a variety of formats including books, periodicals, audiotapes, videotapes, and pamphlets. The formats are chosen for durability, ease of use, and appropriateness for subject, reading level, and age.

PERIODICALS are purchased for all branches and reflect a wide range of subject and reading levels. Most periodicals are indexed in CHILDREN'S MAGAZINE GUIDE.

VIDEOCASSETTES are collected in ½" VHS format. Selection is based on appropriateness to subject, age and interest level. Collected on video are significant features created for children's television, as well as high quality transfers of children's books into film. Some classic children's films are also collected.

AUDIOCASSETTES are collected alone and in tandem with books of the same title. Most audiocassettes and book/cassettes are purchased for the preschool - 2nd grade age group to support reading readiness and early reading skills. Material in these formats are collected for older youngsters as availability, demand, and budget allow.

PAMPHLETS are collected aggressively for all branches as they are considered an invaluable support to reference collections. Subjects generally support the interests of school-aged children, grades 3 and up.

7.7 Children's Collection Scope Levels by Format

DESCRIPTION	TIER 1	TIER 2	TIER 3
Large Print	Popular	Popular	Popular
Audiocassettes	Popular	Popular	Basic
Cassette/Book	Popular	Popular	Basic
Videocassettes	Popular	Popular	Basic
	(in BC and SV only)		
Paperbacks	Basic	Basic	Basic
Periodicals	Popular	Basic	Basic
Reference Collections			
Ready Reference	Basic	Basic	Basic
Core Reference	Popular	Basic	Study

8.0 SPECIALIZED COLLECTIONS

8.1 Local History/Californiana

The Library System's Local History/Californiana (LH/C) Collection has two purposes:

1. To meet the information needs of non-scholarly users (students at the secondary and junior college level and interested adult readers) in their investigations of Santa Cruz County, Central Coast Region, and California history.

2. To collect, store, preserve, and make accessible written and other materials in all formats which record and facilitate the study of the history of Santa Cruz County, the Central Coast Region, and California and its people.

The Library System may undertake other local history archival and collection development responsibilities in cooperation with other agencies, but its primary direction in its own programs shall be to fulfill the two objectives stated above.

Principal support for the development and maintenance of the Local History/Californiana Collection is provided by the McCaskill Trust for Local History, a restricted Library System endowment.

Purpose, Depth, Circulation, and Maintenance of the Collection. The focus of the Local History/Californiana Collection is historical and analytical. This means that materials of current usefulness, such as travel guides, bed and breakfast lists, cookbooks, and drought-resistant planting guides, are *not* included. On the other hand, travel accounts/guides of historic interest (more than 40 years old) *are* included.

Analytical or issue-oriented works focused on California may also be of general interest. In these cases, multiple copies, for both the general and the LH/C Collections, are acquired. Works on social issues, ecology, and the environment are examples of this category. Works concerning issues of current local importance (e.g., off shore oil drilling) are located in the Reference Collection, but may be placed in the LH/C Collection at a subsequent date.

Local government documents, of immediate (5 years) concern to the public, are part of the Reference Collection. Before final disposal, they are evaluated for inclusion in the LH/C Collection.

Other documents and series (e.g., high school yearbooks) are retained, cataloged, and shelved in the LH/C Storage Collection. Histories and other works on particular California cities, counties, and regions are acquired and maintained in the following order of priority:

Santa Cruz County
Central Coast Region
Northern California
Southern California

No more than two copies of a single work are assigned to the LH/C Collection. Last copies of an obviously irreplaceable nature (or unlikely to be accessible elsewhere) are noncirculating. Case by case decisions on each item are made, and circulating and noncirculating items interfiled on shelves.

Literary California. Local Authors (e.g., those resident or strongly associated with Santa Cruz County) are maintained as a separate collection (see 8.3 below), and not assigned to the LH/C Collection. However, those of historic but not necessarily current interest, are maintained in the LH/C Collection.

Other fiction, plays, and poetry about California are maintained and collected, with the understanding that current materials are more accessible to the public in their regular places in the collections. Within reason, all works in a single genre of an author are shelved together. Also, duplicate copies for shelving in both collections are acquired when this facilitates public access.

Artistic California (photography, art, music, dance, etc.). "California" materials generally are housed in the regular collection. However, artists of particular historic interest may be designated for the LH/C Collection, if such placement will facilitate public access. Before any item of Local History or California interest is weeded from the regular collections, it is evaluated for inclusion in the LH/C Collection.

Other Subject Areas. Subject areas which are priorities for immediate collection strengthening include:

Ethnic minorities

Agriculture

Water development and water policy

Santa Cruz County business and industry

Politics

History of local and California women

Local History Ephemera (clippings, theatrical programs, scrapbooks, etc.). If it took place in Santa Cruz County, it is collected, cataloged, and preserved. The Reference department maintains a newspaper clipping file for public access, but its contents are transferred to the LH/C Collection when it is no longer immediately useful.

Local Newspapers and Periodicals. To the extent possible, the LH/C Collection provides access to complete backfiles of all newspapers and periodicals published in Santa Cruz County. These collections are part of the Library System's Periodical Collection, and are in microform or hardcopy, depending upon space and preservation potential. The LH/C Collection does not take responsibility for maintaining hardcopies of each newspaper and periodical. The LH/C Collection supports indexing efforts for each historic newspaper.

8.2 GOVERNMENT PUBLICATIONS are collected from federal, state, and local levels. Some government documents are purchased by the library and some are sent gratis.

State Documents—The Santa Cruz City-County Library System is a selective depository for California state documents and therefore receives many documents gratis from the state. As a selective depository the library abides by the conditions set forth by the state regarding the cataloging, public availability, and disposal of these documents.

Federal Documents—are purchased by the library using the same criteria applied to books and other formats.

Local Documents—are collected at the STUDY level. Related documents such as Association of Monterey Bay Area Governments and local private organizations are collected as needed.

8.3 The LOCAL AUTHOR COLLECTION is a collection of books by authors who live or have lived in our community. The collection is partially supported by gifts from the Friends of the Santa Cruz Libraries, Inc. The majority of titles in the collection are duplicate copies of books housed in the appropriate subject classification elsewhere in the Library System. The object of the collection is to *highlight* for the community the literary efforts of local authors.

8.4 The LARGE PRINT COLLECTION is intended to serve the visually impaired in the community. The collection is made possible primarily through the McCaskill Endowment for the Visually Impaired and through designated gifts. The Large Print collection includes both fiction and nonfiction materials for adults and children.

8.5 LISTENING LIBRARY COLLECTION is intended to meet the special needs of the visually impaired in the community. The collection is made possible primarily through the McCaskill Endowment for the Visually Impaired and through designated gifts. The collection includes fiction, plays, sound effects, poems and nonfiction materials. However, the preponderance of the collection is in fiction, which is a reflection both of community interest and the limited availability of general interest nonfiction works on tape. Materials are purchased in both abridged and unabridged editions.

8.6 MUSIC SCORES AND SHEET MUSIC—The Library System owns a substantial collection of music scores and sheet music which constitute a special resource beyond the scope of most public libraries of comparable size. The collection has been built principally by gift and supplemented by a small trust. The following criteria govern acquisitions of scores, sheet music, and other paper music materials:

1. Selection is based on works listed in A *Basic Music Library*, with particular emphasis on jazz, folk, and popular music. The Library System will also collect study materials on classical masters, music theory, and instructional books on piano, guitar, violin, organ, percussion, and woodwind instruments.

2. The Library System will not attempt to acquire a collection of individual parts of orchestral, choral, or opera scores. However, currently held chamber music and other scores with parts are retained to the extent that they are complete.

9.0 COLLECTION MAINTENANCE

Responsibility for collection development in a given subject includes responsibility for maintenance of those same subject areas. Collection maintenance entails making decisions with regard to particular items to replace, add, discard, rebind, or reassign to another branch.

Why would the library discard a book? With the passage of time, subjects that were in high demand cease to be in high demand and it is necessary to make room for new topics and trends. Also, as time passes, some information is superseded by new knowledge and it is important to keep current on the latest information. Then, of course, some books simply wear out and must be discarded (or replaced or rebound).

9.1 Materials are replaced and copies are added consistent with the Collection Development Plan and are usually limited to works that are still in print. Replacements are made based on the following criteria:

A title which is still in demand

A classic work of fiction or nonfiction

The best available work on the subject

Subject need

Copies of titles already in the collection are added:

To respond to patron need or requests

To make copies of material available at more than one branch

In the case of local history, to allow, when appropriate, for circulating, reference and archival copies

9.2 Materials are considered for rebinding if:

The title is out of print but continues to have value for the collection

Due to the nature of the book's original binding, a rebound copy might have a longer shelf life than editions available in print

9.3 System Storage is an area in the Central Branch used for maintaining titles or copies not necessary for public display (or not suitable due to poor physical condition). Collection maintenance guidelines should be applied to evaluate materials for Storage. Assigning works to Storage is advisable under the following criteria but Storage should not be used to avoid the sometimes tough decision to discard.

> Additional copies of titles which continue to be in demand for use as replacements

> Titles which are significant in a subject area but general use does not warrant them absorbing limited open shelf space

9.4 Materials may be discarded from any collection for one or more of the following reasons. (Materials are not discarded simply because they contain unpopular or controversial opinions.)

> Duplicates bought to satisfy initial heavy demand

> Wholly superseded editions

> Worn out or damaged books that are no longer usable and the items can be replaced with other copies or reprints or when the information content is adequately provided by other titles in the collection

> Dated or incorrect information when it is likely to mislead the user (Historical materials with viewpoints currently considered inaccurate or offensive but representative of their time and place are not discarded on that basis alone.)

> An item which has not circulated in a given period of time. The period of time is determined by the size of the collection in which it resides and the subject matter of the item (see 9.7–9.10).

> Item does not meet the suggested average annual circulation for that subject (or format) area (see 9.7–9.10).

9.5 Disposal of Materials:

> If the material to be discarded is substantial or of potential use to another institution, staff may try to locate a library, school or local group interested.

> If the material has been deemed valuable but outside the collection development plan of this System, staff may seek a buyer for the material.

> Generally, discarded materials are given to the Friends of the Santa Cruz Libraries, Inc. for sale.

9.6 The Collection Maintenance guidelines which follow offer three figures for each subject area (at each Tier Level) to aid the selection librarian in making decisions regarding adding, rebinding, storing or discarding materials.

If the item in question fails to meet one of the criteria below, it should be considered a candidate for weeding or discarding. If an item fails to meet 2 of the criteria below, it almost certainly should be weeded (or discarded). If it fails to meet all three, then it must be weeded unless there are demonstrably compelling reasons to not weed.

However, these standards are meant to inform, not to circumscribe, the librarian's professional judgment. The idea is that we should keep the collection turning over so that it will be fresh, relevant, timely, and *useful*.

WHAT THE COLUMNS MEAN

1. The first column indicates subject (or format) area and its collection scope level.

2. The second column indicates the number of years since the book's latest copyright date, an indication of the *age of the material*. Items in each subject should be no older than the figure given.

3. The third column indicates the maximum permissible *years since the item has circulated*. To determine when the last circulation occurred, see the date of last transaction.

4. The fourth column indicates the minimum *average annual circulation* for items in that subject category. Divide the number of circulation's (transactions) by the number of years since the item has been in the collection (see inventory date).

9.7 Collection Maintenance Levels for Adult Subjects*

Fiction
Fiction, General
Tier 1—Popular	max age n/a	circ within 2 yrs	average 7/yr
Tier 2—Basic	max age n/a	circ within 3 yrs	average 5/yr
Tier 3—Study	max age n/a	circ within 5 yrs	average 3/yr

Mysteries
Tier 1—Popular	max age n/a	circ within 2 yrs	average 7/yr
Tier 2—Basic	max age n/a	circ within 3 yrs	average 5/yr
Tier 3—Study	max age n/a	circ within 5 yrs	average 3/yr

*Editor's Note: Reprinted here are selected examples of how Santa Cruz Public Libraries plan for maintenance of their collections by subject. The full policy contains all subjects, ages, and circulations.

Western

Tier 1—Popular	max age n/a	circ within 2 yrs	average 4/yr
Tier 2—Basic	max age n/a	circ within 3 yrs	average 3/yr
Tier 3—Study	max age n/a	circ within 5 yrs	average 2/yr

Science Fiction

Tier 1—Popular	max age n/a	circ within 2 yrs	average 4/yr
Tier 2—Basic	max age n/a	circ within 3 yrs	average 4/yr
Tier 3—Study	max age n/a	circ within 5 yrs	average 2/yr

Nonfiction

Agriculture/Gardening

Tier 1—Popular	max age 5 yrs	circ within 2 yrs	average 6/yr
Tier 2—Basic	max age 5 yrs	circ within 2 yrs	average 5/yr
Tier 3—Study	max age 7 yrs	circ within 3 yrs	average 4/yr

Anthropology/Archeology

Tier 1—Popular	max age 9 yrs	circ within 2 yrs	average 3/yr
Tier 2—Basic	max age 2 yrs	circ within 3 yrs	average 3/yr
Tier 3—Basic	max age 9 yrs	circ within 3 yrs	average 2/yr

Computers

Tier 1—Popular	max age 5 yrs	circ within 1 yr	average 6/yr
Tier 2—Popular	max age 5 yrs	circ within 2 yrs	average 6/yr
Tier 3—Basic	max age 5 yrs	circ within 3 yrs	average 6/yr

Consumer

Tier 1—Popular	max age 5 yrs	circ within 2 yrs	average 7/yr
Tier 2—Basic	max age 5 yrs	circ within 3 yrs	average 5/yr
Tier 3—Study	max age 5 yrs	circ within 5 yrs	average 3/yr

Earth Sciences/Seismic Activity

Tier 1—Popular	max age 15 yrs	circ within 2 yrs	average 6/yr
Tier 2—Basic	max age 15 yrs	circ within 2 yrs	average 6/yr
Tier 3—Study	max age 15 yrs	circ within 3 yrs	average 4/yr

Environmental and Life Sciences

Tier 1—Popular	max age 5 yrs	circ within 2 yrs	average 6/yr
Tier 2—Basic	max age 5 yrs	circ within 2 yrs	average 4/yr
Tier 3—Study	max age 5 yrs	circ within 5 yrs	average 2/yr

History
   Tier 1—Popular   max age 15 yrs circ within 2 yrs average 7/yr
   Tier 2—Basic   max age 15 yrs circ within 3 yrs average 5/yr
   Tier 3—Study   max age 15 yrs circ within 5 yrs average 2/yr

History, Local
   Tier 1—Popular   max age n/a   circ within 2 yrs average 1/yr
   Tier 2—Basic   max age n/a   circ within 3 yrs average 1/yr
   Tier 3—Compre-   max age n/a   n/a   n/a
   hensive

9.8 Maintenance Levels for Special Formats

Adult Large Print
Fiction, general
   Tier 1—Popular   max age n/a   circ within 2 yrs average 5/yr
   Tier 2—Basic   max age n/a   circ within 3 yrs average 4/yr
   Tier 3—Basic   max age n/a   circ within 4 yrs average 3/yr

Fiction, genre
Mystery
   Tier 1—Popular   max age n/a   circ within 2 yrs average 6/yr
   Tier 2—Basic   max age n/a   circ within 3 yrs average 5/yr
   Tier 3—Basic   max age n/a   circ within 4 yrs average 4/yr

Western
   Tier 1—Popular   max age n/a   circ within 2 yrs average 4/yr
   Tier 2—Basic   max age n/a   circ within 3 yrs average 3/yr
   Tier 3—Basic   max age n/a   circ within 4 yrs average 2/yr

Science Fiction
   Tier 1—Popular   max age n/a   circ within 2 yrs average 4/yr
   Tier 2—Basic   max age n/a   circ within 3/yrs average 3/yr
   Tier 3—Basic   max age n/a   circ within 4/yrs average 2/yr

Large Type Nonfiction
   Tier 1—Popular   max age n/a   circ within 2 yrs average 4/yr
   Tier 2—Popular   max age n/a   circ within 3 yrs average 3/yr
   Tier 3—Popular   max age n/a   circ within 4 yrs average 2/yr

Adult Media
Audiocassette (Listening Library Collection)
Fiction, General
   Tier 1—Popular   max age n/a   circ within 1 yr   average 6/yr
   Tier 2—Basic   max age n/a   circ within 2 yrs average 5/yr
   Tier 3—Basic   max age n/a   circ within 3 yrs average 4/yr

Nonfiction   Nonfiction audio cassettes have the same age guidelines as hardcover nonfiction.

Tier 1—Popular   age (above)   circ within 2 yrs   average 4/yr
Tier 2—Popular   age (above)   circ within 3 yrs   average 3/yr
Tier 3—Popular   age (above)   circ within 3 yrs   average 2/yr

Compact Disc   As a new collection, weeding will be primarily based on condition

Videocassette   Feature and children's videos have long term use and would be weeded primarily on condition. Nonfiction videos have the same age/circulation/guidelines as similar subject matter in print material. Average yearly circulation = 7.

Adult Pamphlets/Government Documents   Works in pamphlet format have the same age guidelines as for hardcover nonfiction. Government documents, in addition to the average circulation guidelines, must be considered vis-a-vis the requirements on this Library as a partial State government depository.

9.9 Maintenance Levels for Children's Subject Categories

Picturebooks and Readers—Primarily on condition
Tier 1—Basic   Average yearly circulation—14
Tier 2—Basic   Average yearly circulation—7
Tier 3—Basic   Average yearly circulation—6

Spanish Language Fiction
Tier 1—Popular   Average yearly circulation—2
Tier 2—Basic   Average yearly circulation—3
Tier 3—Basic   Average yearly circulation—5

Spanish Language Nonfiction—Same age guidelines as for adult subjects
Tier 1—Popular   Average yearly circulation—2
Tier 2—Basic   Average yearly circulation—3
Tier 3—Basic   Average yearly circulation—5

9.10 Collection Maintenance for Children's Materials by Format

Large Print Fiction   Weeded only on condition
Audiocassettes   Primarily on condition
Average yearly circulation—7
Videocassettes   Primarily on condition
Average yearly circulation—35
Paperbacks   Primarily on condition
(browsing collection) Average yearly circulation—6

Periodicals   Holdings for a particular title depend on branch
                     needs and available storage
Reference   Materials in reference are kept as long as present
                     or anticipated need exists

10.0 EVALUATION OF STANDARDS

Coordinators of Adult Services, Children's Services and Reference
Services review subject coverage, collection scope levels and format
selection periodically. Needed changes are made, within the guidelines
provided by the Library's mission statement and collection development
objectives.

The following statistical measure outlined in A PLAN FOR THE
DECADE OF THE 1990's will be used to assess the effectiveness of the
System's collections in meeting the needs of the service population.

Use Rate, calculated by dividing the number of automated circulation transactions by the number of average circulating items in the
collection. The overall collection Use Rate has been set at 5.

Circulation Per Capita, measuring the number of items circulated to
every person in the service area. The standard has been set at 7.5
circulations per capita.

Circulation Per Registered Borrower, measuring the number of items
circulated to registered borrowers. The standard has been set at 15
circulations per borrower.

In-Library Materials Use Per Capita, measuring the number of items
used in all branches but not checked out. Standard will be set based
on sample data collected.

Use Rate By Registered Borrowers: The percentage of registered
borrowers who use their cards during a year should be at least 20%.

Based on this statistical information and any changes in the composition
of the service population, Staff will recommend to the Director of
Libraries revisions to this Plan.

The Collection Development Plan should be reviewed by the Library
Oversight Committee no less than once every five years.

11.0 LIBRARY BILL OF RIGHTS [Not reprinted. See Appendix 1 of this book.]

12.0 BIBLIOGRAPHY

American Library Association. Collection Development Committee. *Guidelines for
   Collection Development*. Chicago: American Library Association, 1979.

Bob, Murray C. "The Case for Quality Book Selection." *Library Journal*, September 15, 1982, pp. 1707–177.

California State Library. *Collection Development Policy*. April, 1989.

Carpenter, Eric. "Collection Development Policies Based on Approval Plans." *Library Acquisitions: Practice & Theory*, Vol. 13, pp. 39–43.

Enoch Pratt Free Library. *How Baltimore Chooses: Collection Development Policies of the Enoch Pratt Free Library*. Baltimore: Enoch Pratt Free Library, 1983.

Evans, G. Edward. *Developing Library Collections*. Libraries Unlimited, Inc., 1979.

Fujimoto, Jan Dee. "Representing a Document's Viewpoint in Library Collections: A Theme of Obligation and Resistance." *Library Resources & Technical Services*, January 1990, pp. 12–23.

Granni, Chandler B. "1988: The Year in Summary: Title Output and Prices." *Publishers Weekly*, March 7, 1989, pp. 36–39.

Hennepin County Library. Collection and Special Services Division. Materials Selection Section. *Collection Maintenance Manual*. Hennepin County Library, 1988.

Output Measures for Public Libraries. Revised edition. Chicago: American Library Association, 1987.

Palo Alto City Library. *Collection Management Policy*. Revised 9/7/88.

Planning and Role Setting for Public Libraries. Chicago: American Library Association, 1987.

Rawlinson, Nora. "Give 'em What They Want." *Library Journal*, November 15, 1981, pp. 2188–2190

Segal, Joseph P. *Evaluating and Weeding Collections in Small and Medium-Sized Libraries: The Crew Method*. Chicago: American Library Association, 1980.

Selsky, Deborah. "Demographic Trends Have Mixed Impact on Book Buying and Reading Habits." *Library Journal*, December 1989, p. 40.

Soltesz, David. "Automated Systems Data in the Service of Collection Development: A Public Library Experience." *Library Administration & Management*, Fall 1989, pp. 209–212

Webb, T.D. "A Hierarchy of Public Library User Types." *Library Journal*, September 15, 1986, pp. 47–50.

Wise, Leona L. "RTSD/RS Gifts and Exchange Discussion Group." *Library Acquisitions: Practice & Theory*, Vol. 12, pp. 419–421.

Worcester Public Library

✻ ✻ ✻ ✻ ✻ ✻ ✻ ✻

Collection Management Plan

CONTENTS

Purpose

Function, Mission and Roles

Principles

Selection, Responsibility and Criteria

Addition or Reconsideration of Library Materials

Collection Development Objectives

Nonfiction

Fiction

Special Collections
　　Dr. Green Collection
　　Grants Resource Center
　　Nonprint Materials
　　Periodicals and Newspapers
　　Rare and Valuable Materials
　　Reference Collection
　　Talking Books Library
　　U.S. Government Documents
　　The Worcester Collection

Collections for Specific Clientele
    Adult Beginning Readers
    Children's Collection
    Foreign Languages
    Young Adult Materials

Weeding and Discarding of Library Materials

Appendices
    Library Bill of Rights and Interpretations*
    Online Information Services Policy
    Reconsideration of Library Materials Form**
    Request for Addition of Materials Form**
    Gifts Policy**

PURPOSE

It is the intent of this document to provide for public understanding of the purpose and nature of the library's collection and to give guidance and direction to library staff for collection development and maintenance.

FUNCTION, MISSION AND ROLES

Function—By City Ordinance, it is the function of the Public Library to provide library services to the citizens of Worcester. And, by contract with the Commonwealth, it provides certain library services to seventy city and town libraries in Central Massachusetts including Worcester.

Mission—The Worcester Public Library provides books and materials, services and facilities for information, individual development and recreation to the residents of Worcester and Central Massachusetts. The Library offers a forum for ideas and is dedicated to freedom of access for all.

Roles—In carrying out this function and mission, the Worcester Public Library developed two major roles. One is to act as an *information and reference center* at the Main Library where the public has access to an in-depth collection of up-to-date and accurate information supplemented by the resources of other libraries through an automated, telecommunication network supported by an

---

*See Appendixes 1, 3, 5, and 6 of this book.
**Not reprinted.

interlibrary delivery system. In addition, Worcester's branch libraries act as neighborhood information centers holding basic reference materials with back-up and extended resources on call from the Main Library.

The other role is to act as a *popular library* where local residents would have convenient access to collections of current and high demand materials through branch libraries, mobile delivery vans and the Main Library.

PRINCIPLES

Certain principles shape the nature and use of the collection. These include:

The principle that the collection contains original, critical and unorthodox ideas necessary for the functioning of a democratic society and therefore public opinion is not the sole guide for the selection of material. It is the library's position that society is at a greater risk through the suppression or censorship of information and ideas than from their free and open distribution.

The principle of free and open use for all. Individual choice is paramount and protected. Materials are arranged in a way to facilitate access to the information. They are not marked or identified to show approval or disapproval of contents. No restriction is placed on their use except for the purposes of protecting them from injury or theft.

The principle that the collection covers the interests and views of all ages. Selection of materials for adults is not restricted by the possibility that children or adolescents may obtain materials some consider inappropriate. The Worcester Public Library supports the American Library Association's Library Bill of Rights, which reaffirms these principles.

SELECTION, RESPONSIBILITY AND CRITERIA

Selection—Selection refers to the decision to retain as well as to add to the collection. It is based upon awareness of the diverse needs and interests of the individuals in this community, balanced against evaluation of material and knowledge of the collection's strengths and weaknesses. The selection process is also shaped by budget, space considerations, and the accessibility of alternative information sources, such as the Central/Western Massachusetts Automated Resource Sharing (C/W MARS) network in which the Worcester Public Library is a participant.

Responsibility—The Board of Library Directors has the legal authority to establish and amend policy. The Head Librarian and staff research, prepare and present draft policies to an appropriate committee of the Board for discussion, revision and recommendation to the full Board for adoption.

Procedures are developed and presented by staff to the Head Librarian for review, revision and authorization.

Collection management under this policy is administered by the Head Librarian and implemented by the librarians working in the Main Library, branch libraries, and outreach services. Suggestions and advice from the general public are welcomed.

Criteria—Materials are measured by objective guidelines. The entire work, rather than individual parts, is evaluated. It is the overall contribution of the work that is critical for acceptance or rejection. No single criterion can be applied to all materials. All acquisitions, whether purchased or donated (see Policy on Accepting Gifts in appendices), are considered in terms of one or more of the following criteria:

Contemporary significance, permanent value or popular interest

Accuracy and reliability

Public recognition of author, editor, illustrator, filmmaker or source vis à vis media, critics, etc.

Relation to existing collection

Price and availability

Format, durability and ease of use

Scarcity of information in subject area

Worcester author or local references.

ADDITION OR RECONSIDERATION OF LIBRARY MATERIALS

The public has a right to request additions to the collection and to question material now in the collection.

During the process of reconsideration, questioned materials remain in the active collection until an official decision is made.

COLLECTION DEVELOPMENT OBJECTIVES

The collection development plan of the Worcester Public Library centers around three levels of service: the Main Library, the branch libraries, and mobile outreach services. This permits the allocation of resources to meet the broad needs of library users.

The collections of the Main Library are designed to serve the residents of Worcester and Central Massachusetts within its primary roles as a reference library and a popular materials library. These collections can be used by individuals either directly or through the branch libraries, mobile outreach services and interlibrary loan to town libraries. They are intended to provide a generally high level of subject strength supporting the broad scope of user interests.

Branch libraries are smaller facilities with collections ranging from 5000 to 25,000 volumes. Branches fill the need for popular materials for the neighborhoods in which they are located. In addition they often serve as the primary library for people whose opportunities to use other libraries are limited, particularly the youngest and the oldest. The Main Library collections and reference staff supplement the resources of the branches.

Mobile outreach services include the Senior Stop van, Kids' Stop van, nursing homes deposits and deliveries to shut-ins. Collection development focuses on the needs of specific demographic groups, with an emphasis on materials in high demand by these user groups. The collections of the Main Library and the branches serve as resources for individual requests or interests.

Definition of Selection Levels - The following terms are used to define both the extent of the existing collection in given subject fields (collection density) and the extent of current collection activity in the field (collecting intensity):

1. Introductory   The fundamentals of a subject which provide the main theories and referrals to other sources.

2. Basic   Overview of a subject, adequate to meet general demand.

3. Extended   Expanded collection with sufficient depth to allow for independent study and practical applications to cover gaps in other area libraries' collections.

4. Comprehensive   Major source material and a broad range of specialized monographs necessary to sustain in depth study.

NONFICTION

The nonfiction collection emphasizes timely, accurate and useful informational materials to support individual, business, government, and community interests. It also emphasizes materials that are current and high-demand. Materials are available for all ages and reading levels and in a variety of formats.

Materials are selected to represent a continuum of opinions and viewpoints when available. Titles with continued value and those of current, accepted authority are part of the library collection. Text books are included when they are the only source available on a subject, when useful to those doing independent study, or when they give an overview of a subject, but are not added in support of a specific curriculum. As a new field emerges, the library attempts to respond with timely additions.

While most non-fiction materials are selected for their utility, others are acquired for their capacity to enrich and entertain.

When choices exist, selection is based on readability, clarity and appeal. Requests from library users are given high priority.

Subject Fields*

The selection levels listed represent collections at the Main Library. No other location exceeds that level of collection. (The classifications are taken from the 20th edition of Dewey Decimal Classification.)

Generalities

000 - 001.63	Generalities & Knowledge	Introductory
001.64 - 006	Computer Science	Basic
010 - 019	Bibliography	Introductory
020 - 029	Library & Information Sciences	Basic
032	English Language Encyclopedias	Basic
050 - 052	General Serial Publications	Basic
060 - 069	Organizations & Museums	Basic
070	Journalism, Publishing Newspapers	Introductory
071	North American Journalism	Basic
080 - 081	General Collections	Introductory
090 - 099	Manuscripts & Rare Books	Introductory

Philosophy & Related Disciplines

100 - 129	Philosophy, Metaphysics and Epistemology	Basic
130 - 139	Paranormal Phenomena	Basic
140 - 149	Specific Philosophical Viewpoints	Basic
150 - 159	Psychology	Extended
160 - 199	Logic, Ethics, Philosophy by Era & Geography	Basic

---

*Editor's Note: Listed here are some examples of how Worcester Public Library assigns subject collection level. The full list is not included here.

Religion

200 - 209	Religion (Philosophy, Miscellany Study and Teaching)	Introductory
210 - 219	Natural Religion	Introductory
220 - 249	Bible, Christian Theology	Basic
250 - 259	Religious Orders and Parochial Activities	Introductory
260	Christian Social Theology	Introductory
261	Social Theology	Basic
262 - 268	Christian Liturgy and Mission	Introductory
269	Spiritual Renewal	Basic
270 - 279	Christian Church History	Introductory
277	Christian Church in North America	Basic
280 - 281	Christian Denominations and Sects	Introductory
282	Roman Catholic Church	Basic
290 - 299	Other and Comparative Religions	Introductory
296	Judaism	Basic

Social Sciences

301 - 304	Sociology	Basic
305 - 306	Social Groups, Culture and Institutions	Extended

FICTION

The collection in the Main Library focuses on twentieth century literature including classic and standard titles, diverse genres and special interests. An effort is made to maintain a collection of pre-twentieth century fiction and lesser used works of literary or research value at the Main Library. There is no single standard for inclusion in the fiction collection. Each work is evaluated in comparison with other fiction works or authors of similar type. Because of the large volume of fiction published, it is possible to purchase only a representative selection with emphasis on major authors and the most popular examples of a genre. Patron requests for materials of this type influence the addition of more copies.

Genre fiction such as mysteries, romances, horror, thrillers, science fiction and westerns are purchased at an extended level at the Main Library. An effort is made to insure access to a variety of titles on school summer reading lists. Short story collections with emphasis on those in the Short Story Index, first novels receiving favorable reviews or publicity, experimental works, and translations of non-English authors are collected at the basic level.

At the Main Library hard cover copies are preferred to paperback because of durability. However, the paperback fiction collection continues to expand because of public preference and because many titles are available only in this format. Branch libraries select a higher percentage of paperbacks.

Large type fiction is extensively collected.

The fiction collections at branch libraries reflect that which is currently popular with their users. Branches maintain a core collection of the classics and draw upon the collection at the Main Library for titles in less demand.

SPECIAL COLLECTIONS

The Worcester Public Library maintains special collections, the development and management of which differ from the general statements in this Collection Management Plan. The Worcester Collection, the Periodicals Collection, the Grants Resource Center, government documents and the Talking Books Library require additional definitions of purpose, clientele served, user needs and scope of collection.

Dr. Green Collection

The Worcester Public Library was founded in 1859 by Dr. John Green, who gave to the city his own library of 12,000 volumes, "as a library of consultation and reference, but to be used only in the library building." His deed of gift further stipulated that no books, "once added to the department by me, (shall) ever be transferred to any other."

These books are never discarded, but books which have no bibliographic value and are damaged beyond repair may be destroyed.

A percentage of the income from the Green Library Fund is used yearly to acquire materials which have reference value. These may be discarded when they become obsolete or worn-out

Grants Resource Center

The Grants Resource Center, an affiliate of the Foundation Center in New York, provides a collection of materials on grant researching, writing and management to assist people in locating sources of funding for their organizations or groups.

Included in the collection is information on local, regional and national grant funding sources. IRS 990's filed for all foundations in Massachusetts are available for research.

Nonprint Materials

The same principles of access and freedom of expression are applied to non-print materials as they are to print materials.

Art Prints. A small collection of art prints, available for borrowing, is maintained. They are selected based on the following criteria:

The work must have artistic merit.

The work will appeal to the general public.

The quality of the reproduction must be high.

The frame must be sturdy and easy to repair and there should be a protective finish on the print surface. Size must be manageable.

Sound Recordings. Sound recordings are made available in formats that are in demand by users, reflect current technology, and conserve space. To this end, purchases are made primarily in audio cassette, although musical recordings are often purchased on compact disc. LP's are purchased only if there is a demand for the material and it is not available in any other format.

Spoken recordings, e.g. recorded novels, plays, how-to's, etc. are selected to parallel most areas of the general collection. Efforts are made to select on a variety of topics and to appeal to a range of interests. Quality of recording and suitability of the subject for aural interpretation are among the selection criteria. Packaging may also affect selection decisions, particularly for multi-part sets. Necessary purchases are made, however, regardless of how the material is packaged.

Musical recordings are selected to provide examples of the best recordings available in a variety of musical styles (classical, semiclassical, rock, jazz, folk, ethnic, and popular). A representative sampling of the works of major composers from all periods of music history is acquired as are recordings of major performers both instrumental and vocal. Quality of recording and quality of performance as determined by standard review media are important selection criteria.

Videocassettes. Videocassette materials are selected chiefly in VHS format. They are acquired by purchase, gifts or free loans, or duplication rights. The Worcester Public Library makes a concerted effort to purchase a wide variety of video materials to meet the needs of a broad cross section of users. The aim is to acquire time-enduring titles, and selections are made in these areas:

NON-THEATRICAL - General interest non-fiction and short fiction works produced for the education and home video markets including items such as documentaries, how-to, self paced learning and instruction, sports, music, health, etc.

FEATURE - Full-length fiction dramatizations including foreign, classic, award winning, and children's features.

Periodicals and Newspapers

Periodicals are serials that are issued at stated intervals, generally more frequently than annually, and which contain separate articles, stories and other writings. Periodicals are an important source of new ideas and topics before such information is available in book form. In addition they provide recreational, how-to, and consumer information. Indexing is an important factor in selecting periodicals. Worcester Public Library seeks to acquire all periodicals indexed in *Readers Guide to Periodical Literature*. While periodicals are originally used for their current informational value, they become a reference source when indexed. Periodicals represent an on-going commitment in terms of subscription costs, storage, and binding.

At the Main Library, the majority of periodicals are not loaned. In general, single subscriptions of a title are maintained. When a periodical is subject to heavy use, an additional copy may be purchased to provide clean, intact issues for binding. Multiple copies of some library journals are purchased to aid in book selection and to provide the staff with current professional information. Periodicals are purchased in microform: to conserve space; to retain titles that are subject to heavy use, loss or mutilation; to preserve rare, fragile or deteriorating material; to fill gaps when the paper copy is missing. Paper copy is retained for periodicals most frequently used and when the actual copies are of historical interest.

The most frequently selected microform format is microfiche and 35mm. The library has a subscription to the Magazine Collection and the Business Collection, which provide general and business periodicals and 16mm microfilm.

The branch libraries loan periodicals of general and popular interest. Selected titles are retained for one year.

The Children's Room at the Main Library purchases informational, recreational and cultural periodicals for children ages 2 through 12. Formats that appeal to children are sought. These periodicals are loaned.

Some periodicals are purchased in languages other than English. These are selected on the basis of availability, a knowledge of the Worcester area population and general interest. These titles also circulate.

The periodicals collection is reviewed yearly for additions and deletions.

Gifts of magazine subscriptions are common and encouraged.

The newspapers of Worcester and the larger Massachusetts cities are the priority purchases followed by the newspapers of other New England cities. Sunday editions of the major city newspapers in the United States are purchased and retained for two months. Recognized major newspapers from around the world are also acquired. Each branch library subscribes to several newspapers and holds copies for one week only.

The following newspapers are retained in microform:

> *Worcester Telegram & Gazette*
> *Boston Globe*
> *Christian Science Monitor*
> *New York Times*
> *The Wall Street Journal*

The Worcester Public Library staff monitor the effect of online data bases on serials acquisitions.

Rare and Valuable Materials

The acquisition of valuable or rare books is not a function of the Worcester Public Library. An exception is made when an item is of bibliographic importance to a particular area of the collection wherein the library has a special responsibility, e.g., the Worcester Collection. The retention of such items already in the collection is governed by the item's bibliographic importance to the library's collection.

This does not preclude the library's acceptance of gifts that might be valuable or rare. Acceptance, however, is made with the understanding that for inclusion in the collection the item must meet the criterion stated above.

Reference Collection

Reference materials are for use in the library. They provide quick, concise and up-to-date information and index other material in the collection. Inclusion in the Reference Collections is determined by factors such as cost, complexity, format, authoritativeness, frequency of use and indexing. Reference works include such standards as encyclopedias, dictionaries, handbooks, directories, bibliographies, etc., as well as more specialized materials which directly support the various information needs of library users. When demand dictates and cost permits, additional copies are purchased for lending.

Materials in CD-ROM format will be selected based on:

• Demand for information contained on product.

• Ease of use, including instructions for end users.

• Cost efficiency

• Space consideration.

Electronic databases, while not developed as a part of the collection, are an integral part of information services the library provides and, as such, funds are allocated for their use. These databases are most notable for their timeliness and efficiency in locating information. (See Online Information Services Policy in appendices.)

Talking Books Library

The collection of the Talking Book Library includes each title on record or cassette produced annually by the National Library Service for the Blind and Physically Handicapped of the Library of Congress. In addition, the Library acquires master tapes of original recordings made by other National Library Service network libraries, and does limited in-house taping on demand.

U.S. Government Documents

The Worcester Public Library is a selective depository library and, as such, is legally required to make all publications received from the government available to the citizens of this region. As a selective depository the library does not receive everything the U.S. Federal Government publishes. Material is selected based on interest and use to citizens of this area and historical value. Since documents cover the whole spectrum for the collection, the documents librarian consults with other librarians when selecting new items.

Depository libraries which are served by a designated regional depository (Boston Public Library) may dispose of any publications which they have retained for at least five years after obtaining permission and receiving instructions for such disposition from the regional depository. Subject specialists are consulted regarding discards that affect their areas.

In addition to the U.S. Government Publications Monthly Catalog and the Cumulative Subject Index to the Monthly Catalog of the U.S. Government Publications (1900–1971), several commercial indexes support the collection. Access to the Monthly Catalog and other document indexes is also available in several databases.

The following special documents series are maintained:

U.S. Congressional Serial Set.

Hearings, consisting of hearings of Congressional committees.

Laws and Regulations, first issued as slip laws and then bound as the "Statutes at Large."

Congressional Record, the daily verbatim record of the activities of Congress, issued daily and cumulative for each Congress.

Publications of popular or current interest in booklet or pamphlet form are duplicated for the pamphlet collection.

The Worcester Collection

The Local History Collection of the Worcester Public Library

The Worcester Public Library collects local history materials and houses them, with the exception of the news clippings file, in the Worcester Room located on the third floor of the Main Library.

The Library acquires material, in all formats, dealing with the city of Worcester. Material about Worcester County is collected when possible. Most of these materials are privately or commercially published, rather than manuscript or archival.

Examples:
City documents, reports published by the city or for the city by private firms.
Annual reports, histories, catalogs of local businesses and institutions - colleges, companies, churches, hospitals, social service organizations, clubs, etc.
Town and city histories for all of Massachusetts and New England.
Descriptive material on Worcester and Worcester County - geography, directories, guidebooks.
Biographical material about people with a Worcester connection; books by local authors.
Newspapers and other serial publications in hard copy and microform. Periodicals published as in-house items by local businesses and institutions are also sought.
Maps and atlases.
Pamphlet files - largely newspaper clippings dating from 1945 to the present. Since there is no index to the local newspapers, this file is the best way of finding current local information.
Pictures, postcards, photographs.

The materials in the Worcester Collection may only be used within the Library. Permission will be given to photocopy most materials.

Access to the Worcester Room is restricted to times when the Worcester Librarian is available. Passes may be issued to long term researchers after an interview with the Worcester Librarian. At all times, staff will retrieve materials for use in the History Department.

COLLECTIONS FOR SPECIFIC CLIENTELE

While the Worcester Public Library has defined its clients as the residents of Worcester and Central Massachusetts, the general statements in the Collection Management Plan apply to adult readers of English. Children, young adults, people for whom English is a second language and adult beginning readers are important users of the library and have collections tailored to their needs.

Adult Beginning Readers

This collection is designed for adults who are beginning to read, adults for whom English is a second language and Adult Basic Education Students. It also serves those who need a simple introduction to a topic in an adult format. Materials focus on grade six reading level and below in a variety of formats. Subjects include fiction and short stories, sciences and history, consumer and general information. All materials are identified with the international library symbol and are available at every library location.

Children's Collection

Materials in the children's collection are selected in response to the needs and interests of young people, recognizing their diverse tastes, backgrounds, abilities and potentials.

In choosing materials for children, age is a determining selection principle. Materials are evaluated for reading level, interest level and treatment of the subject for the age of the intended audience.

For very young children, sturdy "board" books with bright, clear illustrations are selected. When picture books for pre-schoolers are considered, aesthetics (illustration, format) and developmental significance (language, vocabulary, theme) are evaluated. Books for beginning readers are included. For transitional readers, those reading at grade levels two to four, motivational and appealing material is selected. For children through age twelve, the emphasis is on material for voluntary use for personal satisfaction. Timeliness and accuracy are additional criteria for non-fiction materials. The collection supplements the school media centers. Textbooks are not purchased unless they contain better subject coverage than in other books. Some duplication of adult materials is found when they are appropriate for children and young adults. The resources of the entire library are available to children who wish to go beyond the children's collection.

The core of the reference collection is encyclopedias. The standard encyclopedias for children and young adults are regularly updated. Ready reference tools, bibliographies, indexes, and atlases round out the collection. Materials, including journals, supporting professional development are selected for the branch and children's services staff and are available to any interested library user.

Audio visual materials (phono-recordings, cassettes, videos, filmstrips) are selected based on the same criteria as books.

Magazines are selected for their recreational and informational content and often reflect popular trends. They circulate and no attempt is made to retain back issues.

Paperback books supplement the collection and are often duplicates of hardcover editions. This collection primarily contains fiction for middle readers through young adult and ephemeral material on currently popular topics. Visual appeal is also a consideration in selection.

Large print books and foreign language materials are collected to serve children's special needs and interest and are selected based on community interest and availability.

Information on an adult level pertaining to children's literature and material for adults working with children is provided. A specially designated Parents Collection offers a sample of books, magazines and pamphlets on parenting. Books of historical significance in the development of children's literature are retained for use by students. Often they are housed in the closed stack area because of their condition or value.

Multiple copies of Newbery and Caldecott award books are purchased. One copy of each winning book is placed in the non-circulating collection to be available to students.

A pamphlet collection is maintained which includes ephemeral information on difficult-to-locate subjects, current interests, and often asked for topics.

Learning activity games and toys are purchased to enhance children's motor skills, sensory perception and discrimination. Most are kept for use in the library.

The children's collections in branch libraries are selected with the same criteria. The emphasis is on use by children, with students of children's literature referred to the Main Library. The resources of the Main Library supplement the branch library collections.

Foreign Languages

The library's resources include various materials in foreign languages which mirror the ethnic and racial diversity of Worcester with careful consideration given to population shifts, immigration patterns, and circulation statistics. The collection provides general reading materials for people proficient in a language by birthright or by study.

In selecting materials in foreign languages, an attempt is made to buy representative fiction, biography, drama, etc., including the classics, standard authors, modern writers, books describing cultural traditions, and reference material such as encyclopedias and dictionaries. An attempt is also made to buy translated American classics and translations of books about American culture, literature, and history. Additionally, the library tries to provide books suited to the needs of current immigrants.

Magazines are selected for their news, information, entertainment, and cultural appeal, and also for their diverse viewpoints. A small collection of music and language recordings is also maintained.

The following are Foreign Language Collection levels:*

Albanian	Introductory
Arabic	Introductory
Armenian	Introductory
Chinese	Basic
Czech	Introductory
Danish	NA

Young Adult Materials

The library makes available materials in a variety of formats that are aimed at addressing the needs and concerns of young adult patrons. In general, young adult service is geared to the Junior High and High School age, overlapping

---

*Editor's Note: In all, the full policy mentions 30 foreign languages; only a few examples for each level are given here.

somewhat with children's services at one end of range and those for adults at the other. There are, however, many potential users for this material and this factor is given consideration when developing the collection.

Needs of young adults differ in kind and intensity from those of adult users. These users often look to the library for materials and resources to meet academic demands. Young adult materials are selected from the same criteria used in selection of adult materials but with the focus on the experience, maturity, and interests of young people. Branch libraries also maintain young adult collections, featuring paperbacks and periodicals.

The themes in young adult fiction generally center on the struggle to develop an identity and set of values and to find a place in the larger community. The young adult fiction collection consists of material written for and/or appealing to this particular age group regardless of genre. Every effort is made to provide teenagers with fiction that deals with their concerns in open, honest ways, and which meets their recreational and academic reading needs. Issues are explored in contemporary young adult novels, and science fiction/fantasy, historical fiction, mysteries, and westerns written for teenagers.

Teenagers read non-fiction extensively to gain information on topics of concern to them such as personal appearance, sex education, careers/colleges, crisis and coping information, hobbies, music, school assignments, etc. Young adult non-fiction is selected in all subject areas represented in the adult non-fiction collection. Titles are chosen for their timeliness and appeal. The staff makes every effort to purchase factual books which are clearly-written, and attractive in format.

Foreign language editions of English language fiction classics are purchased with young adults in mind. Students whose first language is other than English may find materials available in their native language to assist them in their school assignments.

Pamphlet materials are purchased primarily to supplement books for home-work related assignments. The pamphlet collection includes topical material on youth problems, health issues, science projects, career and vocational information, job-hunting aids, religious and political parties, Cliff Notes and other information aids.

The general reference, audio-visual, and periodicals collections include material for young adults. The resources of the entire library are available to users in this age group.

WEEDING AND DISCARDING OF LIBRARY MATERIALS

To maintain the vitality of the collection, materials are regularly weeded. This is the process of withdrawing of materials which no longer meet the criteria for inclusion in the Library's collection and is an integral part of collection management.

Factors involved in the decision to weed materials are:

- poor physical condition
- superfluous because of duplicate titles or because demand no longer exists
- obsolete, superceded edition, no longer accurate.

This does not sanction the removal of materials because of controversy.

Disposition of library materials is subject to city requirements. Permission has been given for the Friends of the Library to sell the discarded materials with income to benefit the Library.

APPENDIX: ONLINE INFORMATION SERVICES POLICY AT WPL

1. Library Goals and Objectives

    1.1 Operational Goal—To act as the reference and informational center for the City of Worcester and sixty-nine (69) other municipalities comprising the Central Massachusetts Region.

    1.2 Objective—To provide a concentrated collection of materials and specialized staff at a single location, the Main Library, that would service individual and institutional needs for useful, authoritative information, in an environment where one may investigate subject fields and encounter a broad range of information, ideas and interpretations in variety and in depth.

2. Purpose of Online Information Services
    The Worcester Public Library offers online services as an integral part of public information services to support the continuing effort to provide accurate information or materials in response to user requests in an efficient, courteous, impartial and timely manner. Online services provide access to numerous databases containing bibliographic citations, abstracts, statistical tables, full-test of articles, business directory and

financial data. Online databases can often provide information when the printed resources of the library are insufficient to meet the client's needs in terms of 1) time necessary to search the printed materials, 2) complex subject needs that involve combining terms or concepts in the search for information, 3) currency or 4) availability about the subject in the library.

3.   Policies for Online Services

3.1 Online information services represent a complex, technical adjunct to the basic printed reference resources of the library and are to be used when, in the judgment of the reference librarian, the library's printed resources are insufficient to meet the patron's needs. It is not a service to be provided on demand only.

3.2 Online Services are conducted at two levels and call for distinction in treatment.

(1) *Ready Reference Search* - A ready reference search is that which requires little, if any, interaction with the patron in determining the nature of the inquiry and the search strategy that would best provide the answer. This search may be initiated by an inquiry by telephone, mail, or on-site. It is a *no charge* service.

(2) *Extended Search* - Unlike the ready reference, the extended search requires considerable interaction with the patron in the development of strategies to find the best answer in the most cost effective way. It requires a scheduled interview and extended search time.

(3) *Extended Searches* - place significant demands on library resources in the terms of time, personnel and funding (subscription and telecommunication charges). Consequently, it becomes necessary to identify library responsibilities as to the limits, within which the library can use its finite resources for extended searching while at the same time fulfilling its role in the provision of *free* information services necessary for people to function in a democratic society.

Primary Responsibility - Legal obligations, the nature of the library's collection, the variety of the public, the availability of other informational resources in the community, historic use and budgeted appropriations are factors that shape the library's role and policy.

It has been the library's *primary responsibility* to serve those publics who have limited or no informational resource readily and reasonably available to them and to provide, for *free* use, a broad range of information that would meet their general and expressed needs.

It has *not* been the library's *primary responsibility* to act as a substitute resource for the college student, the corporation and the specialist whose organization or institution makes significant provisions for their informational needs.

(4) Given the foregoing, the library will provide *free extended searches* up to $40 of search time costs, per person, per month for *all publics*. This includes holders of valid library cards from the city and regional libraries. Patrons whose search exceeds $40 must pay the difference. In the case of City personnel acting in an authorized capacity no charges will be levied but a record of those charges will be maintained.

(5) Publics (college students, corporate officials, specialists) who seek searches beyond that given to all publics (see #4) must accept search and retrieval costs and scheduling, as determined by library staff.

(6) Searches will not be routinely made on databases that are commonly available, e.g. airline reservations, ticker tape services, etc., and on databases whose connect fees exceed that of Predicasts or for excessive display charges.

PART 3

•   •   •   •   •   •   •   •   •

Partial Library Policies

INTRODUCTION

❖ ❖ ❖ ❖ ❖ ❖ ❖ ❖

T his section presents excerpts from many other libraries' policies which emphasize points that have been made in the introduction and survey chapters of this book. There is no one perfect model that a library can use to ensure for itself a long-lasting and useful document. Instead, there are many possible permutations and combinations of topics that comprise a working and workable collection development policy. This section is divided into chapters representing the possible parts of a policy statement. Within each part, or chapter, public library statements come first, followed by academic library policy excerpts. The order of the topics presented by the chapters is only one of many that a library may choose to incorporate into the organization of its collection development statement. The introduction to this book and the full policies included in Part 2 show other possible arrangements. Although most policies start out with an introduction of sorts, that introduction may contain items as various as a community description, a review of the document, the purpose of the policy statement, or goals, objectives, and mission. Several of the public libraries start their collection development policies with a reiteration of their roles as public agencies, and the academic libraries often introduce policies with histories of the institutions in which they sit.

New to this volume are short commentaries about the parts of the policies presented. It is best to use these commentaries and the policy excerpts as simple guideposts to possible statements for your library. No library can act as an exact model for any other library, because no library is exactly like any other library. The process of writing this collection development policy is in some ways as important as the policy statement that is written. The process becomes the product, and with that process comes understanding of the roles and expectations of the agency or institution. It is a more valuable lesson to learn than can be gained from reading someone else's policy. Below are listed the 61 libraries that contributed policies to this book. They are different in size, in type, in concept, and in theory. Their only similarity is the generosity they showed in sharing these documents with colleagues.

LIBRARIES WHOSE POLICIES ARE REPRINTED IN PART

Many thanks go to the libraries who sent their policies and especially to those below who allowed them to be published in this volume.

Alvin Community College Library (TX). *Selection of Library Materials*, 3110 Mustang Rd., Alvin, TX 77511

Amarillo Public Library (TX). *A Statement from the Amarillo Library Board Governing Materials Selection Policy of the Amarillo Library*, PO Box 2171, 413 E. Fourth St., Amarillo, TX 79189-2171

Athenaeum of Ohio, Eugene H. Maly Memorial Library (OH). *Collection Development Policy*, 6616 Beechmont Ave., Cincinnati, OH 45230-2091

Barrie Public Library (Ontario, CAN). *Collection Development Policy*, 1992. Author: Elizabeth McKay, 37 Mulcaster St., Barrie, ON (Canada) L4M 3M2

Bay State College Library (MA). *Collection Development Policy*, 122 Commonwealth Ave., Boston, MA 02116

Brooklyn Public Library (NY). *Materials Selection Policy*, Grand Army Plaza, Brooklyn, NY 11238

California State University, Chico, Meriam Library (CA). *Collection Development Policies Handbook*, 400 W. First St., Chico, CA 95929-0295

Clearwater Public Library (FL). *Materials Selection Policy*, 100 N. Osceola Ave., Clearwater, FL 34615-6811

Clinch Valley College of the University of Virginia, John Cook Wyllie Library (VA). *Collection Development Policy*, College Ave., Wise, VA 24293-0016

Coffee County Lannom Memorial Public Library (TN). *Collection Development Policy* 312 N. Collins St., Tullahoma, TN 38388

Colusa County Library (CA). *Materials Selection Policy*, 738 Market St., Colusa, CA 94932

Covenant College, Anna Emma Kresge Memorial Library (GA). *Collection Management Policy*, Lookout Mountain, GA 30750

Doane College, Perkins Library (NE). *Materials Selection Policy*, 1014 Doane Dr., Crete, NE 68333-2495

East Gwillimbury Public Library (Ontario, CAN). *Policy for the Selection of Library Materials*, PO Box 1609, Holland Landing, ON (Canada) L9N 1P2

El Paso Public Library (TX). *Proposed Collection Development Policy*, 501 N. Oregon St., El Paso, TX 79901

Fairfield University, Gustav & Dagmar Nyselius Library (CT). *Collection Management Policy*, N. Benson Rd., Fairfield, CT 06430-7524

Fairview Heights Public Library (IL). *Materials Selection*, 10017 Bunkum Rd., Fairview Heights, IL 62208

Florida State University Library, Robert Manning Strozier Library (FL). *Collection Development Statement*, Tallahassee, FL 32306-2047

Flower Mound Public Library (TX). *Materials Selection Policy*, 2121 Cross Timbers Rd., Flower Mound, TX 75028

Green Mountain College, Griswold Library (VT). *Collection Development Policy*, 16 College St., Poultney, VT 05764

Greenville County Library (SC). *Library Materials Selection Policy*, 300 College St., Greenville, SC 29601

Harnett County Library (NC). *Policies and Procedures of the Harnett County Public Library*, 601 Main St., Lillington, NC 27546

Hartford Public Library (CT). *Materials Selection Policy Statement*, 500 Main St., Hartford, CT 06103-3075

Hawaii Pacific University, Meader Library (HI). *Collection Development Policy*, 1060 Bishop St., Honolulu, HI 96813-3192

Homewood Public Library (AL). Lucretia M. Somers, Director, approved by Board on 4/18/94. *Materials Selection Policy*, 1721 Oxmoor Rd., Homewood, AL 35209-4085

James Madison University, Carrier Library (VA). *Collection Development Policy*, Harrisonburg, VA 22807

Jamestown College, Raugust Library (ND). *Collection Development Policy*, Jamestown, ND 58401

Juneau Public Libraries (AK). *Collection Development Policies*, 292 Marine Way, Juneau, AK 99801

Kalamazoo Public Library (MI). *Materials Selection Policy*, 315 S. Rose, Kalamazoo, MI 49007-5270

Le Moyne College Library (NY). *Disaster Policy for the Library*, Syracuse, NY 13214-1399

Loras College, Wahlert Memorial Library (IA). *Collection Development Statement*, Dubuque, IA 52004-0178

Marigold Library System (Alberta, CAN). *Collection Management Policy*, 710 Second St., Strathmore, AB (Canada) T1P 1K4

Meredith College, Carlyle Campbell Library (NC). *Collection Development Policy*, 3800 Hillsborough St., Raleigh, NC 27607-5298

Michigan Technological University, J. Robert Van Pelt Library (MI). *Collection Policy*, Houghton, MI 49931

Mount Wachusett Community College (MA). *Collection Development Manual*, 444 Green St., Gardner, MA 01440

Naval War College Library (RI). *Selection Policies*, 686 Cushing Rd., Newport, RI 02841-1207

New City Public Library (NY). *Collection Management Policy*, 220 N. Main St., New City, NY 10956

Northern Arizona University, Cline Library (AZ). *Cline Library Collection Development Policy*, PO Box 6022, Flagstaff, AZ 86011-6022

Northwestern State University of Louisiana, Eugene P. Watson Memorial Library (LA). *Collection Development Policy*, College Ave., Natchitoches, LA 71497

Norwalk Community-Technical College, Learning Resources Center (CT). *LRC Acquisitions Policy*, 188 Richards Ave., Norwalk, CT 06854-1655

Oakland Public Library (CA). *Book Selection Policy*, 125 14th St., Oakland, CA 94612

Oakville Public Library (Ontario, CAN). *Materials Selection Policy*, 120 Navy St., Oakville, ON (Canada) L6J 2Z4

Ouachita Parish Public Library (LA). *Collection Development Policies*, 1800 Stubbs Ave., Monroe, LA 71201-5787

Queens College, Everett Library (NC). *Collection Development Policy*, 1900 Selwyn Ave., Charlotte, NC 28274-0001

Queen's University Library (Ontario, CAN). *Collection Development Statement*, Kingston, ON (Canada) K7L 3N6

Ripon College Library (WI). *Acquisitions Policy*, PO Box 248, 300 Seward St., Ripon, WI 54971-1499

Rochester Public Library (MN). *Selection Policies*, 11 First St., SE, Rochester, MN 55904-3777

Rosary College Library, Rebecca Crown Library (IL). *Collection Development Policy*, 7900 W. Division St., River Forest, IL 60305-1066

St. Anthony Public Library (ID). *Collection Development Policy*, 110 W. Main, Saint Anthony, ID 83445-2115

St. Clair County Library System (MI). *Materials Selection Policy*, 210 McMorran Blvd, Port Huron, MI 48060-4098

Southwest Regional Library Service System (CO). *Collection Development Policy*, PO Drawer B, Durango, CO 81302-1090

State University of New York, College of Technology at Farmingdale, Thomas D. Greenley Library (NY). *Collection Development Policy*, Melville Rd., Farmingdale, NY 11735

Tomah Public Library (WI). *Materials Selection Policy*, 716 Superior Ave., Tomah, WI 54660-2098

University of South Carolina–Aiken, Gregg-Graniteville Library (SC). *Library Acquisitions and Selection Policy*, 171 University Pkwy, Aiken, SC 29801

University of Winnipeg Library (Manitoba, CAN). *Collections Development Policy Statement*, 515 Portage Ave., Winnipeg, MAN (Canada) R3B 2E9

Viterbo College, Todd Wehr Memorial Library (WI). *Collection Management Policy*, 815 S. Ninth St., La Crosse, WI 54601

Warwick Public Library (RI). *Materials Selection Policy*, 600 Sandy Ln, Warwick, RI 02886-3998

West Springfield Public Library (MA). *Materials Selection Policy.* Materials taken from: Western MA Regional Library System and Leverett MA Library, 200 Park St., West Springfield, MA 01089-3398

William Paterson College of New Jersey, Sarah Byrd Askew Library (NJ). *Collection Development Policy*, 300 Pompton Rd., Wayne, NJ 07470

Winter Park Public Library (FL). *Materials Selection Policy*, 460 E. New England Ave., Winter Park, FL 32789-4493

MISSIONS, GOALS, AND OBJECTIVES

＊ ＊ ＊ ＊ ＊ ＊ ＊ ＊ ＊

A never-ending surprise is the lack of clear mission, goals, and objectives statements in library collection development policies; therefore, it may be helpful to provide some guidelines for understanding and using these important tools of policy development. A *mission statement*, always in keeping with the mission of the parent institution if there is one, should be short, general, and long-lived. The mission of any organization or institution is one that does not change with time unless the entire organization changes. Therefore, the shorter the statement, the less it will be capable of being specific, and the more it will last the life of the institution. In the case of a library, a mission statement need not be more than two or three sentences, and under no condition does this statement need to be more than a paragraph (and a short one at that).

The *goals statements* are a sort of wish list of what the organization or institution would like to emphasize as the role of the library, in broad, though focused, statements of purpose. There should be some ability to meet these goals, all things being equal (which they so seldom are), within the time period of 10 years. These statements often begin with such words as *develop*, *provide*, *encourage*, or *support*. All other policies of the library evolve from the mission and goals statements, and care must be taken in crafting these statements.

The *objectives statements* are attached to specific goals of an institution. These objectives are the ways in which the people of that institution will achieve the goals and mission. They are measurable, specific, determinate, and action oriented.

In the following group are examples of all three types of statements needed to build a working collection development policy. They are not in three distinct groups since the policies from which they are taken often called them mission statements when they were goals, goals when they were objectives, and objectives when they were goals. Each is a well-crafted statement of a particular library at a particular time serving a particular community. The words best paint the picture of the institution that inspired them.

* * * * * * * * *

Marigold Library System (Canada)

Marigold provides a collection that meets the needs of its members.

Brooklyn Public Library (New York)

The Brooklyn Public Library acquires, makes available, and encourages the use of materials in all media which:

- Help people know more about themselves and their world.
- Supplement formal study and encourage informal self-education.
- Meet the informational needs of the entire community.
- Stimulate thoughtful participation in the affairs of the community, the country and the world.
- Give access to a variety of opinions on matters of current interest and encourage freedom of expression.
- Support educational, civic and cultural activities within the community.
- Aid in learning and improving job-related skills.
- Assist the individual to grow intellectually and spiritually and to enjoy life more fully.

Winter Park Public Library (Florida)

To direct the development of the Winter Park Public Library, the Board of Trustees has adopted the following mission statement:

The Winter Park Public Library provides the materials, services, and facility necessary to meet the current and future informational and recreational reading needs of Winter Park's residents. Special emphasis is placed on offering popular materials, and reference materials and services. Resources for independent learning, as well as current, and historic local information are also important. Materials and services appropriate to all ages are available.

In addition to print media, the Library collections include non-print and electronic media. Mutually beneficial, cooperative agreements, which lead to improved library services for the community by avoiding unnecessary duplication, will be initiated by the Library with other area libraries and institutions.

This mission statement is implemented through five goals. The goals are:

Goal I: The Library provides high-demand, high-interest materials of a popular nature in a variety of formats to meet the entertainment and recreational needs of the community.

Goal II: The Library provides reference materials and services that answer the informational needs of the community, or that provide direction to additional sources of information.

Goal III: The Library provides materials and services that enable community members of all ages to pursue practical and/or intellectual self-directed learning independent of the formal educational process.

Goal IV: The Library collects, preserves, and provides access to a variety of types of materials that are by and/or about Winter Park and its citizens in both a current and historic context.

Goal V: The Library evaluates current services and makes plans for new services that will meet the Community's needs now and in the future.

The materials selection policy is based on the mission statement and the five goals.

Harnett County Library (North Carolina)

The purpose or goal of the Harnett County Public Library is to make available to all people in the service area books and other materials that will assist and encourage them

to educate themselves continually and strive to keep pace with progress in all fields;

to become better citizens of home and community;

to be more capable in their daily occupations;

to develop their creative and spiritual capacities;

to appreciate and enjoy works of art, music, and literature; and

to take advantage of library resources and library-sponsored activities that promote the use of leisure time for the evaluation of self-esteem and enhance personal and social well-being.

In order to achieve this goal, the general objectives of the Harnett County Public Library shall be as follows:

A. To assemble, preserve and make accessible, in organized collections, books and related educational and recreational materials in order, through guidance and stimulation in the communication of ideas, to enlighten citizens and enrich their personal lives.

B. To serve the community and county as a center of reliable information.

C. To provide local government officials with information and to perform research as needed.

D. To serve as a center for local history and the preservation of local archives in all forms.

E. To provide a place where inquiring minds may find opposing views on controversial subjects. The library does not promote any particular belief or view, but it should provide a resource where the individual can freely examine both sides on controversial issues or ideas and make his or her own decisions.

F. To support educational, civic and cultural activities of groups and organizations.

G. To provide opportunity and encouragement for children, young people, men and women to educate themselves continually.

H. To seek continually to identify community needs, to provide programs of service to meet such needs, and to cooperate with other organizations, agencies and institutions which can provide programs or services to meet community needs.

I. Provide opportunity for recreation and cultural entertainment through the use of literature, music, films and other art forms.

Southwest Regional Library Service System (SWRLSS) (Colorado)

The mission of SWRLSS is to strengthen, support and equalize member library services by providing leadership and encouraging cooperation among libraries in order to improve public access to information. The goals of SWRLSS are:

Library Development	Increase the knowledge, skills and abilities of member librarians, staff and governing bodies to improve services.
Communication Link	Connect member libraries to facilitate communication with each other and outside entities.
Economics of Scale	Assist libraries to maximize their financial resources through coordinated and cooperative service.

Materials Sharing	Promote the active and reciprocal sharing of library resources.
Leadership	Advocate and define the role of library service in meeting information needs of the 21st century.
System Management	Manage an efficient administrative structure and secure sufficient financial resources to provide services which address member needs.
Public Relations	Increase the visibility of the system and its members.

Loras College (Iowa)

The primary goal of the Wahlert Memorial Library is the support of the undergraduate and graduate academic programs at Loras College. Institutional objectives, as stated in the college catalog, include the "discovery, transmission and integration of knowledge within the liberal arts tradition and within a Catholic environment." More specifically,

1. intellectual development, resulting in a competence in general and professional knowledge, in creative and critical thinking, open-mindedness, and an ability to carry on independent learning;
2. personal development, involving the furtherance of one's identity, emotional maturity and adaptability, and the pursuit of personal goals and values;
3. social development, establishing interpersonal relationships, an awareness of society and a commitment to social needs;
4. spiritual development, stressing the formulation of an intellectual basis for the Christian faith within the context of all forms of human inquiry and values, and manifesting itself in personal and social development.

California State University, Chico

This statement establishes basic policy of the Meriam Library at California State University, Chico, for the development, maintenance, assessment, and preservation of the library's collections. This policy replaces previous statements and draft goals.

> The role of collection management in the University Library is to build and shape collections and to provide access to resources, both local and remote. The management of the collection is the responsibility of the library faculty in consultation with the teaching faculty, the library administration providing support for these efforts.

Collection management provides support for improved access to the library's collection of materials and more effective selection methods through the development of policy statements, collection assessment plans, and procedural guidelines. The selection, acquisition, and discarding of library materials follow guidelines which have been constructed by library and teaching faculty. Periodic assessment of the collection is done to ensure that the library is meeting the demands of its users. Recognizing the increasing strain on resources, a consciously established rationale for priorities in collection management becomes mandatory. Technological advances in information retrieval and distribution offer the promise of improved resource sharing and access to a wider variety of information.

Fairfield University (Connecticut)

The library is a service organization that, through its staff, resources, services, and facilities, supports both the humanistic and professional components of the University's curriculum. It responds to the research and information needs of the entire campus community. It provides instruction in research skills that serve students during their studies at Fairfield University, and in the paths they choose after graduation. It attempts to make the search for information and enlightenment, whether for course work or for personal needs or pleasure, a positive and rewarding experience that encourages an awareness of the usefulness of libraries in the life-long search for knowledge.

Ripon College (Wisconsin)

The acquisitions policy of Ripon College Library is intended to be consistent with the philosophy and objectives of the College, resulting in a solid collection of significant works. The purpose of the policy is to assure the planned and systematic provision of materials for the College to support its curriculum, as well as research and planning related to the curriculum.

Florida State University

The primary goal is to acquire materials which support graduate and undergraduate course work and sustained independent study. The libraries strive to select, acquire, and organize recorded knowledge. The most modern means of access to the collections and to other worldwide databases should be provided. These goals should be flexible and utilize state-of-the-art technology to stay abreast of developing disciplines and new directions of academic research needs.

Doane College (Nebraska)

Perkins Library perceives its particular mission to consist of the following:

1. To select and acquire or provide timely access to as much as possible of the recorded knowledge of mankind as is consistent with the current and anticipated instructional needs of its users.
2. To process and organize the materials with speed, accuracy and economy.
3. To instruct patrons in utilizing the resources of the library, and to provide user access to needed information located elsewhere.
4. To make the collections available to current patrons while at the same time guaranteeing availability of materials to future users through binding, microformatting, climate control, etc.
5. To cooperate with other organizations for the advancement of scholarship and the effective utilization and delivery of resources.

William Paterson College of New Jersey

The *primary goal* of the Library with regard to the maintenance and development of the collection is:

> To acquire and make available those information resources which are needed to support the instructional programs of the College.

The Library will also pursue three *secondary goals*. While these are subordinate to the primary goal, all three demand equal emphasis.

> To acquire and make available those materials needed for research by faculty and administrators which will be frequently used and of long-term value to the College Community.

> To acquire and make available library materials for general information in subject areas not included in the curriculum of the College.

> To collect and preserve all important materials related to the history and development of William Paterson College.

All materials acquired by the William Paterson College Library will conform to the goals of the collection development efforts of the Library.

P U R P O S E

※ ※ ※ ※ ※ ※ ※ ※

Since the time it takes to develop a good collection development policy statement is often long enough to interfere with other work of the library, it is often deemed wise to justify that time with a good reason for having the written document in the first place. A statement of purpose should be a no-jargon account of why the institution needs such a policy in words easily understood by the lay public. (For some statements, those meant for internal use only, the words used to write this justification need not be so general, and more specific terminology would be fine.) The statements included here are those made by libraries, both public and academic, that seek to explain to the staff or the community what the policy attempts to do, and in some cases, how the policy is intended to be used.

※ ※ ※ ※ ※ ※ ※ ※

Winter Park Public Library (Florida)

The purpose of this policy is to help our patrons understand why certain materials are added to the library's collection and others are not. It also serves as the guide for library staff in the selection of materials for the collection.

Barrie Public Library (Canada)

The specific purposes of this policy are threefold.

1. A policy publicly states the principles of selection upon which staff choose materials.
2. A policy assists staff in responding to questions and challenges to the collection from the public about the materials.

3. A written policy statement aids staff in selecting and acquiring a useful, well-rounded collection of materials, and the policy helps staff to ensure that these materials meet community needs.

Flower Mound Public Library (Texas)

A written materials selection policy aids the Library Director in selecting and acquiring a useful, well-rounded collection of books and other materials to meet the needs of the community.

A policy statement helps answer questions by the public regarding the presence or absence of certain materials and helps explain the basis on which materials have been selected.

Fairfield University (Connecticut)

This policy statement is a guide to assist the library in carrying out its collection management responsibilities. Collection management includes not only selection of materials for purchase, both current and retrospective, but also the preservation, replacement or disposal of materials held, as appropriate, and the systematic weeding of obsolete and superseded materials. The immense amount of available materials coupled with the cost of their acquisition make it necessary that the library has a written collection management plan that stresses wise materials selection. Such a policy also provides a statement of principles in support of the content of the library's collections should a selection decision be challenged.

The collection management policy guidelines have been developed by the professional staff of the Nyselius Library, and are open to revision as conditions change. Contributions from the University community are welcomed. Collection management decisions are based on both objective data and the subjective judgments of librarian liaisons, often in consultation with school and academic department liaisons and other faculty. Discipline specific differences in instruction, research, and reliance on library materials must be considered. Objective data to be considered include financial resources available, programs and courses offered, publishing output, enrollment, circulation of materials, interlibrary loans, and comparison with standard bibliographies.

The Nyselius Library Collection Management Policy is intended to clarify the general policies of the library with regard to the principles on which the library's collections are built. A constant shift in user needs, budgetary situations, and other circumstances require that the Collection Management Policy be reviewed regularly. Appropriate revision of the policy will allow for current, flexible, but clearly stated guidelines that are necessary for wise, cost-effective collection management.

James Madison University (Virginia)

This policy is established to assist liaison librarians and other requestors in their pursuit of collection development in the areas of selecting, maintaining, and deselecting all types of materials having instructional and research value in Carrier Library.

It is recognized that there are situations in which it is more effective for Carrier Library to devote resources to providing access to information rather than building collections. Carrier Library is therefore committed to providing access to collections, and information, throughout the region, the United States, and the world. Access extends to print, microform, non-print and electronically delivered information. An effort will therefore be made to participate in both nonprofit and commercial, regional and national research, education, and resource sharing networks and cooperatives. Efforts will also be made to acquire print and electronic bibliographic tools which inform researchers of resources available outside the library and which assist the library in acquiring material located elsewhere.

The policy is also to assist in informing University faculty, administration, students, and other interested libraries and groups of the Library's policies and roles in developing and maintaining our collections.

This policy is purposely left general to allow for individual initiative and judgment in collection development. It is subject to continuing change as new ideas and types of materials become available in the collection development process.

COMMUNITY

❖ ❖ ❖ ❖ ❖ ❖ ❖ ❖ ❖

Libraries seek to place their collections in the context of the communities that they serve. The reasons for this are obvious since everything about the collection depends on whom it is being built for—from the goals, objectives, and mission to the actual selection of materials. Although many libraries do not specifically mention their communities in the collection development policy (some because it is mentioned in planning documents), some provide analysis of whom the library serves within the context of how patrons benefit through the materials that are purchased (and even by what is not purchased), and the collections that are built.

Community descriptions are more often found in the public library sector, and below are two examples of the prevalent types of analyses that are being done today. In a new type of description, the Oakville Public Library and the University of Winnipeg show the "community" as a group of libraries tied together in consortia agreements to serve a much wider community than that of a specific geographic area. This is a significant change from the policy statements of a decade ago, and show the first faint stirrings of what will probably be the next great movement within our field—the library without walls, the institution reaching beyond the near community into the global community.

While academic libraries have been joining networks and consortia for decades, few have tackled the enormous problem of shared resources, and even fewer have attempted or even mentioned coordinated collection development. Until five years ago, coordinated collection development was a dream of many, but a dream without any substance. Slowly, the libraries of the 1990s have had to come to grips with some hard financial realities, and those realities are bringing coordinated collection development into the arena of the possible. True, there are still those big research libraries that think they can buy it all, but those days are really gone for good. The description of the community as a group of libraries under consortia agreements so early in the policy statement shows a real movement in a new direction of cooperation.

❋ ❋ ❋ ❋ ❋ ❋ ❋ ❋ ❋

St. Anthony Public Library (Idaho)

St. Anthony, population 3128, is the county seat of Fremont County, population 10,906. It is on the west slope of the Continental Divide and the North Fork of the Snake River divides the town. With such assets as clean air, clear streams, terrific game hunting, fishing, and enthusiastic people who are raising families in the west, we feel this area has much to offer. Our main industry is agriculture with emphasis on potatoes and cattle. However, we do have several other industries such as lumbering, dairying and other related businesses. The local chapter of the United States Forest Service and the Youth Services Center are also major employers. We have an estimated collection of 24,782 in 1991.

Brooklyn Public Library (New York)

II.   The Community as a Factor in Selection

The prime factors in the community which have a direct bearing upon the selection of materials are: the people individually and collectively, and the adequacy and availability of materials in other community agencies.

1.   The People

The Brooklyn Public Library serves almost two and one quarter million people. Although the numerical population of the borough has not changed substantially in the past several decades, the nature of the community is changing.

There is ever widening contrast between the stable and the unsettled, the affluent and the poor, the student and the dropout. In this time of rising expectation and deepening frustration, tension and conflict, reflected in every aspect of the urban crisis, the community has enormous needs, both expressed and unexpressed. The variety and scope of materials required by such a community, for information, relaxation, stimulation and education, is as broad as the community itself.

There is an ever-increasing number of college and university students and graduates whose needs for materials will continue to be met.

In addition, special purpose materials are required to meet the special needs of segments of the population which have not traditionally been library users. The library will continually search for new and better methods and materials in various media and languages to meet these needs.

2. Other Community Resources

    The library cooperates as fully as possible with other libraries and with community agencies, through groups and organizations whose purposes and activities are related to library objectives. Expanding techniques of interlibrary loan on a city, state and federal level will be utilized to improve service to Brooklyn Public Library patrons. In addition, in order to avoid unnecessary duplication of materials, one factor in selection will be a consideration of the kinds of materials available through other institutions. These include:

    a. Special Libraries—other libraries in the community where materials are available for public or professional use will affect the selection of materials in specialized subject areas. Although materials in all fields will be evaluated for purchase by the library. Purchase of expensive or specialized materials contained in collections like those of the New York Academy of Medicine, The Brooklyn Museum, the Brooklyn Botanic Garden, the Brooklyn Historical Society and the New York Public Library-Research Libraries is generally avoided. In addition, through use of the METRO (Metropolitan Reference and Research Library Agency) referral card, library users can obtain access to other specialized member libraries for specific items.

    b. Educational Institutions—Cooperation with the entire educational community is a basic aspect of public library service. Responsibility for the provision of curriculum-related materials belongs properly to the schools, but the public library will provide materials which supplement and enrich the reference, research, and recreational needs of student borrowers of all ages.

        The same general standards of merit and relevance that apply to all selection will be used to evaluate curriculum-related materials. Extensive duplication to meet mass assignment demands is not feasible, but through the provision of materials in inexpensive formats (pamphlets, paperbacks, periodicals, etc.) the library will attempt to fill some of the gaps which may ultimately be filled by school and academic libraries as they are developed toward adequacy.

Increasingly, agencies and groups, other than schools and universities, are becoming involved in the educational process. The library will support such activities not only through the provision of its materials and services, but whenever possible by cooperating in development of appropriate materials and programs.

c. Facilities for the Blind and Visually Handicapped—In cooperation with the New York Public Library's Library for the Blind, service is provided for the blind and visually handicapped in Brooklyn through agencies of the Brooklyn Public Library.

Oakville Public Library (Canada)

Oakville Public Library within the Library Community

Oakville Public Library is a large library system, centrally located within a library-rich area (Toronto to Hamilton). It is part of HALINET, a network which also includes the public libraries of Burlington, Milton and Halton Hills.

Oakville belongs to the provincially designated Southern Ontario Library Service (SOLS)-Escarpment Area, a group of libraries which extends from Mississauga to Fort Erie. Reciprocal borrowing privileges and a delivery system exist within the Escarpment area. An Interloan network extends throughout the province.

Within a 48 kilometre radius of Oakville are three universities, Ryerson, Polytechnical Institute and four community colleges. Their libraries provide various levels of in-house accessibility to the general public. The National Library in Ottawa and automated data bases provide location information for materials unavailable through local networks.

University of Winnipeg (Canada)

The University of Winnipeg Library is not designated as a research library. It is not a member of the Canadian Association of Research Libraries (CARL) nor of the American Association of Research Libraries (ARL). It is funded as an undergraduate collection. However, because the teaching faculty are required to perform research as part of their contract, some funds allocated to support the teaching programs are used to purchase research materials, especially periodicals.

The Library is situated in the downtown part of the city, within easy walking distance of the Legislative Library of Manitoba and the main branch of the Winnipeg Public Library system. It is also located close to a large number of provincial and federal government libraries that serve a variety of specific constituencies. The Library staff seek to maintain a collection that meets the teaching and research needs stated above, but it is reasonable to expect members of the University community to obtain highly specialized materials from these nearby libraries, either in person or through interlibrary loans.

ALLOCATION OF FUNDS

❄ ❄ ❄ ❄ ❄ ❄ ❄ ❄ ❄

A new issue in collection development policies is allocation of funds. Since this is not a new process in libraries, why is it now showing up in policy statements? There are two reasons for this: one is that more processes that were hidden from the public are now appearing in very public documents; and two, procedures that used to be in manuals attached to policy documents are making their way into the policies themselves.

The following are two laudable ideas to include in policies: (1) the public deserves to know as much as possible about the way their money is being spent, and (2) library administrators need ammunition to fight for funding. Accountability, the byword of the 1980s, has led indirectly to this release of information; that, and the idea that "free" libraries are not free, and that the funding agencies and user groups have a right to know how and why money is being spent, have altered the perception of what a collection development policy should look like.

The second theme behind this new look at how collections are built is to give the public so much information that they will drown in it. An occupational hazard is that librarians are used to doing this in their everyday jobs, and now that philosophy is showing up in written policy statements that contain enormous amounts of extraneous procedural information. Not only does it date the policy statements, which then need reviewing much more frequently than if only policy statements were in them, but the procedural details also detract from the more important policy statements themselves.

Some allocation formulas belong in the policy statement because they give a sense of how the collection is being built (as the examples below do); some do not, as they obscure the policy behind a mesh of too much information with too little knowledge.

❄ ❄ ❄ ❄ ❄ ❄ ❄ ❄ ❄

Marigold Library System (Canada)

Principles of Book Allocation

1. Establish a minimum, a maximum and a recommended number for annual distribution to each library.
   Minimum: 1 book/5 capita or 100 books, whichever is greater, not to exceed 1000
   Maximum: 1 book/3 capita or 1500 books, whichever is less, not to be lower than 100
   Recommended: between 100 and 1500 books per library; depending on the budget and other factors, such as Standards and book rental plans
2. Budget and space permitting, those libraries which do not meet the 1980 Saskatchewan Library Association standard receive a dditional materials.

Saskatchewan Library Association Standard-Book Collections

Population	Book Collection	
	1980	1985
250	1,500	2,500
500	3,000	4,000
1,000	5,000	7,000
2,000	9,000	12,000
5,000	18,000	24,000
10,000	25,000	30,000
	or 2.5/cap whichever is greater	or 3.0/cap whichever is greater

3. If the budget doesn't provide the number of books required, the larger allocations are reduced by a set percentage. No allocation is reduced by more than 25%, and no allocation falls below 100 books.

Doane College (Nebraska)

In keeping with the best thinking of the library profession, the librarian's materials budget shall include not less than thirty and not more than forty-five percent allocated to the Director of the Library or the Collection Development Librarian for library purchases of general periodicals and standing orders, and for the acquisition of special materials not confined to one subject area, or to meet needs not otherwise adequately met by Divisional Allocations. It is here that the goal of "extending the teaching of the College" may be met.

James Madison University (Virginia)

Each year the Acquisitions/Serials librarian reports to the University Librarian on the last year's expenses for serials and the expected cost for the following year. These costs, plus any amount set aside for new serial purchases, are taken from the materials section of the Library budget. The remaining funds are then allocated for monographic purchases through the use of the formula.

The allocation formula, approved by the University Library Committee in 1985, includes among its components factors which are ascertained for each academic department. These include average cost of books, credit-hour productivity at the 100–200 levels and the 300–400 levels, existence of more than one major within a department, reliance of curriculum on the library, and graduate programs.

Library funds are allocated to each department with the expectation that the funds will be encumbered according to a schedule published by the Acquisitions Department. Funds for an academic year may be encumbered as of July 1 and must be fully encumbered by February 1 of the following year to be sure that materials can be ordered, received and paid before the end of the fiscal year.

Monthly reports are sent to each department by the Acquisitions/Serials Department starting in September and ending in March. Each report notes the original allocation, the amount encumbered and spent to date and the amount of requests currently in process. The unencumbered amount is expressed in percentage to enable a quick check to see how a department is progressing toward its goal of 100% by February 1.

University of South Carolina–Aiken

The Director of the Library is responsible for the expenditure of all library funds. A percentage of those funds which are designated for the purchase of library materials is allocated to each academic discipline each fiscal year according to a formula approved by the Faculty and the Administration. It is library policy for each discipline to pay for all periodical subscriptions and standing orders in its particular subject area from its allocation. A general fund which is under the jurisdiction of the Library Staff is reserved for the following: reference materials, standing orders, materials needed to fill in gaps in the collection, materials in subject areas which are not represented in the curriculum, replacement of lost and stolen material, bindery expenses, carry over obligations from the previous fiscal year, general interest journals.

The library allocation formula at the University of South Carolina at Aiken is based upon division of the budget between faculty (60%) and the library (40%). Collection development, then, is a joint effort between divisional faculty and the library.

Major subject disciplines number thirty-two (32), within the College of Humanities, the College of Mathematical, Natural and Health Sciences and the College of Social Sciences and Professions. Each separate discipline has the responsibility to order books and periodicals to support the curriculum. Periodical subscription renewal costs are subtracted from the discipline's allocation; the remainder may be used to purchase books or new periodical titles.

The allocation formula at USCA takes 5 areas into consideration and all 5 carry equal weight in the formula. The 5 are:

1. Library circulation
2. Number of different courses generated
3. Student credit hours
4. FTE faculty, and
5. Equal share

An explanation of the chart below will more fully explain these areas.

DISCIPLINE	EQUAL SHARE	LIBRARY USE	NO. OF COURSES	STU. CR. HRS.	FTE FACULTY	TOTAL
anth	1000.00	19.54 (0.0065)	210.53 (4)	260.19 (0.0867)	250.28 (0.7500)	1740.53
art	1000.00	354.01 (0.1180)	1000.00 (19)	735.96 (0.2453)	620.69 (1.8600)	3710.66
educ	1000.00	2626.45 (0.8755)	1789.47(34)	2003.85 (0.6680)	2129.03 (6.3800)	9548.81
TOTALS	3000.00	3000.00	3000.00	3000.00	3000.00	15000.00

Total appropriation is 25000

Total faculty share of allocation is 15000

Sum of allocations by acronym is 15000

Each discipline is assigned an acronym (see the "discipline" column). Next, the faculty share of the allocation is divided by 5, giving each "column" or variable group an equal total value. In the example, each column has a value of $3000. The "equal share" column is divided by the number of disciplines to determine the equal portion. EDUC's (Education) equal share would be $1000, since there are three acronyms in the example.

The "library use" column is based on library circulation statistics which are kept for books and periodicals, for the previous fiscal year. In the example, EDUC had 87.55% of the total circulation. Therefore. EDUC would receive 87.55% of the value of the "library use" column ($3000) which would amount to $2626.45.

The "number of courses" column requires the most difficult data collection. This number is the total number of separate courses that "made" for fall and spring semesters of the previous year. Multiple sections are not counted; labs are counted once; independent studies are counted once. The numbers are manually tallied, using the *Registration Summary*, which is generated by the Registrar's Office. In the "number of courses" column there is a total of 57 courses. Each course receives a dollar value (1/57 of $3000). This dollar value per course is multiplied by EDUC's number of courses (34 % $52.631579), giving a value of $1789.47.

The "student credit hours" column is based on figures from a report generated by the Computer Services Division. EDUC's student credit hours amount to 66.8% of the total student credit hours for the previous fall and spring semesters. This results in EDUC receiving 66.8% of the value of the column ($3000) or $2003.85.

The final consideration is "FTE faculty." These figures are also based on the previous fall and spring and are compiled by the Office of the Vice-Chancellor for Academic Affairs. The total number of FTE faculty (8.99 in the example) is divided into the value of the column ($3000). Each FTE faculty then has a dollar value. This dollar value is multiplied by the number of FTE faculty in the discipline, resulting in that discipline's dollar value for the column. EDUC has 6.38 FTE faculty and each had a dollar value of $333.704116, resulting in $2129.03 for the discipline.

The final total per discipline is arrived at by adding the values of each column, i.e. equal share ($1000) + library use ($2625.45) + number of courses ($1789.47) + student credit hours ($2003.85) + FTE faculty ($2129.03) EDUC's total share of the allocation would then be $9548.81. In the example the total book and periodical budget was $25,000, with the faculty shares amounting to $15,000.

SELECTION POLICY

* * * * * * * *

Many libraries begin the actual selection portion of the collection development policy statement with their philosophy of selection. The selection statement tries to give the reader a sense of how libraries select materials given the other parameters that will be shown in the policy. It is here that a library will mention the age-old question of demand versus quality, as if these two were opposing viewpoints on a continuum in the selection process. Any procedures of note will be mentioned in the selection statement which perhaps will hint at the larger world of lending, networking, and coordinated selection may lurk in this introductory paragraph. Sometimes the library has prioritized its entire selection process, and the beginning sentences of the selection portion of the document will point this out. As the mission, goals, and objectives were the introduction to the entire policy statement, this selection statement is the introduction to all of the parts of selection to follow.

* * * * * * * *

St. Anthony Public Library (Idaho)

For budget reasons we can acquire only a limited number of the thousands of books published annually. We are forced to select carefully. Our selection is based upon principle rather than personal opinion, reason rather than prejudice, and judgment rather than censorship.

East Gwillimbury Public Library (Canada)

Materials selected conform to the interests, needs and abilities of the community the library serves, but aren't restricted by them. Consideration is given to the fact that interests may not come into existence without the material to create it. The Library has the responsibility to foster interests as well as sustain it within bounds of budgetary restraints.

Brooklyn Public Library (New York)

In a world in which change is so rapid and pervasive, the library's obligation extends beyond meeting present conditions. The library must also strive to anticipate future needs of the community. Books have always been, and will continue to be, a proper concern of the library, but ever greater amounts of information are now being contained in other forms. As research continues in the field of communication, and as the community changes and develops, the library must be a media center, acquiring appropriate materials, regardless of form, and integrating each into its total services.

Clearwater Public Library (Florida)

The Library is dedicated to meeting the information needs and expectations of all citizens and population groups in the Community. It is recognized that patrons use a wide array of Library materials and consider reference and referral assistance to be basic services of the Library. A trained and dedicated staff uses available resources to plan and deliver Library service in a creative and responsive manner. Special emphasis is given to children's services in order to stimulate early and lifelong interest in reading and learning activities. The Library recognizes the contribution of business to the well being of the community and provides information to meet corporate needs. There are four primary purposes that Library activities support: reading, viewing, and listening materials for general knowledge, cultural enrichment, education and recreation; authoritative and timely information in support of daily living, occupational needs, educational pursuits, and intellectual curiosity; introduction of the youngest members of the community to reading and learning activities; and materials/services for business and industry.

Naval War College (Rhode Island)

The Library shall use its funds for (1) current purchases; (2) rounding out the collection (scope); (3) filling in gaps (retrospective). The amount of materials purchased is in direct proportion to the size of the Library's budget in any fiscal year.

Meredith College (North Carolina)

Priority

Priority for additions to the library collections are the following, in descending order:

1. materials supporting the curriculum
2. standard reference tools
3. materials contributing to a balanced collection
4. materials supporting research of the Meredith faculty, administration and staff
5. materials for recreational reading

Norwalk Community-Technical College (Connecticut)

The following are considered the primary resource needs of the Norwalk Community-Technical College Learning Resources Center:

a. Reference materials, general and for specific fields covered by the curriculum
b. Material concerning each field of the curriculum
c. Periodicals to meet curriculum needs and the reading interests of students
d. Materials for individual enjoyment and enrichment

RESPONSIBILITY FOR
SELECTION
❋ ❋ ❋ ❋ ❋ ❋ ❋ ❋

Among the most interesting questions in the entire range of selection issues in libraries today is (1) who is responsible for choosing the material that goes into the collection, and in legal terms, (2) on whose authority are these decisions made? Those are two separate questions, just as who is legally responsible, and who actually chooses the materials are often two distinct entities. In the public library sector, the board of trustees of the library is often the legal party upon whose shoulders rests the responsibility for selection of the library's materials. They do not, however, select that material. Somewhere in the body of the document should be a mention that the body legally responsible for the materials in the library invests that responsibility in the director who then assigns certain librarians, staff, etc., for the actual selection of that collection. That gives public libraries a certain protective hierarchy if anything goes wrong in that area. It also gives a clear chain of command for procedural questions that may need to be answered for patrons requesting information about why certain books were purchased and others not. It should be a clear statement, and libraries have chosen to give sometimes brief statements about this chain and sometimes a longer explanation as to not only who, but how and why the responsibility is divided the way that it is.

In academic libraries, the question of selection responsibility is more complex because there have traditionally been two groups who vie for the honor of being the primary selectors of materials for the college or university library: the faculty and the librarians. In most institutions the two share this responsibility but in a number of places it is squarely in one camp or the other. From what is in written collection development policies reviewed for this volume, most university libraries rely on their professional library staff to do the actual selection but ask the faculty of the institution to keep their eyes open and to order what they believe the library should have. In some college libraries, it is the other way around. There are many articles that will argue for one way or another, but no research has confirmed the overwhelming need for it to be one way or the other. Faculty tend to know more about their subjects, but look at the library in terms of their specific subject's narrow focus. The collection tends to be more unique if faculty does the selection, but more full of gaps as well. If librarians do the selection, the collection tends to be better balanced and cover curriculum needs better, but be more homogeneous. This statement of responsibility, therefore, for both public and academic libraries, is extremely important.

❋ ❋ ❋ ❋ ❋ ❋ ❋ ❋

Greenville County Library (South Carolina)

The Board of Trustees of the Greenville County Library determines the Materials Selection Policy for the library system. The responsibility for administering this policy rests with the Director of the Library. The actual selection of materials is accomplished by staff members who are assigned responsibility for selection in specific subject areas under the direction of the Deputy Director.

Northern Arizona University

Responsibilities: The primary responsibility for the selection of materials to be incorporated into the Cline Library collection is shared between the academic faculty and library subject specialists. NAU staff and students are provided with the opportunity to make recommendations for the selection of materials.

Green Mountain College (Vermont)

The responsibility for the selection of materials lies in theory with all of the members of the faculty and the professional library staff. However, the ultimate responsibility for materials selection and the development of a strong collection rests with the librarian, who oversees the growth and maintenance of the collections s/he determines that the core collection is maintained and that new acquisitions reflect the needs of the students, the faculty and the goals of the institution.

Ripon College (Wisconsin)

Responsibility for the selection of library materials lies with both the librarians and the faculty. The librarians are in a position to observe the quality and balance of all subject areas, and they oversee the selection and purchase of materials in all subject areas. The departmental faculty will bear primary responsibility for recommending the acquisition of materials in their subject fields. Departments are expected to recommend library purchases which will develop the entire field of their disciplines. Faculty are encouraged to take a strong interest in developing the collection in their various disciplines by using rigorous discrimination in their selection of materials to be added to the library holdings. Students, staff and administrative officers may also submit recommendations for purchase to the library staff.

Hawaii Pacific University

UNIVERSITY LIBRARIAN. The ultimate responsibility for selection of books lies with the University Librarian, who operates within a framework of institutional policies established by the Board of Trustees and the President of Hawaii Pacific University.

LIBRARIANS. Responsibility for selection of books is delegated by the University Librarian to the librarians, who will assume selection responsibilities for assigned subject areas.

UNIVERSITY FACULTY. It is recognized that faculty can make a significant contribution to the development of a collection by recommending books. Members of the on-campus and off-campus career, limited-term full-time, and adjunct faculty may make recommendations for the purchase of books. An on-campus faculty-initiated recommendation is to be forwarded to the appropriate curriculum coordinator, who then forwards the recommendation directly to the librarian responsible for selection in that subject area. Recommendations from off-campus faculty are to be forwarded to the Vice President and Dean for Satellite Programs, who then forwards the recommendation to the librarian responsible for selection in that subject area. All faculty-initiated recommendations will be evaluated by the selection criteria presented below. The University Librarian reserves the right to delay purchasing action for budgetary reasons, or refuse any recommendation due to the inappropriateness of the book.

LIBRARY SUPPORT STAFF. The library support staff are encouraged to participate in the selection process, and may make recommendations for the purchase of books to that subject area.

UNIVERSITY STAFF. Full-time members of the University staff may make recommendations to the Library for the purchase of books.

STUDENTS. Students may make recommendations to the Library for the purchase of books.

Any recommendation from the library support staff, university staff, and students should be made on a MEADER LIBRARY SUGGESTION CARD available at the library service desks. All recommendations will be reviewed by the appropriate subject area librarian and the University Librarian, who reserve the right to refuse a recommendation for budgetary reasons, or failure to meet the selection criteria presented below.

Northwestern State University of Louisiana

Responsibility for Selection and the
Selection Process

Anyone, including students, may recommend materials for selection by the Library, except in the case of recommendations for additions to special collections. The primary responsibility for selection, however, rests with the teaching faculty and librarians of NSU. Further, the faculty shall ensure that the Library has the materials needed to further the educational mission of the University. Faculty members are expected to recommend materials which serve to support the courses they teach and which supplement the general library collections appropriate to their disciplines and specialties. The Library will attempt to acquire through interlibrary loan or facsimile transmission those materials needed for research by students, faculty, or University staff which cannot be secured through purchase or which fall outside the collection guidelines. U.S. Government publications that are not available in Watson Library will be acquired through interlibrary loan from the Regional Depository at Louisiana Tech for patrons who request them.

Queens College (North Carolina)

Selection of Library Materials

All faculty and College administrators are encouraged to submit requests for both print and nonprint materials which fall within their areas of expertise and which conform to the collection policies presented in this document. The cost of these materials will be charged against the appropriate departmental allocation.

In an effort to assist the teaching faculty in the selection of appropriate materials for the library collections, each member of the library faculty is assigned to work as a liaison for several departments. Liaison assignments are based, in so far as possible, on the subject specialties and interests of the librarians. Each department chair is asked to appoint a member of the departmental faculty to serve as that department's representative to the Library. The liaison librarian and the departmental representative will work together to encourage faculty to submit requests for new acquisitions and to resolve any problems or questions concerning Library policies and procedures from the departmental faculty. In addition, the departmental representative should apprise the liaison librarian of any anticipated changes in the curriculum which would impact on Library use.

In general, requests for new acquisitions should be submitted to the Library through the departmental representative. Department chairs may ask that they sign all requests before they are sent to the Library, and the Library will make every effort to honor such requests. All departmental requests should be routed first to the liaison librarian, who will in turn hand them over to the Acquisitions Manager for processing. The liaison librarian will work with the departmental representative, the department chair, and the teaching faculty, to resolve questions concerning the appropriateness of specific materials for the collection. The final authority and responsibility for the development of a sound collection rests with the Director of Everett Library.

Doane College (Nebraska)

Selection of Material

A.   The Director of the Library has over-all responsibility for the development of the library collections, but the building of an adequate materials collection must depend upon use of the specialized knowledge of all members of the academic community, and part of the responsibility for developing a strong and well-balanced collection is shared by the groups below:

1.   The advice and active participation of faculty members is necessary, and it shall be the responsibility of the members of each discipline to recommend purchase of the best materials in support of their various disciplines, with reference always to their courses as they are or will be taught at Doane College.

2. Because the librarians are in the best position to observe the overall growth and development of the collection and because the Director of the Library is ultimately responsible for the quality and balance of the total collection, the professional library staff shall use the general library allocation to select materials in all subject areas.

3. While many of the books added to the library are selected by the faculty, recommendations for materials from students of the College should be encouraged. Serious suggestions will be considered carefully and an effort made to include all worthwhile pertinent titles in subsequent book orders.

COLLECTION LEVELS

❋ ❋ ❋ ❋ ❋ ❋ ❋ ❋ ❋

Y ears ago, academic libraries came up with the idea of dividing their selection decisions by subject and then by the level of intensity that they were going to collect in each of the areas. A reason for this approach might well have been the introduction of approval plans into the selection process of academic libraries. The Resources and Technical Services Division of the American Library Association (now the Association for Library Collections and Technical Services [ALCTS]), came up with a detailed collection intensity level definition scheme which libraries have used from that day forward. Far be it, however, for libraries to accept such a scheme without playing around with it and making it their own. So, although many of the concepts and the words are similar, the collection levels below are slightly changed, rearranged, or rewritten so that librarians are able to add their small touches to the process.

Although selection levels certainly started out with academic libraries, they proved so useful in the selection process that public libraries began to see if they could adjust them to fit a public library setting. The first library of note to do this was Cuyahoga County Public Library, in Ohio. Since that time other libraries have changed the way that collection levels have been defined, and more and more public libraries appear to be attempting to define their collections in these terms.

❋ ❋ ❋ ❋ ❋ ❋ ❋ ❋ ❋

East Gwillimbury Public Library (Canada)

This collection is designed in general for the lay person and materials whose subject treatment goes beyond the university undergraduate level will, in most cases, not be considered appropriate to the goals of the general collection.

El Paso Public Library (Texas)

A. Basic - A highly selective collection which serves to introduce and define a subject.
B. Intermediate - A collection adequate to maintain knowledge of a subject for generalized purposes and independent studies through the undergraduate level.
C. Comprehensive - A collection which includes all significant and relative works about a subject area for a defined field.

Queen's University (Canada)

Levels of Collecting

The level of collecting represents the areas of concentration in which programmes are offered, related directly to the level of teaching and research, e.g.: undergraduate degree, masters programme, doctoral programme and post-doctoral research. Individual faculty members may be involved in research in areas not specified in any programme, and/or at a level beyond that necessary for the programme given. Thus they may require library materials in areas not necessarily reflected in the collection policy statements of the department or to a depth different from that stated in the policy.

These individual research interests may eventually be recognized for teaching and research and thus be incorporated into the collection policy statement at a later date. However the faculty members' interests may change, or the faculty may leave this university before such recognition is achieved.

That is why the fullest consultation between librarians, library representatives, department heads, and deans if necessary, is essential in establishing the degree of support to be offered to acquisitions for individual research.

Level A

Exhaustive assembling of unique collections, including all printed editions plus archival and MS materials. Normally such collections would cover a very small subject area, e.g.: Political parties in Kingston in the 1840's.

Level B

Intensive collecting in specialized scholarly fields in order to support doctoral and post-doctoral research with a high degree of adequacy. Virtually all printed materials in English are sought and there is fairly intensive collecting in other western European languages. In addition to printed and micro-text material, level B may include manuscripts or other special capabilities. For example, in literature in addition to drafts, manuscripts, letters, diaries, first editions, translations, commentaries and definitive editions of an author, there is collected material by and about those who influenced the author or were influenced by him, as well as extensive material on the social and cultural history of the time. This level allows for indefinite expansion of the research program, but the cost is still counted and regional and national resources are considered. Collecting attempts to be fairly comprehensive but not exhaustive.

Level C

Beginning research level. Collecting material at a level advanced enough to cover basic requirements for graduate studies at least to the master's level. Includes fundamental works of scholarship, comprising primarily books and other published materials in western languages or in a language especially relevant to the subject or language being taught (e.g.: French, Spanish, Russian, etc.). Little manuscript or other non-print material is included except in narrowly-defined fields or for special needs. All important secondary sources in relevant subject areas would be included, as would research studies, definitive editions and first editions where important. Areas being collected at level C should have all major reference works for the subject and the important periodical publications. This level is expected to supply the majority of material required for research up to the master's level, but at level C collecting is still quite selective and considerable consideration is given to regional and national resources. Catalogues of other libraries would be purchased at this level. There is considerable reliance on interlibrary loan or photocopy purchases from other libraries.

Level D

Maintains a collection advanced enough to support undergraduate instruction effectively and to support the needs of the four-year program. Material for courses numbered 300 to 500 would be collected at this level. It includes reference material of all kinds, files of basic journals, a wide range of subject indexes and bibliographies and all the more important secondary sources. Definitive editions, works of criticism and analysis, important monographs and research studies which "tell something new" would be included as would conference proceedings and important publications of research societies.

Level E

Assembling a core collection of basic works. Those materials without which no college or university library should exist. The standard materials required for undergraduate curricula and the general works needed for a balanced college collection. Into this category would fall fundamental reference anthologies, collections, general periodicals, and some major subject periodicals. Materials listed in Choice's Opening Day collection and in Books for College Libraries is mostly at levels D and E. Material for courses 010 and 299 would normally be collected at the first level.

Northwestern State University of Louisiana

Levels of Collection Intensity

The selection of materials for Watson Library should be based upon the following levels of collection intensity or depth:

1. RESEARCH LEVEL provides major source materials required for thesis research and graduate level papers. Types of materials would include research reports, major reference works, specialized monographs, serials, indexes and abstracts. Collection for the following areas (which offer graduate degrees) should be pursued at the research level:

Art	Music
Education*	Nursing
English	Psychology
History	Student Personnel

*Including the programs listed at the Study Level and Counselling and Guidance, Educational Administration/Supervision, Reading, Secondary Teaching, and School Psychology

2. STUDY LEVEL provides materials adequate to support study on the undergraduate level. The collection at this level should contain basic monographs, representative journals, and key reference tools. In most instances these materials should provide definitions and fundamental concepts. Materials such as bibliographies and subject dictionaries and encyclopedias should be acquired. Collection for the following areas (which offer undergraduate degrees or emphases) should be pursued at the study level:

Accounting	Industrial Technology
Advertising Design	Journalism

Agriculture
Animal Science
Anthropology
Aviation Science & Technology
Biology
Business Administration
Chemistry
Computer Information Systems
Computer Science
Drafting Technology
Education*
Electronic Engineering Technology
Equine Science
Foreign Languages**
Forestry
Geology
Home Economics
Industrial Management

Mathematics
Medical Technology
Military Science
Office Administration
Philosophy
Photography
Physical Education
Physics
Plant & Soil Science
Political Science
Radiologic Technology
Social Science
Social Work
Sociology
Space Science
Speech
Theatre
Veterinary Technology

*Art Education, Business and Office Education, Distributive and Business Education, Early Childhood Education, Elementary Teaching, English Education, Education in Health-Physical Education and Recreation, Industrial Arts Education, Mathematics Education, Music Education, Science Education, Social Science Education, Special Education, Speech Education, Vocational Home Economics Education
**French, Spanish, German

3. BASIC LEVEL provides materials which serve to introduce and define a subject and in which few selections are made beyond very basic reference books, monographs and representative journals. The basic level collections will offer some support for those areas in which Northwestern offers no major, but does offer coursework, or for which each library should have a representative collection in order to support a broad liberal education.

OTHER CONSIDERATIONS. In addition to subject-specific materials, Watson Library should actively collect appropriate materials of an interdisciplinary nature. English-language materials should predominate, though an adequate selection of foreign-language dictionaries and foreign-language materials sufficient to support the University's language course offerings should be ordered. Major emphasis will be placed on materials covering the United States and Western Europe. Other geographical areas will be covered at the basic level.

Northern Arizona University

Levels of Collection Intensity

The Cline Library recognizes that levels of need differ from subject to subject. The level of curriculum support desired may not be consistent with budgetary constraints. Therefore, collection development efforts cannot always be maintained at the established level.

Level 0: *Out of scope*
Materials are not collected in this area.

Level 1:
Only fundamental reference works with basic information on a subject will be acquired. Reference works will include encyclopedias, dictionaries, and general bibliographies.

Level 1A: *Minimal; uneven coverage*
Unsystematic representation of subject.

Level 1B: *Minimal; well chosen*
Only fundamental reference works with basic information on a subject will be acquired. Few selections will be made beyond very basic works.

Level 2A: *Basic Informational and General Interest Collection*
A basic information and general interest collection is a highly selective one which would introduce a subject not represented in the University's curricula. Such a collection would include basic reference sources; a selection of basic texts, bibliographies, and handbooks; seminal works of recognized writers, and a minimum number of representative journals. Material will normally be in English. The collection would not be sufficiently intense to support courses in the subject (Approved 3/29/90)

Level 2B: *Advanced, Information and General Interest Collection*
An advanced basic information and general interest collection will support students in basic lower division courses as well as basic information and general interest needs. It will include materials on a wider range of topics with more depth, some historical materials, and a broader reference collection. (Approved 3/29/90)

Level 3A: *Basic Undergraduate Collection*
A Basic Undergraduate Collection is adequate to support fully all courses at the lower division undergraduate level. It would include a good collection of reference and bibliographic sources, all basic works and complete sets of works by the most important writers in

the best editions, critical works about important writers, selected secondary sources, and a well balanced selection of basic journals. The majority of these materials would be in the English language. A good selection of currently published basic monographs such as those represented in *Choice* best books lists would be included. (Approved 3/29/90)

Level 3B: *Advanced Undergraduate Collection*
An Advanced Undergraduate Collection is one which will adequately meet the needs of students in baccalaureate and independent study at that level. It would include a comprehensive collection of reference sources including indexing and abstracting services, and extensive bibliographic and biographical sources. In addition to comprehensive coverage of fundamental works of scholarship, it will include a wide selection of retrospective works, all key journals on primary topics, and selected other journals. Materials will be primarily in English. (Approved 3/29/90)

Level 3C: *General Research Collection*
A General Research Collection is one which will support all courses at both the baccalaureate and master's degree level as well as independent research at this level. It will be sufficient for imparting knowledge about the primary and secondary topics of the field. In addition to the above a collection at this level will include a substantial collection of the works of secondary figures, a significant collection of periodical titles on both primary and secondary topics with extensive backfiles, access to appropriate machine-readable data files, and works providing an in-depth coverage of research, techniques and evaluation in the field. While primarily in English the collection will include materials in other languages as appropriate. (Approved 3/29/90)

Level 4: *Comprehensive Research Collection*
A Comprehensive Research Collection is one which will support independent study and research by students and faculty in programs where the Ph.D. degree is offered or anticipated in the near future. It should include as complete an assemblage of current and retrospective materials of scholarly value as possible and extensive holdings of serials with complete runs, primary source materials, and other documents. It will include comprehensive coverage of reference sources, critical and biographical works, bibliographies, and other materials.

Level 5: *Exhaustive Collection*
An Exhaustive Collection is one which is intended to be one of the largest, best developed collections in the world. No limitations will be placed upon collecting efforts because of format, language, context, or age. Any budgetary constraints will be considered temporary. At this time, only the Colorado Plateau Collection falls in this category.

To provide specific guidance to persons selecting materials in the various subject areas, collection intensity levels have been assigned to the LC Classification Schedules. To further assist selectors, the level of the collection as it currently exists is also listed. This is a continuing process. This section is expected to change more often than the rest of the policy. It is, therefore, included as an appendix to facilitate this process.

SELECTION CRITERIA

* * * * * * * *

Perhaps the most important part of any collection development policy is selection criteria. The reasons why materials are purchased can be found in this section, and it is increasingly important for the public that supports libraries and the patrons who use libraries to know where their money goes and how the decisions are made.

Often the criteria section is broken up into a number of different sections which reflect the different kinds of materials that a modern library is now supplying to the public. Whereas it used to be that the criteria for selection could be nicely divided into those criteria used for nonfiction materials and those criteria used for fiction materials (and they are different from each other), now the library staff is faced with criteria for formats as widely different as videos, electronic software, microforms, periodicals, archives, not to mention specific and controversial subjects such as witchcraft and sex, or in fields such as psychology, science, and religion.

Although this section can contain both general and specific criteria used by the library, often just the general criteria are mentioned and specific criteria are saved for a later section on the specific format or subject area. The general criteria are mostly known by now, but different libraries have different ways of constructing them, and so below are a number of examples of how criteria have been formulated in specific libraries. Sometimes the different format criteria are included here, and sometimes they are not. If the criteria are included in this section, then this is where the section was found in the original policy document. Likewise, if criteria are included in another section, such as "Formats," that is because the library chose to put it in that other section.

One library in this section called its criteria section "Criteria for Selection or Withdrawal of Library Materials." This is the only library that actually took note of the fact that these two processes are, at its very heart, the same process. The criteria used to choose material are the same that are used to discard it from the collection. What differs, after all, is the community for which it was selected versus the community for which it will be rejected, and the time it was selected versus the time it will be discarded. The process and the criteria remain the same.

❊ ❊ ❊ ❊ ❊ ❊ ❊ ❊ ❊

St. Clair County Library (Michigan)

Criteria for Selection or Withdrawal of Library Materials

The library staff shall use the following general criteria in the selection, duplication, replacement and withdrawal of library materials:

> Demand for the material
> Usefulness and appeal
> Appropriateness of format, content, and style
> Value of the material in relation to the whole collection
> Availability of special materials in more comprehensive library
>   collections in the area
> Currency and accuracy of the material
> Space and budgetary considerations

Homewood Public Library (Alabama)

The permanent book collection should reflect a strong, accurate and up-to-date reference collection, a broad fiction collection of classics and standard titles, and basic non-fiction titles covering a wide range of subject areas for the researcher and the recreational reader.

Selection of materials will be influenced by:

(a) Anticipation of and response to continuing and changing needs and interests of the community and of individuals.
(b) Current and historical significance.
(c) The attention of critics and reviews.
(d) Budgetary considerations.
(e) Physical limitations of the building.
(f) Need for additional or duplicate materials in the existing collection.

(g) Availability of materials in the Public Libraries of Jefferson County System, through interlibrary loan, and in special or more comprehensive library collections in the area.

(h) Patron demand.

(i) Professional judgement.

Tomah Public Library (Wisconsin)

Items having widespread demand may or may not meet the general and specific criteria contained in this policy. However, demand is a valid factor in book selection and it shall be considered an important factor in cases such as books on best seller lists for which there is persistent local demand.

Kalamazoo Public Library (Michigan)

Criteria for Materials Selection

Each resource must be considered for its value, its format, and the audience for which it is intended. No single criterion is applicable to all purchase and access decisions. Some resources may be judged primarily for their artistic merit, scholarship, or value to humanity; others are chosen to satisfy the informational, recreational, or educational interests of the community.

Librarians apply their judgment and experience in selecting materials according to the criteria listed below. All criteria do not apply to each item. Works of imagination are judged by different standards than are works of information and opinion. Works that present an aspect of life honestly are not necessarily excluded because of frankness of expression. Materials are judged as a whole rather than on isolated passages. In considering individual titles in the selection process, librarians consult reviews, bibliographies, and other evaluative sources. However, the library generally purchases all current best sellers, giving higher priority to demand than to reviews or other relevant criteria. The criteria include.

- suitability of physical form for library use;
- suitability of subject and style for intended audience;
- present and potential relevance to local interests and needs;
- appropriateness and effectiveness of medium to content;
- number and nature of requests from the library district public;
- historical significance;
- importance as a document of the times;

- relation to existing collection, alternative formats, and other material on the subject;
- reputation and/or significance of the author/artist and publisher/producer;
- authority, competence, and purpose of the author/artist;
- attention of critics, reviewers, and the public;
- comprehensiveness and depth of treatment;
- objectivity;
- clarity, accuracy, logic of presentation, and/or ease of use;
- representation of a minority point of view;
- relevance to the experiences and contributions of diverse populations;
- artistic presentation and experimentation;
- quality of illustrations;
- originality;
- vitality, readability, or ability to sustain interest;
- effective characterization;
- authenticity of historical or social setting;
- value of resource in relation to its cost.

Electronic resources enhance the library's collections by providing convenient access to expanded and consolidated information. Locally mounted databases and gateway services enable the library to provide new technologies, which are becoming essential tools for information delivery. All criteria (above) relevant to the selection of materials in traditional formats apply to electronic resources as well. However, because machine-readable formats require nontraditional means of acquisition, storage and access, some additional criteria must be considered:

- ease of access and number of access points;
- hardware and software requirements, including maintenance;
- vendor support and contractual requirements;
- comparison of content with other formats available;
- networking capabilities;
- ownership of product;
- staff training and/or client assistance requirements.

Warwick Public Library (Rhode Island)

Fiction

A novel should do at least one of the following things: excite the imagination, stretch the mind, arouse emotion or delight the senses. The aim of the fiction collection is to do all four. Fiction is evaluated on the basis of the following criteria: artistic merit; true representation of the aspect of life chosen by the author to describe; effectiveness in sustaining the reader's interest; a plausible plot; structural soundness and clarity of style; and vitality and consistency in characterization. In selecting fiction, consideration is also given to reader demand and the popularity of the author.

East Gwillimbury Public Library (Canada)

1. GENERAL CONSIDERATIONS.
   a) Suitability of subject and style for intended audience.
   b) Compatibility of material with library facilities and use.
   c) Present and potential relevance to community interests and needs.
   d) Appropriateness and effectiveness of medium of content.
   e) Insight into human and social conditions.
   f) Importance as a document of the times.
   g) Reputation and/or significance of author or producer.
   h) Skill, competence and purpose of author or producer.
   i) Budgetary considerations.
   j) Availability of material within the East Gwillimbury Public Library System, through interloan or through special or more comprehensive library collections in the area.

2. SPECIAL CONSIDERATIONS FOR THE EVALUATION OF WORKS OF NON-FICTION.
   a) Authoritativeness.
   b) Comprehensiveness and depth of treatment.
   c) Clarity, accuracy and logic of presentation.

3. SPECIAL CONSIDERATIONS FOR THE EVALUATION OF FICTIONAL WORK.
   a) Creativity, novelty.

b) Story content.

c) Appropriateness of style.

d) General literary acceptance.

e) Intentions of author and/or publisher.

f) Reader demand.

g) Authenticity of setting.

4. CONSIDERATIONS FOR SELECTION OF MATERIALS OTHER THAN BOOKS.

The same philosophy and standard of selection which apply to the selection of materials other than books.

a) NEWSPAPERS. Newspapers are selected to meet reference and research needs of patrons to provide current information, and to satisfy casual interest in current events. Local, national and foreign newspapers are supplied upon sufficient demand and within budget and space limitations.

b) PERIODICALS. The selection of periodicals will be made using the same criteria as the other materials. The library will endeavor as a long range policy, to develop a collection consistent with the availability of indexes in the various subject fields. As far as possible, in order to preserve content and conserve space, back issues will be kept in microform.

c) VIDEOS. The selection of videos will be made using the same criteria as other materials.

Ouachita Parish Public Library (Louisiana)

Certain factors influence the selection of library materials. Among these are:

1. The importance of subject matter to the collection;
2. Timeliness or permanence of the work;
3. Authoritativeness;
4. Objectivity;
5. Availability of material in the system, in other libraries or in print;
6. Popular appeal;
7. Skill, competence and purpose of author;
8. Representation of opposing views on subjects of interest to the people;
9. Price;
10. Historical value;
11. Relevance of material to special collections;

12. Attention of critics, reviewers and public.

Imaginative works serve a vital purpose in the life of children and need to be judged carefully.

Specific Criteria for the Evaluation of Works of Imagination

1. Artistic presentation and experimentation;
2. Vitality and originality;
3. Effective characterization;
4. Sustained interest;
5. Authenticity of historical or social setting;
6. Representation of important movements, genres, trends or national cultures.

Librarians and staff in the Children's Service are responsible for the selection of material. The Division Head for Children's Services for the system has the final responsibility and authority in the selection of material for this collection, subject to the ultimate responsibility of the Director.

Greenville County Library (South Carolina)

Criteria for Selection

Criteria used in the selection process include the following:

(1) each type of material must be considered in terms of its own merit and the audience for whom it was intended. There is no single standard which can be applied in all cases when making an acquisition decision. Some materials may be judged primarily in terms of artistic merit, scholarship, or their value to humanity; others are selected to satisfy the informational, recreational, and educational needs of the community.

(2) a small proportion of the materials evaluated is subject to widespread or substantial local demand. Items having such demand may or may not meet other criteria contained in this policy. In any case, the volume and nature of requests by members of the public will be given serious consideration. As the social and intellectual climate of the community changes, however, materials which originally were not recommended for purchase may become of interest.

(3) the Library does not act as an agent for or against a particular issue. The disapproval of materials by one individual or group should not be the means of denying those materials to all groups if, by library selection standards, they belong in the collection.

(4) materials which present aspects of life honestly will not be excluded because of frankness of expression or illustrations. Materials will be judged as a whole rather than on isolated passages.

Rochester Public Library (Minnesota)

Standards for Selection of Adult Nonfiction

1. The Library acquires materials of both permanent and current interests in all subjects, based upon the merits of a work in relation to the needs, interests, and demands of the community. Each item is evaluated as a whole and not on the basis of a particular selection. While a single standard cannot be applied to each work, the following general criteria are used in selecting materials for purchase:

- Significance of subject matter
- Timeliness and/or popularity of a subject or title
- Reputation or qualifications of author, artist, or publisher
- Local interest (subject, author, or publisher)
- Availability of materials on the subject, provision or alternative viewpoint
- Level of difficulty
- Critical review
- Imprint
- Purchase Price
- Technical characteristics, i.e., quality of paper, typography, binding
- Suitability of format for library use
- Suitability and usefulness of subject and style for the library's intended audience
- Present and potential relevance to community needs and preferences
- Importance as a document of the times
- Relationship to the existing collection and to other titles and authors dealing with the same subject
- Popular demand
- Historical value
- Permanence, timelessness
- Quality of writing, style of writing
- Availability of similar material within the community and other area libraries

- The appearance of the title or author in special lists and bibliographies
- Literary merit as expressed by reviewers
- Originality
- Accuracy and authenticity of information presented

Each of these criteria may not and need not be used to evaluate each item, but they are applied as general guidelines for consideration of all materials.

- Uniqueness or special features
- Social significance
- Relevance
- Inclusion on standard bibliographies and indexes
- Currency of information
- Permanent value as a standard work

Standards for Selection of Adult Fiction

Standard library reviewing media are used as the basis for selecting adult fiction since library staff cannot obtain and judge each title directly. Staff selectors' judgments are thus based on prior evaluation by reviewers. Review sources relied upon include the following:

Booklist, Book Review Digest, Fiction Catalog, Kirkus Reviews, Library Journal, Minnesota Reviews, New York Review of Books, New York Times Book Review, Publisher's Weekly, Title Index of Current Reviews, Wilson Library Bulletin.

Also used are book review sections of local, regional, and national newspapers and news magazines.

Given the above, however, a number of basic standards are applied as appropriate. (There is no single standard which can be applied in all cases.) Some titles and/or authors may be judged in terms of artistic merit, scholarship, or their value as documents or documenters of the human condition. Others are judged according to the expressed educational, informational, cultural and recreational needs and preferences of the community. Additions to the adult fiction collection are considered on the following bases, not necessarily in this order and including but not limited to:

- suitability of physical format for library use;
- suitability and usefulness of subject and style for the library's intended audience;
- present and potential relevance to community needs and preferences;
- insight into human and social conditions;

- importance as a document of the times;
- relationship to the existing collection and to other titles and authors dealing with the same subject;
- reputation or significance of authors;
- popular demand;
- historical value;
- cost;
- permanence, timelessness;
- quality of writing, style of writing;
- availability of similar material within the community and other area libraries;
- the appearance of the title or author in special lists and bibliographies;
- literary merit as expressed by reviewers;
- originality;
- authenticity, truthfulness;
- characterization;
- representation of important literary trends.

Alvin Community College (Texas)

Criteria Used for the Selection of Books and Other Materials:

1. Availability of funds;
2. Nature and frequency of patron requests;
3. University parallel and occupational-technical education curriculum requirements;
4. Lack of bias or prejudice;
5. Recommendations in selection of media;
6. Non-textbook forms of materials;
7. Up-dates subject field knowledge;
8. Subject content applicable to the undergraduate level;
9. Authoritative and competent presentation; and
10. Relation to the existing collection.

Athenaeum of Ohio

Specific criteria for the selection of individual titles

1. Anticipated use.
2. Accuracy.

3. Authority of the author.
4. Timelessness of the publication.
5. Strength of present holdings in study area.
6. Literary quality.
7. Cost.
8. Contribution to the field of knowledge.
9. Reputation of the publishing house.
10. Level of treatment.

This list is not in order of priority.

Hawaii Pacific University

General

Criteria to be used in selecting library books include:

1. Importance of subject matter in relation to the University's educational goals and the curriculum.
2. Timeliness or permanence of the material.
3. The author's reputation and significance as a writer.
4. Authoritativeness as reflected in recommendations or adverse criticisms by respected authorities or book reviewers.
5. Relative importance in comparison with other similar types of materials on the subject.
6. Clarity of presentation and readability.
7. Reputation and standing of the publisher.
8. Price.

Michigan Technological University

Selection Guidelines

The following guidelines should be considered in selecting and adding materials to the collection:

1. **Subject matter and scope**
   Does the material suit the purposes of the curriculum for which it is intended. Will it serve the interests of students in more than one curriculum?

2. **Treatment**
   Does the subject suit the need of students studying the discipline? Is it introductory? Is it speculative? Is it scholarly, technical, or popular? Is there partial or complete coverage? Is it current or retrospective?

3. **Validity/Accuracy**
   Is the material indexed? Does it present fact or opinion? What are the author's qualifications? What is the publication date? What is the reputation of the publisher? Is the material based on primary or secondary sources? Is it based on observation or research?

4. **Point of view**
   Is the material partisan/sectarian? Is it fair? Is it a contribution to community values/citizenship? Does it challenge and promote thought? Does it show unredeemable bias?

5. **Elements of quality**
   What elements make the material the best of its type for addition to the collection? What degree of creativity is shown? Is the format suitable for the message? Is there freshness in the presentation? Are there similar publications?

6. **Literature**
   Does the material add understanding of personality, human nature, and the human condition? Does the work represent the best of its author or genre? Representative works of an author of current and lasting interest or genre should be selected. Study editions with notes should take preference over standard editions. Anthologies of poetry, drama, etc., should take preference over individual works. Usage should be a criteria for selection.

7. **Format**
   Format should include consideration of introductory material, print, indexing, paper, and binding. Are these suitable for the material? Is size a factor? Are there standard format items which could substitute? What is the quality of the illustrative material?

8. **Price**
   Is price reasonable compared to other materials in the same subject area? May an item of lower cost substitute? May paper cover meet our needs in preference to hard cover?

Green Mountain College (Vermont)

The major criterion for the addition of materials to the library collection is the relevance of the material to the educational program of the college. Additional criteria to be evaluated include the following.

1. anticipated use
2. accuracy and reliability
3. reputation of author or editor
4. cost
5. timeliness
6. current strengths and weaknesses of present holdings in the subject area
7. reputation of publisher
8. level of treatment
9. format
10. literary quality

Critical reviews from professional journals and other reputable sources will be used in assessing the quality and value of a particular item. The following reviewing journals will be consulted regularly for new materials: *Choice*, *New York Times Book Review*, *Library Journal*, *Wilson Library Bulletin* and *Booklist*. In addition, the book review sections of the professional journals to which the college library subscribes in education, leisure studies, parks administration, gerontology, psychology and sociology will be checked by the professional library staff and by any interested faculty as each issue comes out for pertinent new publications.

APPROVAL PLANS

* * * * * * * *

Although some public libraries are beginning to use approval plans, perhaps differently than their academic counterparts, the only surveyed libraries to mention them in the collection development statements were university libraries. Since it is known that many more libraries actually use approval plans, it seems odd that so few would mention them in the statement. The reason for this could be that some libraries do not think a statement on the use of approval plans belongs in a collection development policy, but it does. All policies that relate to the building of the collection belong in this statement, and approval plans certainly qualify. Why some libraries seek to hide the fact that they use such plans is baffling, but perhaps they believe that selection is such a professional task that to admit to using an approval plan might somehow lower them in their colleagues' estimation. Developing an approval plan that works, and then operating one that runs smoothly is far more professional than spending inordinate amounts of time choosing books for the collection when there is so much else to do in running an academic library.

* * * * * * * *

California State University, Chico

Because it is essential to acquire a large portion of recently published academic books in subjects relevant to the university's program in a timely fashion, the library encourages participation in appropriate approval plans. An approval program can provide breadth, depth, and currency to the collection.

Criteria for evaluating such plans include:

A. Timely shipments of new books without need to identify and order individual titles.
B. Comprehensiveness of coverage according to profile.
C. Reasonable discounts and book prices.
D. Delivery of appropriate books in good condition.
E. Willingness of jobber to modify approval profiles, accept returns, and provide management reports.

Florida State University

Fundamental to a library's acquisitions efforts is the goal of obtaining a broad range of monographic materials in the most timely manner possible. No more efficient procedure exists for accomplishing this goal than the maintenance of a comprehensive approval program. The FSU Libraries have an approval plan with Blackwell North America which supplies newly published works from the United States of America and Canada, and selected works from the United Kingdom. Subject descriptors and profiles for each discipline were originally set up by FSU faculty and library staff. Various subject profiles are adjusted periodically with faculty and librarian input. A detailed analysis of subjects is contained in Blackwell North America's *Thesaurus*.

GIFTS AND
MEMORIALS
❋ ❋ ❋ ❋ ❋ ❋ ❋ ❋

Although not strictly a method of selection, acquiring materials through gifts and exchanges (more often gifts now, since exchanges are labor intensive and therefore too costly to pursue), could be considered another facet of the selection process. Certainly all of the criteria that are promulgated for the actual selection of materials for the collection must also be met for those items that come to the institution through the agency of a gift or donation.

There is another problem with gifts that has been with libraries since day one, and that is how to acknowledge them. With the Internal Revenue Service rulings on appraisals stemming from the 1970s problems with presidential papers and deductions, libraries have gotten much more careful about what they will provide in the way of proof for tax audit purposes. Most libraries will provide little more than a count of how many items were given and when. The American Library Association has performed a service for the profession by creating an appraisal of gifts statement which many libraries append to their collection development policies.

The gift policy portion of a collection policy is one of the two places most likely to contain a sample form that the patron would complete; this form relates the library's policies with the acceptance of any gifts. (The other place in a collection development policy that typically contains a sample form is the section that discusses intellectual freedom and censorship. The form is usually called Reconsideration of Library Materials.") Libraries are beginning to look into fund raising through gifts of materials and money as an important part of running a modern library, and gift statements are becoming more specific as to what a gift consists of and what the library is willing to provide the donor in the way of recognition. Often the donor is leaving the library something in his or her will or a memorial gift in someone else's name. Libraries have been named after very generous patrons who have donated millions to an academic institution and been rewarded with such recognition. Future financial support trends point to fund raising, with gifts remaining a traditional mode of support.

* * * * * * * * *

Oakville Public Library (Canada)

Donations Policy

The Library encourages and welcomes gifts of money for the purchase of collection and other Library materials, equipment, and for the improvement of Library facilities.

The Oakville Public Library rarely accepts gifts of books, periodicals, audio visual materials, toys and other materials for the collection and does so only with the understanding that the Library may do with them as it sees fit. Gifts of materials for the collection are subject to the same principals and standards of selection as outlined in the Materials Selection Policy and applied to all materials added to the Library's collection. Because of limita-tion of space, budget and staff, the Library reserves the right to accept or discard, at its discretion, any unsolicited materials sent to any location of Oakville Public Library. The Library cannot guarantee that any gift will be part of the collection or kept permanently.

Once accepted, donations including collection materials, are the exclu-sive property of the Oakville Public Library and are, therefore, subject to all Library rules, regulations and procedures. Those making monetary donations may wish to recommend how their contribution(s) are to be used. The Oakville Public Library will comply with such requests whenever possible. However, the Oakville Public Library reserves the right to commit donations to services and projects in keeping with its priorities.

Coffee County Lannom Memorial Public Library (Tennessee)

A. Memorials

1. The library accepts monetary contributions as memorials, either for books to be purchased and designated memorials or to be added to the library's Memorial Fund. Because of the need for co-ordination of book purchases to meet the reading needs of the public, the donor of a book is requested to designate the subject area for selections which would be appropriate. A large stock of new books is kept at the library from which memorial books may also be selected. Because the library does not need multiple copies of titles, it will be necessary for the final selection to be at the discretion of the librarian.

2. Used books cannot generally be considered worthy memorials. In the case of books on Tennessee or by Tennesseans, if the books are in good condition or if the donor will finance the professional restoration of the volumes, they will be placed in the library as memorials. This category is the only acceptable exception.

3. A Register of donors to the Library Memorial Funds will be kept on display at the Library. Money thus contributed will be used to purchase specific library items needed by the library, at the discretion of the librarian and the Library Board.

B. Donated Materials

1. Books or other materials will be accepted on the condition that the Library Board has the authority to make whatever disposition it deems necessary. If the library cannot use them in its collection, applying the same criteria it would to new materials, it reserves the right to sell the items to benefit the Library Fund.

2. The libraries of Coffee County may accept special collections of papers and documents which may be of interest to and used by the general public being served. In addition, all such collections must be arranged and stored in such a manner as to facilitate their use. All such materials will be considered reference and as such will not be loaned outside the library. However, the libraries shall not accept responsibility for maintaining privacy of any personal or group records as all library material is for the benefit and use of the general public. No restrictions will be placed on duplicating materials within these collections.

3. Gifts of money, real property or stock will be accepted if conditions attached thereto are acceptable to the Coffee County Library Board.

4. Personal property, art objects, portraits, antiques, books and other museum objects will be accepted only at the discretion of the Board.

5. The library will not assign a monetary value to the items donated. If requested, the library will give patron a receipt for the number of items donated, along with date and signature of library personnel.

Harnett County Library (North Carolina)

IV. Gifts to the Library

Gift material will be accepted with the understanding that the books or materials may be added to the collection, sold, exchanged, given to other libraries, or discarded. Gift items will be added to the collection in normal sequence because separate collections limit the use by the public and complicate the location of materials. Gift items will be acknowledged and may be designated by a bookplate.

Restricted Gifts are those to which the donor has attached terms, conditions, and purposes. These may be quite specific, such as "for the purchase of the 1900 Census for North Carolina" or very general as "for audiotape cassettes."

Nonrestricted Gifts are those to which the donor has not attached terms, conditions, or purposes.

It is the prerogative of the library to accept or reject any gift. Gift cash may be spent without budgeting or appropriation. Checks made out to the Harnett County Library will be turned over to the "General Fund" of the county, not to the library; so donors who wish to make a gift specifically to the library are encouraged to make the gift to the Friends of the Harnett County Public Library. If restricted, a check of cash must be spent according to the donor's conditions. If nonrestricted, it may be spent on authorization of the library board within the scope of its statutory authority for any library need.

The library would be pleased to receive gifts, either restricted or nonrestricted, or cash to be spent for books or other realistic library needs.

A. Materials of Predetermined Value—In Memory of, In Honor of, and Other Gifts

1. Patrons wishing to make arrangements to purchase or to give new library material should be referred to the library director—whether for in-person, telephone, or mail inquiries.

2. A Gift or Memorial Material Request form should be completed before the patron leaves or hangs up the phone. Patrons may request a specific title or form of information or they may suggest certain subjects or areas for selection by library staff. They may give money at the time of inquiry, send money in an amount they determine, or request to be billed for the amount of the purchase. Restrictions of county laws make it advisable for gifts to be directed to the Friends of the Harnett County Library, rather than to the library itself.

3. If a donor needs a suggestion for a gift, the library director can refer this request to technical services. If new material is given instead of money, that material along with the gift form is sent to the technical services department.

4. The library director immediately sends the proper recognition form to the donor, to the family of the deceased, or the person being honored and to any others noted on the form.

5. If material needs to be ordered, the technical services staff will order the material. If the donor is to be billed, this will be done at the time material is ordered.

6. Checks or cash are given to the library director to be deposited in the library's gift fund.

7. When the material arrives, a gift plate is attached and the items sent on for cataloging and processing.

8. After all procedures are completed technical services sends the completed gift form to the library director's office where it is kept on file.

B. Historical and Other Valuable Materials

Items of historical or community interest will be referred to the library director for consideration. The library board and the library director will be responsible for recommending the acquisition of the material and will follow through on the proper handling of the items.

C. Materials of Undetermined Value

This group of gifts represents the greatest volume of gifts received by Harnett County Public Library.

D. Used Materials

1. No used gift materials requiring pick up service will be accepted sight unseen.

2. Final decisions on acceptance of used gift materials rests with the library director. All used gift material questions should be referred to the library director as soon as they come up.

E. Unordered New Materials

1. When unordered new gift materials are received through the mail, they go to the technical services department, which acknowledges their receipt.

2. When unordered new materials are accompanied by an invoice or a notice of billing, they will immediately be brought to the attention of the library director so that a decision about returning them can be made at once.

F. Income Tax Deductions

The following applies when, and only when, a patron requests a receipt indicating monetary value of the gift material voluntarily presented to the library:

All such requests are to be referred to the library director, since persons requesting receipts intend to use them to verify a tax deduction on their income tax returns. A Gift Form (see next page) is given to the donor, thanking him for his gift, and he is advised to fill in the form himself and assign a monetary value to his gift.

GIFT FORM

I/We hereby transfer and deliver all of my/or rights, title and interest in and to the property described below to the Public Library of Harnett County as an unrestricted gift, along with whatever literary rights I/We may possess to this property.

Dated this _____ day of _____ 19 _____

1. _____
   Signature

   _____
   Address

2. _____
   Signature

   _____
   Address

3. _____
   Signature

   _____
   Address

The Public Library of Harnett County hereby accepts and acknowledges as an unrestricted gift the collection or item(s) described below and agrees to administer it/them in accordance with its established policies.

Dated this _____ day of _____ 19 _____ :

Accepted by: _____
             Signature

             _____
             Title

Description of the collection: _____

_____

_____

_____

Loras College (Iowa)

Gifts

The library will accept gifts of monographs, journals, manuscripts, and other print materials appropriate to the collection. The library accepts gifts only on the condition that it may appropriately exchange, dominate, sell, or discard those items that cannot be added to the collection. Before accepting gifts on behalf of the library, staff members must ensure that donors understand and agree to this condition. If there is any question about accepting a gift, the final determination rests with the Director of Library Resources.

The staff member accepting a gift must complete the Donor Agreement Form. Official acknowledgment of the gift is made by the acquisitions assistant. Guidelines for evaluation of gifts are the same as those for selecting purchased materials.

The library cannot make appraisals. It abides by the Statement on Appraisal of Gifts, approved by the Board of Directors of the Association of College and Research Libraries.

Gifts of money may be used by the library to purchase library materials, equipment, or services. Donors of monetary gifts may designate the use of those funds for specific purchases through negotiation with the Director of Library Resources.

Florida State University

Gifts

The libraries welcome any gift which may contribute to their development or services. They must conform to the general selection guidelines previously mentioned in the policy and to the following stipulations:

A. All gifts are final. By the act of donation, the donor permanently relinquishes all rights to ownership and dispensation. The libraries shall not be held accountable for the property donated beyond the accountability required by the State of Florida for state property.

B. The libraries reserve the right to dispose of gifts to its best advantage. Such disposition may include:

1. Retention in the libraries.

2. Transfer to other departments of the University.

3. Transfer to another institution within the State University System of Florida.

4. Donation to other local, national and international institutions or organizations.

5. Sale.

6. Routed to Property Records if the gift is not needed in the libraries' collection.

C. In accordance with the donor's request, appropriate recognition will be given to gifts retained in the libraries by affixing book plates, labels, or plaques to gifts showing the donor's name, and if applicable, the name of the person in whose honor or memory the gift was made.

D. The libraries will not set aside a special location for gift materials or affix labels, signs, or plaques to physical facilities indicating the presence of these materials. The libraries will not accept restrictions on usage of the materials which are contrary to general Library policy.

E. The libraries cannot appraise gift materials for tax purposes.

F. The libraries accept cash donations to be used for the purchase of library materials, equipment, or services, and will honor the donor's wishes regarding the nature of materials or services to be purchased, provided such purchases are in accordance with the needs of the libraries.

G. Gifts and donations will be acknowledged in writing by the Director of libraries.

H. Any material that bears the ownership markings of another institution and does not have any indication of having been writhdrawn from that institution's collection will be returned to the proper institution when possible.

I. Reproductions or photocopies of copyrighted works will not be accepted unless evidence of compliance with the copyright law (Title 17, U.S. Code) and its prevailing interpretations are provided.

CLIENTELE

❀ ❀ ❀ ❀ ❀ ❀ ❀ ❀

Often libraries mention specific groups of users in their policy statements. This may be because library materials specific to their needs form a special or large segment of their collection, and they wish to bring this particular group to the attention of the readers of the policy. In the case of public libraries, children and young adults certainly form this type of group. In the case of academic libraries, students often form this type of group. Below are such policy statements. Pay special note to the public library's reading of its responsibility to students in the town, and note that these younger populations are not the only ones that may need special treatment.

❀ ❀ ❀ ❀ ❀ ❀ ❀ ❀

Colusa County Library (California)

User Groups: In addition to the requirements of the general public served, materials will be selected to meet the needs of business, the professions, government, and community organizations. Materials selection will also include consideration of the needs of the homebound, the visually, physically and mentally disabled and those individuals with learning disabilities. The needs of adult beginning readers and of people for whom English is not the principal language will also be considered. Both the adult and young adult collections will serve as supplementary sources for student use, but materials selected for students must also be useful to the general reader. Textbooks will not ordinarily be purchased as the public library is not designed to provide school library service. Although school curriculum demands are considered, the public library should be a supplement not a substitute for the development and use of school library resources.

Barrie Public Library (Canada)

A mission of the library is to serve the educational needs of the citizens of Barrie and contracting townships. It is the responsibility of those institutions engaged in formal education to provide materials which support their curriculum; the provision of library resources that are not related to the curriculum, yet needed for an effective school program are also the responsibility of these institutions.

Ouachita Parish Public Library (Louisiana)

Books for young adults are selected with the aim of helping them find self-realization, live useful, well-adjusted lives in the community, and know and understand the world at large.

Greenville County Library (South Carolina)

The specific aim of the children's collection is to provide a wide variety of materials on many different conceptual levels to meet the diversified needs, interests, tastes and backgrounds of children through grade 7, or age 12. These materials should provide enjoyment for children and meet their personal information needs. In the words of the Public Library Association's Standards Committee Task Force on Children's Service, these materials should "further their search for understanding of self and environment; satisfy their need for aesthetic experiences; develop pride in their heritage and an understanding of other cultures; improve their ability to make critical judgments; and develop their verbal, visual, and aural communication skills." The observance of any restriction desired by parents on the use by their children of materials selected according to these criteria will be the parents' responsibility. In order to provide for children of different abilities, some adult and young adult materials are acquired. Additional materials are provided for adults to acquaint them with juvenile materials and the development of appropriate skills in children.

Green Mountain College (Vermont)

Clientele

The college library should meet the needs of its students from its own collections for general information. Recognizing the college's uniqueness in its small size and its isolated location, the college library will use all recognized means of interlibrary cooperation to assist its students in locating materials for specific academic and educational needs. Informational needs of the faculty and staff will be served through our own collections as well as those of other libraries. Efforts will be made to serve the needs of faculty and staff in graduate programs; however, with limited fiscal and human resources, persons engaged in this work should expect to do most of their research at the library of the institution where they are enrolled.

LEGAL ISSUES AND INTELLECTUAL FREEDOM
❋ ❋ ❋ ❋ ❋ ❋ ❋ ❋ ❋

There are numerous legal issues that appear in policy documents, most notably intellectual freedom and censorship. Most policies express the library profession's opinion of these guiding principles, many in the form of allegiance to the American Library Association's Library Bill of Rights and its many interpretations. Given the importance of intellectual freedom principles, that seems a rather skimpy way of declaring one's values. The collection development policy is the perfect place for the library to present a thoughtful discussion of its own interpretation of intellectual freedom. These statements should include discussion of values, principles, ethics, the public good, the public trust, democracy, the American Way of Life, and where libraries fall in the scheme of things. Instead of reiterating someone else's wording only, more libraries should write the kind of statements included below.

Included among the following statements are a few from our neighbors to the north, whose constitution and government give them rights we so long have thought of as being exclusively ours. Quoted is Canada's Charter of Rights, not all that dissimilar to the United States Constitution's Bill of Rights, upon which the ALA's Library Bill of Rights is based.

Although they present legal issues that should be in policy statements, copyright and other intellectual property laws are seldom mentioned in collection development statements. There appears to be no good reason for this, except perhaps that no one yet knows where libraries stand in this arena. Another area where librarians have yet to develop policy statements is in copyright of materials such as journals or original papers, which appear on the Internet, for instance. The profession hasn't come to terms with any electronic information sources in relation to intellectual property rights.

Last but not least, many libraries mention confidentiality as a right of their users and back it up with laws on the books, some going so far as to print the laws upon which such legal statements are based. Patrons in most states have the right to privacy in dealings with libraries, but most libraries do not spell this out in their documentation.

❋ ❋ ❋ ❋ ❋ ❋ ❋ ❋

Homewood Public Library (Alabama)

Widely diverse points of view, including controversial and unorthodox subjects, will be available in the collection. Inclusion in the collection does not imply library approval or agreement with the contents. The Board of Trustees and Staff recognize that some materials are controversial and that any given item may offend some patrons. Selections will not be made on the merits of any anticipated approval or disapproval, but solely on the merits of the work in relation to building the collection and to serving the interests of all the patrons.

The Board of Trustees upholds the principles set forth in the *Library Bill of Rights*, as amended January 23, 1980.

Oakville Public Library (Canada)

Oakville Public Library Board endorses the Statement of Intellectual Freedom established by the Canadian Library Association in 1974. Amended, November 17, 1983 and November 18, 1985.

It is as follows:

> All persons in Canada have the fundamental right, as embodied in the nation's Bill of Rights and the Canadian Charter of Rights and Freedoms, to have access to all expressions of knowledge, creativity and intellectual activity, and to express their thoughts publicly. This right to intellectual freedom under the law is essential to the health and development of Canadian society.
>
> Libraries have a basic responsibility for the development and maintenance of intellectual freedom.
>
> It is the responsibility of libraries to guarantee and facilitate access to all expressions of knowledge and intellectual activity, including those which some elements of society may consider to be unconventional, unpopular or unacceptable. To this end, libraries shall acquire and make available the widest variety of materials.
>
> It is the responsibility of libraries to guarantee the right of free expression by making available all the library's public facilities and services to all individuals and groups who need them.
>
> Libraries should resist all efforts to limit the exercise of these responsibilities while recognizing the right of criticism by individuals and groups.

Both employees and employers in libraries have a duty, in addition to their institutional responsibilities, to uphold these principles.

With this endorsement, Oakville Public Library recognizes that the selection of library materials is predicated on the library patron's right to be informed, and similarly, his/her freedom from censorship by others. Selections for this library will not be made on the basis of anticipated approval or disapproval, but solely on the merits of the material in relation to the building of the collection and to serving the needs and interests of users.

This library holds censorship to be a purely individual matter and declares that, while anyone is free to reject for himself books and other materials of which he/she does not approve, he/she cannot exercise this right of censorship to restrict the freedom of others.

West Springfield Public Library (Massachusetts)

The library neither approves nor disapproves the views expressed in materials included in the collection. The inclusion of an item is not to be considered an endorsement, official or otherwise, by the library.

Materials are not marked or identified to show approval or disapproval and no materials are sequestered, except to protect valuable or rare items from injury or theft.

Responsibility for the reading, viewing and listening of children and young adults rests with their parents or legal guardians. Access is not restricted by the fact that children may obtain materials their parents consider objectionable.

Freedom of expression, specifically the right to publish diverse opinions, was proclaimed in the Bill of Rights to the United States Constitution to be essential to the democratic form of government. A public institution committed to the principles of intellectual freedom, the library recognizes its obligation to provide as wide a spectrum of materials as possible. Selection cannot be restricted by the possibility that certain materials might be considered objectionable by some readers on moral, religious, political or other grounds.

The library endorses the principles of the Freedom to Read and Freedom to View Statements and the Library Bill of Rights adopted by the American Library Association June 18, 1948 amended February 2, 1961 and January 23, 1980. All documents are incorporated as part of this selection policy.

Titles are selected on the basis of content as a whole and without regard to the personal history of the author. Important works of major political, social and religious movements are included. In no case is any item included or excluded merely because of the race, nationality, political or religious views of the author.

The library cannot exclude all materials that could conceivably result in mental or physical injury to some individual, since theoretically any material could be harmful to someone if improperly used.

It is essential in a free society to provide access to all library materials. No restrictions are placed on what anyone may read, view, or listen to. Individuals or groups may occasionally question the inclusion of an item in the collection because of fear or doubt about the effects of the material on impressionable persons. Although the library understands this concern, it is the library's position that the risk to society is far greater if public access to ideas and information is restricted.

The library is opposed to the removal from its shelves, at the request of any individual or group, of materials which have been chosen according to the materials selection policy. In addition, the library will oppose efforts on the part of an individual or group seeking to have materials added to the collection which are contrary to the selection policy.

Northern Arizona University

Censorship: The Cline Library recognizes that the free access to ideas and full freedom of expression are fundamental to the educational process. To this end, we subscribe to and comply with the American Library Association Library Bill of Rights and Freedom to Read Statements. The collections will be available to all patrons of the library. The collections should offer the widest possible range of viewpoints regardless of popularity of items or viewpoints or the sex, political philosophy, religion, national origin, or notoriety of their proponents.

The selection or retention of material will not be made on the basis of viewpoint, frankness of language, or the controversial manner an author may use in dealing with scientific, religious, sexual, political, social, moral, or economic issues. Where there is controversy or disagreement concerning the truth of particular ideas, issues, or beliefs, the Cline Library will attempt to provide a wide selection of materials encompassing the major views.

The Collection Development Officer with the advice of the Collection Development Committee will respond to all questions concerning the propriety of specific materials place in the Cline Library collections. Persistent criticisms from persons or groups will be referred to the University Librarian and the Faculty Library Committee.

Covenant College (Georgia)

Intellectual Freedom and Censorship

In a Christian academic library, there is always the danger that a particular subject area in the collection may not represent diverse points of view on a subject. This may be true because of the selection of materials from a Christian perspective and/or if an academic department has some other particular approach to their discipline. It is important for the library faculty to work with the department faculty to be aware of such tendencies and to fill in the gaps, if even to a limited extent.

There is always the tendency to succumb to pressure not to purchase certain controversial materials for the collection. This is especially true of materials inconsistent with and/or hostile to a Christian worldview. It is important to point persons with such tendencies to the Statement of Purpose of the college and the mission statement of the library. Having only materials compatible with a Christian worldview would not serve the purpose of a Christian liberal arts education, although a Christian worldview is essential to properly understanding our culture as a whole, as well as the separate academic disciplines, education in Christian perspectives only is too narrow for the purpose of Covenant College. In order to bring a Christian worldview to bear upon culture in general as well as specific disciplines, knowledge of our culture as a whole and current thinking in specific disciplines is, of course, necessary. Controversial materials, as such, are not to be avoided in collection development.

Someone raising an objection to a book or other material in the library will be asked to provide a written explanation of their objection, citing specifics from the material in question. The written complaint will then be given to the Faculty Library Committee for review and recommendation. The librarians, in consultation with the Academic Dean, will make a decision taking into consideration the recommendation of the Faculty Library Committee. The decision and the recommendation of the Faculty Library Committee will be communicated to the complainant. No action will be taken without a written complaint which cites specifics from the material in question.

Harnett County Library (North Carolina)

The library will protect, as far as possible, the privacy of any patron who uses the library and not make any inquiry into the purposes for which a patron requests information or books. Records which may be required in lending books or answering reference questions are for the sole purpose of protecting public property. Under no circumstances shall the staff of the library ever answer to a third party about what a patron of the library is reading or calling for from the library's collection. Furthermore, it is the policy of the library not to yield any information about its patrons or their reading to any agency of government, whether local, state or federal, without an order from a court of competent jurisdiction.

New City Public Library (New York)

In accordance with New York State Law, the Library protects each user's right to privacy regarding information sought and materials borrowed. A copy of the law is attached, Appendix G.

APPENDIX G
NEW YORK STATE CIVIL PRACTICE LAW AND RULES

§ 4509. Library records

Library records, which contain names or other personally identifying details regarding the users of public, free association, school, college and university libraries and library systems of this state, including but not limited to records related to the circulation of library materials, computer database searches, interlibrary loan transactions, reference queries, requests of photocopies of library materials, title reserve requests, or the use of audio-visual materials, films or records, shall be confidential and shall not be disclosed except that such records may be disclosed to the extent necessary for the proper operation of such library and shall be disclosed upon request or consent of the user or pursuant to subpoena, court order or where otherwise required by statute. (Added L.1982, c. 14. § 1; amended L.1988, c. 112, § 1.)

Doane College (Nebraska)

Reaffirming Perkins Library's concern for intellectual freedom and for readers' rights of privacy, the library will not disclose to anyone the names of, or other information regarding readers and will not identify materials called for or examined by them.

No library records shall be made available to casual members of the public, the press, or any agency of State, Federal or Local government, except pursuant to such process, order, or subpoena as may be authorized under the authority of and pursuant to Federal, State or Local law relating to civil, criminal, or administrative discovery procedures or legislative investigatory power.

The Library Committee and Library Director shall resist the issuance or enforcement of any such process, order or subpoena until such time as a proper showing of good cause has been made in a court of competent jurisdiction. Moreover, any costs incurred by the library in any search through patron records, even under court order, shall be chargeable to the agency demanding such search.

CONSORTIA

* * * * * * * *

If not mentioned in the communities statement, networks, consortia, and other cooperative arrangements are usually mentioned toward the end of the policy statement. This is because these agreements affect the building of the collection in ways that the public might not understand, and which both benefit and hamper the public's use of the collection. Some materials are not purchased because a member of the consortia already has them or has promised to purchase them, and the library must purchase some materials because it has commitments to the consortia. Library patrons have the right to know what effects such arrangements have on them and the use of their library and any member library's collections.

* * * * * * * *

Juneau Public Libraries (Alaska)

The Juneau Public Libraries' operating assumption of a single collection in three locations is based on active resource sharing and extensive cooperative reliance. Although the Douglas and Valley libraries began as relatively independent and autonomous facilities, they are now closely linked with the downtown Juneau library. Collection development is centralized for the public library system as a whole.

Juneau Public Libraries became in Fall of 1985 one of three founding members of the Capital City Libraries (CCL) group, along with the Alaska State Library and the Library of the University of Alaska Southeast. This local resource-sharing group produced its first cooperative citywide catalog on microfiche in December 1985. The CCL's online public access catalog became operational in December 1986, followed by the integrated circulation system with shared patron file in February 1987. The Juneau-Douglas High

School Library joined the CCL group and entered its holdings onto the citywide online database in the fall of 1988. Members of CCL meet regularly to coordinate collection development activities.

Membership in Alaska Library Network facilitates resource-sharing among libraries of all types within the state. A statewide microfiche catalog is produced on a regular basis.

The Juneau Public Libraries contracted for full participating membership in the Western Library Network in July, 1983. This provides the library with an extensive resource-sharing arrangement throughout the Pacific Northwest region. The shared catalog is online.

With access to materials dramatically improved systemwide, citywide, statewide, and throughout the Pacific Northwest region, one result is less need for duplicate titles, more ability to broaden and strengthen the system's holdings with unique titles.

Use of these bibliographic databases and other cooperative arrangements such as the statewide conspectus have great impact on collection development. They give Juneau Public libraries the ability to support both core and special interest collections at a reasonable level, while increasing coordinated and cooperative reliance on other libraries for materials in areas of peripheral concern.

Florida State University

In order to maximize University resources and to enhance cooperative use of expensive acquisitions the libraries support an extensive InterLibrary Loan program. The University Libraries are a part of the State University System of libraries and are members of numerous cooperative organizations. Each of these organizations aids in the sharing of materials to the advantage of faculty and students. In the selection of expensive library materials, consideration is given to their accessibility through interlibrary loan agreements and through library networking.

Mount Wachusett Community College (Massachusetts)

The rapid growth of the published literature and the diverse interests of the college preclude the library from meeting all the varying needs of its users with its own collection. This policy acknowledges the need to increasingly rely on cooperative resource sharing activities because of the growing impossibility of building a totally comprehensive collection. The vast bibliographic data base of OCLC usually provides the M.W.C.C. library with quick access to location information for interlibrary loans. Our cooperative efforts with other libraries in the Gardner area (facilitated by membership in the NCMLA as well as CWMARS) will enable the library to share resources more effectively. Further, networks provide for the cooperative acquisition of scarce and expensive material.

Fairfield University (Connecticut)

The library is a member of Bibliomation, an area non-profit organization that provides automated services to libraries in several areas of Connecticut, a member of the Southwestern Connecticut Library Council (SWLC), and participates in the Online Computer Library Center (OCLC), a national bibliographic utility providing cataloging, bibliographic searching, and interlibrary loan services through Nelinet (New England Library Network).

Cooperative collection development agreements with area libraries are not generally effective for a library supporting primarily an undergraduate curriculum and a limited number of graduate programs. Reference librarians collaborate with their colleagues at other area libraries to locate resources needed by our patrons that are not available in Nyselius Library. Decisions regarding the disposition of gifts, the initiation of new periodical subscriptions or the cancellation of existing subscriptions, and the purchase of expensive sets may include consideration of resources available at other area libraries. ReQuest, a CD-ROM database produced by the Connecticut State Library containing the book holdings of over 200 libraries and the periodical holdings of more than 300, is used, along with our GEAC circulation database containing the holdings of over 45 libraries, to access the holdings of Connecticut libraries for collection management purposes.

Jamestown College (North Dakota)

Cooperative Collection Agreements

Only two formal cooperative collection agreements exist between Raugust Library and other libraries in our region.

The first involves the Curriculum Library. Our Curriculum Library has been designated the state resource for children's materials, and as such receives about 500 children's books per year on permanent loan from the State Library. We bear the expense of cataloging, shelving, and lending these materials, but as they are gifts to the State Library from various publishers, we do not have any control over the selection process. This has not been a problem, as all the books have been new and of very high quality, but as it is an element which we cannot control, the quality, of the program should be evaluated periodically to see if it is still meeting our needs.

The second agreement involves cooperative purchasing of the books indexed in the ESSAY AND GENERAL LITERATURE INDEX. Each library subscribing to this index receives a monthly listing of materials chosen for inclusion. The academic libraries in North Dakota have divided responsibility for purchasing these materials alphabetically among themselves; Raugust Library is responsible for anything beginning with the letter K (4.2% of the materials indexed). This is not an onerous burden, and the materials nearly always fit our library well.

There are various informal agreements with other libraries as well. The Alfred Dickey Public Library purchases what might be described as more general or popular materials, oftentimes things outside our curriculum areas, and our patrons who desire these items are referred downtown for them. Conversely, the public library sends patrons who need more scholarly materials to the college library. The directors of these two libraries do not feel that competition in these areas would benefit either library or either primary patron group. In one area, at least, the public library has a better collection than the college library, even though it is an area which we teach—namely, small business administration. Their collection has grown out of the need to provide assistance to the businesspeople of Jamestown, and our students have benefitted from it. It makes no sense to duplicate this collection when the public library is only a mile away from campus.

Given the geographic isolation we deal with, cooperative agreements are not easy to sustain. The only other one is very informal and involves the State Library again. This simply states that if a book is borrowed on interlibrary loan more than twice during a year, the State Library should be notified so that it can buy a copy for back-up. We have invoked this policy only twice in the past eight years.

MINITEX, which is the regional network of which we are a member, is currently starting work on plans for regional collection development. This movement is in its infancy, and will need to be watched for further developments.

COLLECTION
MAINTENANCE
❋ ❋ ❋ ❋ ❋ ❋ ❋ ❋ ❋

The opposite of selection is maintenance, and the part of the policy that deals with maintaining the collection has become increasingly more important as the price of materials has skyrocketed, and the need to protect the basic assets of the library's collection becomes ever more important. Since libraries can no longer purchase everything needed by everyone in their community, protecting what they have becomes a priority.

In the case of binding, replacement, preservation, disaster preparedness, etc., protecting the actual material becomes paramount to the professional. In the case of weeding, protecting the quality of the collection is considered the highest good. Clogging shelves with damaged or out-of-date materials reflects very badly on the library, and therefore, on the community that the library serves whether it be the town, city, or even the university. In most public libraries, weeding means getting rid of certain materials for the benefit of space and more accessible browsing for the patron. In the case of the academic library, it may mean second level access to little-used materials, or actually sending some material to warehouses that service a number of individual libraries.

There are two areas of collection maintenance that are relatively new to policy statements—disaster planning and preservation programs. These issues, which did not appear in the last edition of this book, really show the shift in emphasis towards protecting the collection a library already has, from a former emphasis of selecting whatever a library needs. With the knowledge that our most prized paper collections are slowly being eaten up from the inside, libraries are beginning to invest in programs to preserve their existing material. Although few libraries mention this in their statements, preservation procedures are present in most academic libraries. Although no such statements were found in public library collection development policies contributed for this book's compilation, the larger public research libraries probably have them in another policy or procedural document. Smaller public libraries have yet to face the problem since their collections are supposed to be turning over every ten years, and materials still last that long. However, even the smallest of libraries have some collections they wish to save (perhaps local history or town archives); so it may come to pass that even very small libraries may become involved in preservation programs.

❊ ❊ ❊ ❊ ❊ ❊ ❊ ❊ ❊

Warwick Public Library (Rhode Island)

The library recognizes the need to continuously evaluate its collections in response to the changing nature and needs of its community through the deselection, replacement, and duplication of titles.

Deselection of library materials is an integral part of collection development. An active and continuous deselection program is essential in maintaining a viable and useful collection. The following categories of materials should be considered for deselection: worn or mutilated items, duplicate copies of seldom used titles, materials which contain outdated or inaccurate information, superseded editions of specific titles, and materials no longer of interest or demand.

While the library tries to maintain copies of standard and important works, it does not automatically replace all materials withdrawn due to loss, damage or wear. Decisions concerning the replacement of individual items are based on the following considerations: demand for the specific item, the number of copies held, the existing coverage of the subject within the collection, the validity of its contents, the availability of the title for reorder, and the cost of mending versus the cost of replacement.

Duplication of materials is governed by popular demand, importance of the material, and budgetary limitations. For popular works such as bestsellers, the library takes into account the number of reserves as a guideline for purchasing additional copies.

Hartford Public Library (Connecticut)

Maintenance of the Collection—General Principles

Maintenance of the collection, which includes discarding, replacement, rebinding and repair, requires the same careful study and attention as initial selection. The department and agency heads are responsible for maintaining their collections, including carrying out the Library's continuing program of discarding.

The Library withdraws books and other materials from its general and special collections to maintain the usefulness of these collections and to make most effective use of available space. The same judgment and discretion used in building the collections are required in determining which materials should be removed. Principal reasons for the removal of materials are irreparable condition, obsolescence of contents, and reduced demand requiring fewer copies of a work than when originally purchased.

The Chief Librarian, in consultation with department heads and subject specialists, is authorized to remove materials of minimum or modest value. When it seems appropriate to staff and the Chief Librarian to remove items of greater value (e.g., rare books, manuscripts, prints) final approval is obtained from the Board of Directors.

Materials of little or no value or in very poor condition may be destroyed. Those which may still be useful elsewhere are made available to schools, libraries and other appropriate non-profit institutions.

Materials with market value, including unaccessioned gifts as well as deaccessioned items, are made available for purchase by the public through special sales conducted by the Friends of the Hartford Public Library and on a continuing basis from a browsing area in the Central Library. Materials of high value are offered to dealers and may be auctioned if market conditions warrant.

Under no circumstances will the Library's unwanted materials be sold to anyone, including especially Corporators and staff, through other than public sale.

Harnett County Library (North Carolina)

Collection Maintenance

Harnett County Public Library recognizes the need for continuous evaluation of its collections in response to the changing nature and needs of its community; this collection maintenance is accomplished through the weeding (i.e., removal from the collection), replacement, and duplication of its titles.

WEEDING is a necessary adjunct of selection; the criteria applied to acquisitions form the basis for weeding the collection.

Materials are regularly discarded from library collections; they are withdrawn because they are out-of-date, because they are so badly worn or damaged that they cannot be bound or mended, because it is cheaper to replace them, or because they are once-popular works that are no longer used. Space, the cost of replacement, and the appearance of the collection are factors in these decisions. Although the library tries to have copies of all standard and important works, it does not attempt REPLACEMENT of every copy withdrawn due to loss, damage, or wear. Community interest and the availability of newer or other format materials will be the primary considerations. Since books rapidly go out of print, many specific titles simply cannot be replaced. Withdrawn materials may be sold at a public sale by the Friends of the Harnett County Public Library and proceeds used to buy additional materials.

The library gives serious consideration to the number of requests for an item as a guide for DUPLICATION. Since duplication must not be at the expense of important but less-demanded materials needed for the permanent collection, popular demand, importance of the material, and budgetary limitations will be the determining factors.

Since the problems of mutilation, damage and loss of library materials occur regularly in the libraries, it is necessary to establish guidelines to ensure that the libraries' services will not be impaired.

A. DEFINITIONS

The terms mutilation, damage, and missing are defined as follows:

- mutilation—the wanton removal of pages or parts of pages from library materials. Also any writing or marking in books.

- damage—wear on library materials caused by negligence of the user; or, normal deterioration due to heavy use by patrons.

- missing—absence of library materials which are not charged out, and cannot be located through a systematic search of the collection.

B. WHY THERE ARE GUIDELINES ON REPLACING MATERIALS

The specific purpose of the guidelines regarding mutilation and damage to materials are as follows:

1. to reduce the occurrence of abuse through user education, improved loan services, adequate copies for heavily used materials, the reserve book system, security check, and faculty cooperation.

2. to establish procedures for reporting and recording damaged books and materials.

3. to act promptly in replacing or repairing materials.

4. to improve the cooperation among all agencies using county-owned books and materials.

5. to develop statistical reports required for anticipating needs of seasonal materials; predictable term paper researches, etc.

C. GUIDELINES FOR REPLACING MATERIALS

1. The initial handling of mutilated or damaged library materials is that the circulation librarian or shelver places these materials in the designated area for further evaluation by the library director. The

replacement or withdrawing of missing materials shall be attempted periodically.

2. Replacement—while the library tries to have copies of all standard and important works, it does not attempt to replace each copy withdrawn because of loss, damage or wear. Decisions will be based on the following criteria:

   ■ demand for the specific item

   ■ number of copies held

   ■ existing coverage of the subject within the system

   ■ availability of newer and better materials on the subject

   ■ price of the replacement copy

   ■ coverage of relevant subject matter in standard indexes

3. Factors in the decision to rebind are:

   ■ value and use of the title

   ■ possibility of replacement

   ■ physical condition, including quality of paper, margins and illustrations

   ■ cost of rebinding versus cost of replacement

   ■ number of copies available

D. CONTINUOUS MAINTENANCE IN THE CHILDREN'S COLLECTION

Because the library recognizes that information is ever changing and that out-of-date material on a subject is often worse than no material at all, the children's collection will be continuously revised and weeded.

The following types of material are considered for withdrawal when evaluating the collection:

1. Materials in poor physical condition.

2. Slow-moving titles not in standard sources such as the Children's Catalog.

3. Subjects no longer of interest.

4. Multiple copies of things no longer in demand.

5. Old editions replaced by later revisions of nonfiction titles.

In weeding, care will be taken to retain local material as well as books by local authors—in both adult and juvenile materials.

Ouachita Parish Public Library (Louisiana)

Reasons for Collection Weeding

To Improve the Collection. Careful, dependable weeding will enhance the readability and up-to-dateness of the collection, thereby building public trust. It has been said that many patrons feel that library books are selected by experts and the mere fact that the book is in the library lends authority to it. To foster and insure this reputation, weeding is a necessity.

To Save Space and Money. Weeded materials no longer cost money for cleaning, binding, mending, extra stacks, extra files, and all the other hidden costs of maintenance and space, none of which are cut by lack of use. Crowded shelves can be avoided. There can be more space for tables and chairs for in-house research, study and entertainment. The library can present the open friendly appearance that is the goal of every librarian.

To Save Time. Collection weeding will save time for patrons and staff. Crowded shelves, full of ragged books with torn markings, cost time if one is trying to use the collection for research or looking for a particular book or trying to shelve books. Use of the card catalog is impeded by drawers too full with cards. An overload of useless books increases all library housekeeping.

To Make the Library More Appealing. Attractive new books will replace ragged and unattractive volumes as a result of weeding.

To Provide Feedback on the Collection's Strength and Weaknesses. Systematic weeding increases staff knowledge of the collection. This can be extremely helpful in collection building practices.

Bay State College (Massachusetts)

Replacement of Missing Titles

Missing titles are replaced within two years, or immediately as needed, dependent upon the needs of the collection. All replacements are at the discretion of the library. If the item is deemed unnecessary or outdated, the item will be withdrawn. If books are recovered after withdrawal from the collection, they will be evaluated as if they were gifts.

Alvin Community College (Texas)

Alvin Community College Library Weeding Policy

General policies:

1. One complete weeding of the library will take place once a year.
2. Money available for replacement and/or binding will be considered.
3. Works containing outdated or inaccurate information will be weeded, unless they have intrinsic value.
4. Older editions will be replaced by newer ones, and the older edition discarded.
5. In the case of classics, older editions and translations will not be weeded except for unused multiple copies.
6. Excess, unneeded duplicate copies of seldom used titles will be discarded.
7. The last copy of a work authored by a faculty member will not be weeded.
8. If an item has not circulated in the previous 10 years, it will be considered a prime candidate for weeding.
9. If a book is in such poor physical condition that it would take longer than 15 minutes to repair, it will be considered for bindery or replacement.
10. The usefulness of an item to a particular group or individual will be considered.
11. The relation of the item to other books in the subject area will be considered. If the work is the last book in a subject area, and the area needs to be covered, newer editions or titles will be acquired.
12. The historical depth of the overall collection will be considered. As a community college where scholarly research is not performed, depth and breadth of the collection will be attained in very few areas.
13. Newspapers and periodicals replaced by microforms will be weeded and discarded.

California State University, Chico

Disposal of Discarded Library Materials

After collection development librarians, in consultation with the teaching faculty, have identified which materials are no longer needed in the Meriam Library collections, disposal of the material is necessary. The Office of the Chancellor memorandum LSD 81-24/BA 81-44 allows state university libraries, keeping disposal costs at a minimum, to use local discretion to recycle, trash, or destroy said materials or they may be sold to the general public, i.e., students, faculty, campus personnel, and citizens at large, at open non-exclusive local campus book sales. All proceeds shall be used to purchase library replacement collection material.

Given these options, it is recommended that the following procedures be adopted:

A. Books and Periodicals

    1. Discarded materials and unwanted gifts may be sent to Campus Property Management for disposal or given to the Friends of the Library to be sold at their book sales.

    2. All library materials bearing California State University, Chico, property stamps shall be clearly marked DISCARDED.

B. Nonprint Resources

    1. Dispose of nonprint media materials as appropriate for the format of the item discarded.

       a. Films may be returned to the distributor for credit or may be used by the IMC Media Preparation Area for experimental, educational, or demonstrational purposes.

       b. Audio cassettes or video cassettes will be erased and the tape used again as appropriate.

       c. Other nonprint materials (e.g., games, kits, slides, sound recordings, transparencies, etc.) will follow disposal guidelines set down for printed materials.

Mount Wachusett Community College (Massachusetts)

Weeding Policy

I. Definition:

Weeding constitutes the removal of outdated, superseded, damaged or duplicated material from the collection.

Materials weeded from the reference collection may be placed in circulation if considered of lasting value.

II. Purpose:

1. To reevaluate the collection in conjunction with the selection of new and replacement materials in order to keep the collection viable and useful.

2. To delete unnecessary, out-of-date materials from the shelves.

3. To alert faculty and librarians to areas of weakness in the collection.

4. To identify work materials in need of replacement, binding or repair.

III. Responsibility:

Primary responsibility lies with the librarians, although advisement from pertinent teaching faculty may be sought where appropriate and available. Faculty are allowed college service credit for assisting with weeding the collection in their subject areas.

IV. Guidelines:

Criteria for Withdrawal of Materials

A. Physical condition beyond repair—

1. To be replaced if they meet selection criteria and are available.

2. To be rebound if valuable and if possible or kept protected if valuable and still useful.

B. Excess number of duplicate copies—

1. When deemed no longer needed for the academic program.

2. Exceptions include popular works and literature for which demand may fluctuate.

C. Superseded editions—

1. A "next-to-last" edition may be kept depending on subject, length of time between editions, circulation, or extent of revision.

2. Some reference works will be kept in all revisions according to guidelines in the "Reference Collection Development Policy."

3. Those with material cumulated in a newer edition.

D. Materials not suitable for the collection (i.e. graduate level in a program not taught at M.W.C.C.).

E. Outdated Material—

1. Anything more than 5 years old should be checked in a standard bibliography and retained if included in it or if deemed still useful.

2. Exceptions are the Humanities subject areas, crafts and gardening.

F. Insufficient use will be considered but not used as a sole factor.

G. Broken sets or runs—

1. If missing volumes are needed for sets to be useful but are not available or are too expensive to be purchased.

H. Journals—

1. Broken runs of unindexed journals.

2. Broken runs of older journals of little use or no longer purchased or published.

3. Older issues replaced by microfilm.

Some Criteria For Not Discarding

A. Local author or faculty member, or local topic.

B. The subject matter of the book is unique and is out of print.

C. The illustrator is famous, or the book contains unusual photographs or illustrations.

D. The book enjoys a fair circulation.

E. The book is a prize winner (Pulitzer, NBA, etc.).

F. The book is analyzed in a standard index (EGLI, etc.).

G. The book is source material.

H. The book is part of a series.

I. The book has an excellent extensive bibliography which is still useful.

J. The book reflects the mores of a period.

When To Weed

A. As necessary, when damaged or outdated titles are found through shelf-reading, preparing bibliographies, etc.

B. According to program review:

1. After the initial weeding of unnecessary duplicate copies, a schedule will be arranged according to the program review schedule, until entire collection has been done once.

2. Using that schedule as a guide, once the entire collection is completed, 25% of the collection will be weeded each year, so that the entire collection is weeded once every four years.

C. The reference collection should be weeded every year.

D. Periodicals should be reviewed every year as the periodical list is updated.

Procedures:

1. Weeding action taken on damaged, superseded or duplicated books (found through shelving, shelf-reading, inventory, etc.) will be assessed on an individual book-by-book basis. A decision will then be made as to whether the item should be discarded, kept, or repaired.

2. Weeding action on books missing in inventory or excessively overdue from the previous year(s) will be assessed on an individual book-by-book basis. A decision will then be made as to whether the item should be replaced or withdrawn.

3. Books:

   a. Go through s.1. and check dates, prominent authors, "classics" or recognizable items.

   b. Mark "keep," date, and initial those to be kept. Pull cards for those to be discarded.

   c. Go to shelves with book truck, pencil, scrap paper for notes, and s.1. cards for books to be pulled.

   d. Pull books to be considered for withdrawal, including any that s.1. cards were not pulled for; make notes if necessary.

   e. Bring truck to office area for other librarians to review.

   f. Check bibliographies or consult faculty when necessary.

   g. Return those to be kept off the shelf, or set aside for repairs.

   h. Those to be discarded should be stamped "DISCARDED" and book cards should be pulled. Write down call numbers for any without cards and pull s.1. cards if not already pulled.

   i. Count those discarded and add to list of books discarded.

   j. Pull card sets for discarded books.

   k. If discarding duplicate copies, mark s.1. card "W" and date next copy number withdrawn and then refile s.1. card.

   l. Contact North Central Corrections Institution to see if they want any discards, then send list to state surplus warehouse.

4. Magazines

   a. Using magazine list, check shelves to match dates to be held and those received on microfilm.

   b. Paper copies are kept for the most current full year we receive microfilm, for the same title, therefore providing an overlap for paper and microfilm for one year. All remaining older paper copies are discarded.

c. Discard to faculty if marked on check-in card, otherwise discard.

d. Broken runs or discontinued subscriptions should be decided on an individual basis for discard. If warranted, notify other college libraries of their availability.

Inventory Policy

Procedure
The following procedure will be used for the annual inventory of the M.W.C.C. Library (at the conclusion of the Spring semester):

1. Shelf read book collection.
2. Check shelf list against books on shelves (1 person reading last line of call no. aloud from shelf list, 1 person silently reading call numbers on books).
3. For shelf list cards with no books:

    a. check circulation file and overdues

    b. if found, refile in shelf list

    c. if not found, keep separate as missing

    For books with no shelf list cards:

    a. shelve books in cataloger's office

    b. check file of cards for previously missing (withdrawn) books

    c. if cards are found, and the book is to be kept, count as new book on sheet and refile cards

    d. if cards are not found and book is to be kept, catalog using OCLC and treat as a new book (count on sheet)

    e. if cards are not found and book is not being kept, stamp book "discarded" and put on shelf with free books

    f. if cards are found and book is not being kept, discard all cards, stamp book "discarded"

4. Follow same procedure for non-print collection.
5. At conclusion of inventory, count no. of missing (and not accounted for) books and non-print materials by subject category. Give figures to Library Director to add to statistics. Figure % of missing books by dividing the number actually missing by the total current book count.
6. Check shelf list cards for missing books to decide whether:

a. books will not be replaced—pull all cards and file cards in missing books file

b. books will be replaced and are available in BIP—order books, mark, reorder, date on shelf list card, then refile in the shelf list

c. books should be replaced but are not available in BIP—Library Director will choose the substitute and decide which books should be reordered immediately. Other slips will be filled with P.O.'s. Pull cards for books to be replaced and file with cards for missing books.

7. Procedure no. 6 should be repeated for the books which were charged out and not returned from the previous year. They should be counted* as withdrawn by subject category on the total count sheet at this time (and cards filed in missing file), but they should not be counted as "missing."

*Keep an additional separate count of books overdue over a year and withdrawn.

Replacements

The library will not automatically replace all materials withdrawn from the collections because of loss, damage or wear. Decisions to replace an item will be based on the following considerations:

1. Demand for the specific titles to support the curriculum.
2. Number of copies held.
3. Existing coverage of the subject within the collection.
4. Availability of newer and better materials on the subject.

Titles in the collection reported missing will be promptly replaced if needed for teaching or research, if they are obtainable. Literary works and recognized titles in all subject areas will be replaced one year after reported missing, if still in print.

Missing serial volumes should be replaced on microfilm; missing pages of a serial issue will be replaced by clipped-in photocopies. Microfilms missing during annual inventory will be replaced automatically in the same format. Missing pages of a book will be replaced by clipped-in photocopies.

Binding, Mending, and Discarding

Decisions will be made continuously on how to handle worn books; whether to mend, bind or withdraw them. Each decision is based on the actual condition of the book, the number of duplicate copies in the collection, the current validity of its contents, availability of the title for reorder, and the cost of mending versus the cost of replacement. In making such decisions, these guidelines will be followed by the librarians:

1. Withdraw books under the guidelines in the weeding policy.
2. Assuming the title is still available, replacement with a new copy is preferable to rebinding if costs are comparable. In cases where rebinding will not restore the book to a condition suitable for normal library use, the books should be replaced. Books which are worn and cannot be rebound due to overly narrow margins should also be replaced with a new or good second hand copy.
3. Binding is preferable to mending if a title is expected to have long-term usefulness and if an inordinate amount of mending is required.
4. Mending will be done only when need is detected early. In general, most pamphlets and paperbacks which are in poor condition should be discarded.
5. In some instances, an irreplaceable title of importance must be retained regardless of condition. Special handling will be given such a title.
6. Cataloged paperbound titles will usually be bound before circulation to withstand library use.

Le Moyne College (New York)

Disaster Policy for the Library
Emergency Steps

1. **On Call:**

   Director of the Library   Home Number:
   Administrative Asst to Director   Home Number:
   Public Services Librarian   Home Number:

   The Security Guard will contact the person responsible.

   If there is a person on duty in the library, they will contact the Security Office immediately.

   The responsibility of the person contacted is to come to the library as soon as possible and assess the problem.

   Water Damage - Flooding or water coming from the ceiling:

   a. Ceiling - cover shelves and books immediately with plastic sheeting.

      Flooding - remove books from shelves being affected and use vacuum to remove water.

    b. Call the emergency repair person and crew in to remove the books from the shelves. If they are not wet they can be boxed immediately and removed. If the materials are wet they are to be spread on a table away from the danger area.

2. **Emergency Kit.** Should be accessible at all times and stored in an area away from mechanical rooms and water pipes. The Security, Physical Plant and Library Staff need to know where this is kept.

    EMERGENCY KIT CONTENTS:

        Plastic sheeting cut to size for covering shelves and books
        Boxes or collapsible plastic crates
        Packing tape
        Scissors
        Waterproof markers
        Cloths
        Chemical light stick (need demo)
        Vacuum to remove water (large tank)

3. If water is spraying on the books, the first step to take is to cover the shelves with plastic sheeting until the problem can be repaired and manpower available to move the books off the shelves. Time is a very important step and can prevent major loss of materials.

4. The Physical Plant personnel who are on twenty-four hour call are to be contacted to come in to remove the books/materials when a disaster arises. The Security Staff is responsible for contacting these men.

5. After the initial disaster is over the Physical Plant is needed to come in and clean up the affected area.

6. A workshop is needed periodically to make the Security, Physical Plant and Library Staff aware of the steps to be taken in the case of an emergency.

7. The Treasurer's Office will be contacted and insurance company notified of the disaster. I checked with Bob Satterlee and our present insurance has a $10,000 deductible for one given incident.

The Director of the Library will assess the damage and decide what steps will be taken to restore the materials. There are many options depending on the amount of money available to restore damaged books.

If a water disaster occurs the first major step is to get the books to a cold storage facility as soon as possible. We will have to make arrangements with one of these companies to take the books immediately if a disaster should occur.

James Madison University (Virginia)

Carrier Library is dedicated to preservation through a variety of efforts. In accordance with these efforts, the Library actively supports the use of alkaline paper for publishing. The decision to purchase soft cover instead of hard cover editions of titles is part of this preservation orientation. The binding available through our commercial binder is much more durable and protective of the contents than is the mass-produced hard cover product. Openability for photocopying also may be improved through the rebinding process. The extra cost for this binding is more than compensated for by the difference in price between hard cover and soft cover editions.

The temperature and humidity of Carrier Library is constantly monitored. The Library strives to maintain an environment most beneficial to the maintenance of the collection and the comfort of its users within the limitations set by building constraints. Physical handling of the collection is done in accordance with proper preservation procedures. Education of the staff and users through signage, displays, and other media is constant.

Items in the Library's collections may incur damage while in use. The Library staff encourages users to report any damage when it is discovered. In addition, Loan Services staff may notice the damage during handling. In all cases damaged items are sent to the mending technicians for repair. Repairs are done in accordance with the best preservation techniques. When the damaged item is considered by the mending technicians to be of questionable value, or the necessary repairs are impossible without limiting access to the contents, the item is considered for deselection or replacement. As time permits, the mending technicians are examining the entire collection to identify those items needing repair.

The Music Library parallels the processes and programs described above, with the Music Librarian acting as the person in charge of preservation programs and utilizing a group of trained students as mending technicians. The entire collection is being examined and evaluated by the librarian and is being brought up to current standards by the technicians. All newly added materials are protected at these standards as well.

Michigan Technological University

J. Robert Van Pelt Library Preservation
Program Statement

Goal: To maintain and preserve the library collections in original or in reproduction format in order to provide access to information for our users and to protect unique materials. Priorities will be determined by our collection policy and the limitations of available resources.

Objectives
1. To assess the severity of deterioration of materials in this library.
2. To assess the subject areas in which the problems occur.
3. To determine preservation priorities based on our collection policy.
4. To determine needs and changes required for conservation and preservation in our building and facilities.
5. To develop ongoing programs which will serve to alleviate and monitor the problems.
6. To inform ourselves and our users of preservation needs, issues, and practices.
7. To budget time and money to support the program.

Content of the Program
1. Survey: extent of need, costs (using expertise of the statistics areas of the Mathematics Department).
2. Administration: by the Collection Development function of the library.
3. Processes and procedures: to be an integral part of all staff activity.
4. Educational activity: directed to all Library staff and the campus community.
5. Disaster plan: to be defined.
6. Facilities and buildings: old and new, to be analyzed and planned to include conservation and preservation needs and requirements.
7. National participation: to include planning and standards as set by the Association of Research Libraries.

Current Strengths Upon Which to Build
1. Collection: focused (science/engineering-related: 24% monographs, 48% serials), old, unique, relatively small, high percentage of serial/ journals.
2. Electronic linkage: FOCUS, UPRLC, OCLC permits regional, national, and international participation.
3. Expertise on campus for assessing needs.
4. Education of staff.

J. Robert Van Pelt Library Preservation Committee 1990

Conservation/Preservation Repair Levels

Level I.

No action by Binding/Repair. Return book to designated location. To include:

Worn paperback; worn spine/slightly torn

Worn cloth binding/slightly frayed

Journal issues: individual issues with torn covers (front and back) or separated—repaired by Stack Supervisor at the Circulation Desk

Level II.

To Repair/Binding. Included:

Stapled binding

Torn/separated cover

Magnetic strip exposed

Torn spine

Loose pages/signatures

High circulation (cf. FOCUS or date due slip)

Level III.

To Collection Development. Included:

Non-repairable or unable to be rebound

J. Robert Van Pelt Library Collection Evaluation and Preservation Committees

Keep Codes

The following codes are used for library materials which have been reviewed by the Collection Evaluation Committee and which are to be retained in the collection.

Code Decision

1. Keep indefinitely in present form in usual location. Implies: Use no extraordinary means of preservation. We understand eventual deterioration will occur.

   a. high use.

   b. I.L.L. use.

2. Keep because we have it.

   a. may not be widely held.

   b. is in the periphera of academic subjects pertinent to MTU.

   c. may be old but still in-print (indicates continuing worth).

  d. periphera academic subject, listed in BCL.

  e. historical value.

3. Keep in box.

4. Keep. Pertinent subject area.

  a. rebind.

5. Acidic, crumbling.

6. Rare, or close to rare (5 or less OCLC holdings).

7. Illustrations of pertinent or unusual worth.

8. Out-of-print.

9. Classic.

  a. old.

  b. listed in BCL, any edition.

  c. listed in subject bibliographies.

10. MTU Unique/primary research source:

  a. Pre-1920 mining, metallurgy, general or technical trade engineering book or journal.

  b. If illustrated, keep in original format.

  c. Monitor for deterioration.

  d. Eventual candidate for preservation reformatting.

These codes will be entered into NOTIS in the "notes" field of the particular item record. Examples:

  3.10.a Keep in box; MTU unique/primary research source; Pre-1920 mining book.

  2.d. Keep because we have it; listed in BCL-periphera subject.

Circulation Preservation Procedures

The Circulation Department includes the following as part of its Preservation Procedures:

1. As part of their initial training students will view the video on Preservation entitled, "Use and Abuse: The Role of Staff and Patrons in Maintaining General Library Collections."

2. When discharging materials students should examine each item to determine whether it may need repair:

  a. Check physical appearance of each book.

    b. Open up the book to see if pages are coming out or if it is falling apart.

    c. Anything with a stapled binding should go to the Stacks Manager.

If the student assistant determines that the item warrants repair it should then be given to the Stacks Manager.

3. Books to go to the Stacks will be placed on the book trucks standing up. If they are too large to be stood up, they will be placed on the book trucks on their spines.

4. Walk Stacks "Preservation Style".

    a. Loosen books so they are not squeezed tightly on the shelves.

    b. Be aware of books in dire need of repair.

    c. Straighten up books on shelves and pick up any books which may be lying on the shelves.

5. Dusting is an important part of the library's overall cleanliness. Dust has a damaging effect on library materials. Dusting is to be done on a regular basis, especially the bottom shelves of the stacks.

6. Books too large to be stood up on shelves need to have the spine down on the shelf and a call number label placed on the upper left side of the front cover for easy identification.

7. Students Assistants will be informed of the damaging effects of food and drink upon library materials. Patrons will be asked to remove any food or beverages brought into the building.

8. Hands should be kept clean at all times.

9. Bound volumes of materials should be copied using the Xerox 5042 Library copiers which are designed with an "edge" to preserve book bindings.

10. Carpeting or foam is placed in the Reserve Book Drop and Outside book drop to prevent damage to materials.

11. Stools are placed in the available locations for ease in shelving and reshelving materials.

S U B J E C T S

* * * * * * * * *

There are still some subject areas where special considerations in collection development need to be taken. Already mentioned in the section on legal issues are some controversial areas, and it might be wise to include them in a separate area dealing with just such issues. There are some subject areas, though usually not controversial, which are also in need of separate explanations—such as recreational reading materials in an academic library, and scholarly items in a public library.

For an example of what might be seen in a full-blown policy, see those that are reprinted in full in Part 2. Below are policy statements about fields which are relatively noncontroversial, but which, with many others, would consti- tute an entire collection selection process, area by area. In the case of a library with an approval plan, all areas would have this type of treatment; in the case of a library without an approval plan, some areas might be set aside and discussed because they are in some ways unusual or unique in that library's situation.

* * * * * * * *

James Madison University (Virginia)

Law Library

The Laird L. Conrad Law Library was created in 1974 by a joint arrangement between James Madison University and the Harrisonburg-Rockingham County Bar Association. Materials owned by the Bar Association are available for long-term housing in the Law Library and are incorporated into the Leonardo online system. All materials held within the Law Library are either the property of the Bar Association or are University-owned titles which were approved for inclusion by the Bar Association's Joint Law Library Committee. Other law materials are housed in both the circulating and reference collections. Requests for additional titles are submitted to the Joint Law Library Committee. Law Library materials do not circulate.

Northwestern State University of Louisiana

Recreational Reading/Best Sellers

A Reading Area has been established in the lobby of the first floor of Watson Library to provide a selection of recreational reading for the NSU community. Science fiction, popular fiction, mysteries, biographies, and selected non-fiction books are displayed on the Reading Area shelves. Currently, a core collection of classics and standards in these areas is augmented at regular intervals by materials received through a best seller approval plan. The Reading Area should be reviewed on an on-going basis for materials to be returned to the regular stacks or to be weeded from the collections.

Ephemeral items, such as Harlequin Romances and other formula fiction are not purchased. Further, such items, when acquired by gift, should not be added to the Reading Area or the regular library collections.

Warwick Public Library (Rhode Island)

Parapsychology

In acquiring works on astrology, fortune telling, witchcraft, extrasensory perception, hypnosis, and related areas, the same selection criteria are applied as to other nonfiction items. Because of the nature of the subjects, the extraordinary demand for materials, and the prolific output in these areas, selection must be especially careful and special attention paid to the authority and reputation of the author and publisher. Purchasing multiple copies of a well-written or much-in-demand item is preferable to acquiring dubious titles just to increase the size of the collection.

Oakland Public Library (California)

The Black History Collection is an interdisciplinary collection of books designed to support the reference and research needs of the Oakland community and to promote a greater understanding of the Black experience.

The collection's major geographical focus is the United States, although other areas, especially Africa, are represented. Although there is no chronological limitation, the collection focuses on materials covering the experience of Black Americans during the 19th and 20th centuries. The collection is designed for the use of the general public; esoteric or academic texts are not included. Fiction is not generally collected but classic or groundbreaking titles may be included. Poetry and drama are collected in anthologies.

The Black History Collection does not circulate. Circulating copies of most books in the collection, however, are also available in the reference sections and in many branch libraries. Circulating copies of standard titles are replaced regularly, as needed. Core reference titles, such as *The Negro Almanac* and *Who's Who in Black America*, are not duplicated in the circulating collection, although additional reference copies may be placed in other sections.

Science Fiction

The science fiction collection is being expanded. Classic titles that are missing are being replaced; series are being completed; fantasy titles are being collected. In this genre many classic titles are available only in paperback. Exciting new authors often publish only in paperback. Mass market paperbacks, therefore, are frequently reinforced and catalogued in this genre to improve accessibility to the works of these authors.

One third of the new titles are fantasy; two thirds are basic science fiction.

Selection Policy: Computer Books

The Main Library's computer book collection addresses the needs of students, small business, jobseekers, consumers and home computer users by providing access to circulating materials on the most popular and widely used microcomputers and software programs. Primary emphasis is on materials that introduce and explain major computer languages, elementary and intermediate programming, word processing, spreadsheets, telecommunications, database management and graphics to new and experienced users. Many items purchased for circulation are also included in the reference collection. Titles cataloged reference concentrate on consumer "blue books," software directories and out-of-print material.

New City Library (New York)

Some subject areas worthy of special discussion are:

Sex Education: The Library provides books and other materials that explain human physiology, development, and reproduction in plain language. Material is also selected that addresses sexual orientation, birth control, abortion, and the ethical/moral issues surrounding these topics. As with all issues of potential controversy, the Library attempts to provide variety and balance of viewpoints.

Pamphlet Materials: 1. Pamphlet selection follows the general policy outlines for other items. Since this material is inexpensive and frequently free, useful pamphlets are acquired in multiple copies. They supplement books and magazines. Because many pamphlets are issued for advertising or propaganda purposes, great care is used in their selection. A balance of viewpoints on controversial issues is sought; polemical treatment is avoided. Acceptable pamphlet material has the issuing agency or publisher clearly identified.

Paperback vs. Clothbound: When paperback and clothbound editions of a given book are released simultaneously, paperbound is usually chosen for reasons of economy. Exceptions may include: classics; collected or major works; and materials by popular authors or on popular subjects where demand is expected to endure for many years. To aid durability, paperback originals may be reinforced in-house or sent to a bindery.

Local Authors: Plays by, and biographical works about, New City playwright Maxwell Anderson are shelved in the Rockland Room. Works by other local authors are, in general, acquired according to their own intrinsic merits, evaluated by the same criteria applied to other works of fiction and nonfiction, and shelved in the general book collection.

Picture Books: Generally designed for the preschool or primary grade child, picture books may be either fiction or nonfiction. They are distinguished by the art work which may be integrated with, or take precedence over, the text. The quality of illustration and format are of equal importance to the literary quality.

Greenville County Library (South Carolina)

Religion: Because religion is one of the deep concerns of humanity and theology is one of the major intellectual disciplines, the library attempts to provide accurate and objective information on beliefs and practices of various religions, denominations, and sects. Its selection is broad, tolerant, and without partisanship, consistently directed toward choosing the best books in regard to authority, timeliness, and good literary quality. Since users vary widely in background, an effort is made to choose materials to fit differing needs while avoiding both very specialized and oversimplified materials.

Fiction: The novel is a dynamic literary form which is subject to change and innovation by writers to suit their differing aims. While the library collects representative novels of the past, it also has the responsibility of making available contemporary works portraying many aspects of current society. Style of writing, characterization, philosophy, or social commentary may make a work a worthwhile acquisition.

Since each novel is ordinarily judged on its individual merits, no attempt is made at completeness in the library's holdings of an author's works. Exceptions are made, however, for the great novelists of the past and for outstanding contemporary novelists.

In selecting fiction, the library has set up no arbitrary, single standard of literary quality. An attempt is made to satisfy a public varying greatly in formal education, social background, and taste. Under these circumstances fiction selection does not mean choosing only the most distinguished novels but also the most competent, pleasing, and successful books in all categories of fiction writing in an effort to meet current literary standards and public demand.

South Carolina Fiction Cooperative: As a member of the South Carolina Fiction Cooperative, the library assumes responsibility for maintaining on a permanent basis a last-copy circulating collection of adult and juvenile fiction titles written by authors whose last names begin with GLASQ through GORD. Within its area of responsibility the library maintains last copies of its own fiction and also adds last copies received from other public libraries in the state when these titles are not already included in the libraries in the state when these titles are not already included in the library's collection. Guidelines for the South Carolina Fiction Cooperative, established in 1986 as a joint effort among all public libraries in the state, determine the content of this collection. Light romances are excluded in accordance with these guidelines.

F O R M A T S

* * * * * * * *

In the group of policies surveyed, collection development policies now include all formats of library materials, from those that are very traditional, say, periodicals, reference books, or archives, to those that have just come of age within the last few years—electronic sources. In a collection development policy, if the format has specifics about its selection, acquisition, maintenance, or even servicing, it should be separated out in its own paragraph or two. Aside from standing out in the policy statement, if it is a particularly difficult format to use, expensive compared with others, or so new that few people are yet using it, this part of the document will help to put it into perspective for the audience of library users. Among the issues that most libraries want to emphasize in their policy statements are (1) the restriction of purchase of certain formats (e.g. textbooks, multiple copies) and (2) the reporting of reasons for those restrictions to the public in writing. Backed by a board or other official sanction, this type of written policy clarification will support librarians when issues are raised from their communities.

* * * * * * * *

Audiovisual Materials

Tomah Public Library (Wisconsin)

Because the Tomah Public Library functions in a rapidly changing society, it must keep flexible attitudes toward changes in communicative materials, in relation to both new forms and new styles of expression. It must be, for example, responsive to the increased output and improved quality of such forms as recordings, films and paperbacks. Materials in these forms are selected when they are suitable in content and effective in treatment; they are judged in terms of their own kind of excellence and the audience for whom they are intended.

Fairview Heights Public Library (Illinois)

Videocassettes will be purchased to support the non-fiction and classics portion of the library collection. Adult entertainment items will not be purchased.

Amarillo Public Library (Texas)

Spoken Word

Books on tape is the preferred format for entire works, particularly when the work is contained on two or more cassettes. Multiple copies of such works are purchased selectively for study, as needed and as budget allows (e.g., Shakespeare). Such works are no longer purchased in LP format.

The books on tape collection emphasizes fiction, including recent bestsellers, mystery and intrigue titles, older works by both popular and critically acclaimed authors and selected classics. Currently, purchases are limited to sets that are complete in one album and cost not more than $100.

Excerpts and condensations of novels and plays, as well as short stories, are purchased for the cassette collection. These works are generally contained on a single cassette.

Also purchased for the cassette collection are collections of speeches, old radio programs, motivational works (e.g., *Think And Grow Rich*), documentaries and interviews on current issues, health and psychology and both the King James and the Revised Standard versions of the Bible. Works on selling and real estate are not purchased at this time.

Videocassette Selection Policy

There is a growing awareness of film as a vital source of information and as an art form in today's society. Films provide the citizen with information about his work, his community, the world, and his place in it. The Library, in accordance with the general Materials Selection Policy, will acquire videocassettes that will meet the educational, informational, cultural, and recreational interests of the people of Amarillo. To fulfill this purpose, the Library will maintain a carefully selected collection of representative materials of permanent value and of current interest. Thus, instructional films, how-to films, children's visuals, documentaries, plays, management and training tapes, nostalgia, and feature films emphasizing timeless subject matter as well as classics are appropriate to this collection's scope. Amarillo Public's video collection will evolve to fill an important gap in the community in the provision of film access too difficult to locate subjects and films of merit that are no longer available from current suppliers.

For budget reasons, the Library can acquire only a limited number of the many video items issued annually. Selection is based upon principle rather than personal opinion, reason rather than prejudice, and judgment rather than censorship. To assure the acquisition of quality video materials, the following characteristics will be considered in relation to each title requested:

Favorable Reviews   The videocassettes to be acquired will be those materials which, in the opinions, of reputable reviewers or experts within the subject area, present ideas and information in an accurate and well-organized manner and which employ a style of presentation appropriate for the medium, the subject matter, and the intended audience.

Appropriateness of the Subject to the Collection

Appropriateness to the Interests and Skills of the Intended Users

Technical Quality   The technical quality of purchased videos shall meet professional standards, i.e., sound formats should be clear and visual formats should be in focus and have consistent and accurate color tones.

Authority and Competency of the Film Maker

Cost

The library recognizes that many materials (print and nonprint) are controversial and that any given item may offend some library user. Selections will not be made on the basis of any anticipated approval or disapproval but solely on the merits of the work in relation to the building of the collection and to serving the interests of the citizens of Amarillo.

Oakland Public Library (California)

Selection Policy: Videos

The purpose of the Oakland Public Library's video service is to develop and maintain a well-balanced collection of videocassettes for the home use of its users. As with all library materials, the basic standards governing purchase decisions are technical quality, timeliness, social significance and public demand. Materials are collected that appeal to the educational and recreational needs of the broadest range of the Library's users.

Video cassettes are selected to strike a balance among a number of subject categories, with emphasis on:

> Feature films, both current and classic
> Videocassettes for children
> Documentaries, including athletic events
> Cultural performances, including concerts, operas, plays
> and music videos
> Informational videocassettes, including health, exercise,
> travel and language instruction

All videocassettes under consideration, except titles priced under $40.00 and feature films seen by at least two committee members, are previewed to ensure adherence to the stated selection criteria. In addition, published reviews and the evaluations of the East Bay Motion Picture and Television Council are consulted prior to purchase. Gifts are subject to the same selection guidelines as purchased videocassettes.

Videocassettes in languages other than English are purchased only when English language subtitles are included.

Videocassettes are purchased in VHS format only.

The Library subscribes to the American Library Association's Library Bill of Rights and will oppose any effort to remove a videocassette from the collection that was acquired under its video selection policy.

New City Library (New York)

Books-on-Tape

In addition to the general criteria listed in the main text of the collection management policy, selection for this collection is based on quality of interpretation and technique, plus the value of sound in conveying the subject matter to the listener. The collection contains fiction and nonfiction. Either may be purchased in bridged or unabridged versions, depending upon availability and price relative to other criteria. This collection is not necessarily intended for use by the visually or physically disabled. The New York State Library for the Visually and Physically Handicapped maintains an excellent collection of talking-books for qualified citizens. Applications are available at the adult Information Desk.

Abridged Material. With the exception of some books-on-tape, and of some large-print books, the Library rarely selects condensed or abridged versions of materials when the complete version is available and affordable.

Videocassettes

A. General Statement
The library collects videocassettes in order to serve the audiovisual needs of the community. The collection avoids specialized material, and strives to serve the largest number of people. Selection of adult videos is guided by a general design to maintain a one-third/two-thirds split between nonfiction and feature films, emphasizing quality and specifically acquiring videos less likely to be available through commercial outlets. The collection does not include material purchased specifically for school or college curriculum use.

B. Selection Criteria

1. There is no single set of criteria that can be applied to all videocassettes. Some items are judged primarily in terms of artistic merit or documentation of the times, while others are selected to satisfy the recreational and informational needs of the community. Stress is placed on acquiring videos of contemporary significance and permanent value.

2. Consideration is given to popular demand, the relationship of the video to the existing collection and to other videos available on the subject, its importance in film history, and the cost of the video relative to its value. The collection includes videotapes of cultural, recreational, and instructional worth. The collection acknowledges serious use, while also recognizing the legitimacy of entertainment.

3. The Library seriously considers suggestions from the public, but acquisitions are limited to works for which an acceptable level of quality has been determined in one or more of the following ways:
- By the opinion of qualified reviewers in recognized, authoritative review sources
- Through recognition by awards given by critical or artistic organizations, institutes or associations
- In-house review evaluation by the department head or delegate

4. If an artist, in seeking realistic representation of the human condition, includes material that is sexually candid or dialogue with vulgar diction, such inclusion will not be considered reason for rejection if the video otherwise meets standards for acquisition.

5. General quality criteria also include the following:
- Present and potential relevance to community needs and interests
- Insight into the human condition
- Accurate presentation of factual information
- Use to intended audience
- Public demand resulting from the attention of critics and reviews
- High-quality performances and accurate content
- Technical skill in production
- Provides a presentation most effectively or appropriately delivered by the video format
- Provides information or offers a presentation that is unique to or only available in video format

Juneau Public Libraries (Alaska)

Videos for home use are offered for checkout at the downtown and Douglas libraries.

Materials in video format are collected, as are materials in all other formats, to meet the informational needs of the general public.

A considerable number of video rental outlets are in place in the Juneau area, and Juneau Public Libraries concentrate on meeting needs which commercial suppliers do not meet. That is not to say that the library will never overlap any of the offerings of any of the local video retailers. Rather, the library's primary focus will be on categories of material for which there is little or no commercial availability within Juneau. Special consideration will be given to subjects most effectively presented in visual form, such as drama and dance (both how to and great performances), quality features, documentaries and classic works originally created for the film medium. For children's materials, the library will prefer presentations based on original illustrations and high-quality children's literature.

Because hardware is available in over 50% of U.S. homes and is available for rent locally from commercial video outlets, VCR's and monitors are not offered for loan from the library's media services.

Brief guidelines for selection are:

1. Avoid substantial competition with video store stock. Omit recent feature films.
2. Avoid duplication of ASL video holdings.
3. In choosing nonfiction, prefer subjects more effectively conveyed visually than in print, e.g. dance, sports, opera, drama.
4. In choosing for juveniles, prefer those juvenile titles based on original illustrations and high quality literature. Omit commercially oriented juvenile materials, such as cartoons with licensed characters (e.g. Smurfs) for which purpose is to market other products.
5. Provide wide variety of materials, including film classics, non-current feature films, foreign films, science, how-to, travel history, PBS materials.
6. Prefer titles with low to moderate (usually home video) price, e.g. a 60-minute tape for $39 to $79 maximum.
7. Pay higher prices for Public Performance Rights only for compelling reason (e.g. for college credit courses).

Northwestern State University of Louisiana

Formats

All formats of information should be considered for selection, providing the content falls within the guidelines set forth in this document. Consideration should, however, be given to the condition and durability of the materials. Materials which require special handling or which are delicate may not be appropriate for our collections. Some may be candidates for binding or other treatments which will increase their durability and, therefore, their usefulness to Watson Library and the University Community.

Non-print materials will be added to the collections according to the same criteria as materials in print formats. At the present time, emphasis is placed on audiocassettes, videocassettes, compact disks, and various microformats. In light of new and developing technologies and the progressive obsolescence of some established technologies, other formats may be proposed for addition to the collections if they meet the guidelines of this Collection Development Policy. In addition, the following should be considered in the selection of non-print materials:

1. Availability of hardware needed to use the item
2. Cost
3. Timeliness
4. Technical quality
5. Aesthetic appeal
6. Ease of use

Hawaii Pacific University

Filmstrips—Silent

Filmstrips will be considered an archaic media form. This collection will not be developed further except if suitable materials are unavailable in another form, and use of the filmstrip is deemed essential to meet the instructional objectives of a particular course. Any new acquisitions will be converted to slides.

Weeding. The LAC Director will periodically examine all audiovisual materials in terms of relevance to user needs and selection criteria POLICY. In order to maintain active, up-to-date, useful collections.

Factors to be considered include:

1. lack of use;
2. physical condition; and
3. accuracy and datedness of information.

Selection Criteria

The primary obligation of the Learning Assistance Center is to uphold the doctrine of freedom of the press and to encourage independent thought in an academic environment. The Learning Assistance Center subscribes to the American Library Association's Bill of Rights (as amended, 1980).

Criteria to be used in selecting audiovisual material include:

1. Importance of subject matter in relation to the University's educational goals and curriculum.
2. Timeliness or permanence of the subject matter.
3. Quality of the material as reflected in recommendations or adverse criticisms by respected authorities or reviewers.
4. Relative importance in comparison to other similar types of materials on the subject.
5. Clarity of presentation of subject matter.
6. Reputation and standing of the producer.
7. Price.
8. The number of courses in which the material can be used.
9. The number of course sections per year in which the material can be used.
10. The number of times the material will be used for a single class, (i.e., a single showing, daily, frequent LAC assignments, etc.).
11. The typical number of students enrolled in a course for which the material is intended.

12. Whether the material is listed on a course syllabus which is followed by all instructors teaching a course, only on some instructors' syllabi, or is listed only as supplemental material.
13. Availability of other audiovisual materials in the collection for the course(s).
14. Whether the recommendation is from an individual instructor or from all instructors teaching a particular course.
15. Whether the material is in a format that can be predicted to remain in use for at least the next ten years.

Computer-Based Resources

Florida State University

CD-ROM Databases

Criteria for selection include the extent to which a new database enhances the library's bibliographic access to information, improves the overall collection, or is relevant to the curriculum. Decisions are based on availability of hardware.

Hawaii Pacific University

Electronic Information Sources

1. *On-line Sources.* As policy, Meader Library will subscribe to selected on-line database services which extend the scope of the collection and provide statistical, bibliographic, and full-text access. Subscription will be based on ascertained need, considering faculty, staff, and student needs. At present, on-line services available locally and from the mainland U.S. will be considered. Addition of on-line services from sites other than those identified above will be considered on a case-by-case basis.
2. *Compact-Disc-Read-Only-Memory (CD-ROM).* As policy, Meader Library will pursue the acquisition of CD-ROM products which will either enhance the availability of information, or act as a substitute for the printed format when cost effective. The products may be either bibliographic access, or full-text in nature. In general, acquisition emphasis will be given to those products which are supportive of the Social Sciences, particularly in business-related areas.

Queens College (North Carolina)

Electronic Resources

Increasingly, journals are being published and distributed in electronic format through networks like the Internet. The Library will assist faculty and students in locating electronic serials and in accessing the information they contain. However, the Library will not attempt to archive electronic journals for future access at this time.

Viterbo College (Wisconsin)

Electronic Services: CD-ROM Programs, Online Searches, Subscriptions

Electronic materials are well suited to information which becomes dated quickly. Science materials are often expensive in print and are soon dated. Materials may include full text, abstracted text or index only. All three types of materials will be considered for purchase. In some cases electronic text can substitute for print materials.

Selection criteria (In addition to the criteria used for print materials these criteria apply specifically to electronic media)

- Is the program user-friendly?
- Are source materials available in the library for indexed items?
- Are journals indexed of a quality and quantity appropriate for Viterbo students and faculty?
- Are full text materials available?
- Do entries include abstracts?

California State University, Chico

Electronic Resources

The following policy statement on electronic media reflects the University Library's desire to build collections and improve access to materials through a comprehensive and current collection development policy. It is intended to elaborate on newer technologies which the library is currently using or will use in the future. In keeping with the library's overall collection development policy, materials will be collected or accessed based on its intrinsic merits and relevance to the instructional programs at CSU, Chico, regardless of format.

An electronic resource is defined as any resource which requires computer access. Electronic resources may be located either on-site or off-site. Electronic resources include, but are not limited to, citation or full-text information, software and multimedia programs.

On-site means the items (computer discs, tapes, programs, databases, etc.) are housed somewhere on campus, usually in the library but possibly at another campus location such as the Computer Center. These items may be available at one location only (e.g. the library) or may be available at many different campus locations (e.g. computer labs, dorms, classrooms) via the network. In some cases "on-site" items may even be available to users off campus who dial into the campus network. On-site refers to an item's location, not necessarily its availability.

Off-site means that access is provided, usually over telephone lines, to data (programs, databases, etc.) that is physically located at a distance from the campus. examples of off-site databases are Lexis/Nexis, CARL Uncover, and census files held at other CSU campuses.

Citation databases provide citations to sources of information (books, journal articles, government documents, etc.) rather than the actual text or information. Full-text databases include complete articles, reports, documents, and any other resources which provide actual text and information.

Whether serial or monographic in nature, acquisition of electronic resources must parallel collection development policies currently practiced and stated elsewhere in the *Collection Development Policies Handbook*. The most important priorities are: a) to support and supplement the CSU, Chico, curriculum; b) to support current research programs related to academic disciplines at CSU, Chico; c) to build support for anticipated instructional needs. Other collection needs can be considered once the above priorities have been satisfied.

Guidelines

Resources which provide unique access to information at the appropriate subject, content and cost levels for our users, and reference tools, such as abstracting and indexing services, that provide access to current and retrospective citations and full-text databases, will receive the highest priority for subscription, purchase, delivery, and access.

The library retains ownership of all materials purchased with library funds, including funds allocated to Colleges, Centers and Departments. Although computer technology and electronic media are evolving at a quick pace, the library will endeavor to invest in hardware and software for electronic resources which are enduring and not transient in nature.

Impact on staff for maintenance, support, and training of new resources will be considered.

Acquisitions

Before ordering, the library will consider the following:

- Has the product been previewed?
- Are the protocols already in use in the Meriam Library or does the resource use similar, easily learned commands and/or protocols?
- Are the equipment and infrastructure for distributing and maintaining the electronic resources already in place? Electronic resources must be compatible with the software/hardware available in the library. Equipment for use and maintenance must be in place before subscription, purchase or access.
- Do copyright and licensing agreements restrict the use of the software of other electronic media? The library will avoid signing licensing agreements restricting the use of electronic products by multiple users. The library will comply with Copyright Law and advise users that responsibility for copying, and any infringement thereof, resides with the user.

Collection Development

Resources will be acquired with the intent of supporting the curriculum.

New products which enhance awareness or accessibility of the library's current holdings of journals, books, and other resources will be given priority.

Library faculty, in conjunction with the Systems Office, will determine the most appropriate location and circulation or access policies for resources housed in the library, such as software, CD-ROMs, etc.

Requesters should consider the following specific criteria when evaluating electronic resources. Elements of evaluation include, but are not exclusive to, these selection criteria:

- Uniqueness of content, capabilities or features
- Subject relevance
- Currency
- Accuracy, authoritativeness, and completeness of database
- Cost/benefit considerations
- Interdisciplinary applications
- Offers added value over other formats
- Ease of installation and maintenance
- Ease of access, use, and instruction
- Frequency of updates or newer editions
- Downloading is possible and easily performed

- Compares favorably with print and other electronic products
- Availability of archival copies and replacements
- Reasonable storage and maintenance costs
- Availability of hardware and workstations to support product
- Ability to network
- Availability of user manuals and other documentation
- Availability of support services by vendor
- Local staffing to install, maintain, and train users

William Paterson College of New Jersey

Microcomputer Software

All requests to purchase microcomputer software must be made on a Microcomputer Software Request Form. The Library acquires those types of software packages which supplement the Curriculum Materials Collection as well as college level computer-assisted instruction packages which support the general College curriculum. These include tutorials, educational games, simulations, and drill and practice exercises as well as some multi-purpose packages such as word processing, data management, spreadsheet, statistical packages, etc. Only software that is compatible, in terms of memory size, language and peripherals, with hardware in the Library will be purchased.

Microcomputer Software, especially software which has not been favorably reviewed or which costs more than $100.00, will be previewed and evaluated by members of the Microcomputer Committee prior to purchase. The committee consists of the following members:

Librarian in charge of Library software applications, Chair
Head of the Audiovisual Department
Curriculum Materials Librarian
Associate Director for Collection Management
Associate Director for Readers Services
Head of Collection Development
Supervisor of Audiovisual Services

The requestor, and the appropriate Dean and librarian coordinator will also be invited to preview and evaluate the software. A member of the teaching faculty may be called in to provide technical expertise or subject expertise. The Committee follows the general guidelines for nonprint materials to assure the acquisition of quality microcomputer programs. Additional factors that will be taken into consideration in the selection of software are:

- Appropriateness of the subject to the curriculum and the collection
- Evidence of field testing and favorable reviews

- Availability of backup copies from the publisher or authorization for the Library to make copies
- Reputation of publisher in terms of providing notification of new versions, replacement copies of damaged programs, and warranties on program bugs and defects

The committee may make an affirmative decision even when a requested title does not have all of these characteristics. However, it is unlikely that it would approve the purchase of a title that did not possess the first two characteristics.

The Library will duplicate all uncopyrighted Curriculum Materials software and add these to the circulating collection. In the case of copyrighted materials, the Curriculum Materials Librarian, in consultation with the Collection Development Librarian, will consider cost and desirability of purchase of a second copy on a per item basis at the time of initial purchase.

Clinch Valley College of the University of Virginia

Computer Software

Computer software acquired by the Library must fall within the following categories:

1. Educational games and simulations;
2. Application programs for office use, e.g., spreadsheets, database management systems, etc. and for mathematical applications;
3. Graphics programs;
4. Expert systems shells;
5. Multimedia software, e.g., hypertext.

The Library will acquire one copy of each software package. Faculty must justify the purchase of such software. The cost of this material will be deducted from the requestor's fund. All software packages are to be used for a specific project only and/or as a review tool to assist students with their projects. However, if all students in a class are required to use a specific software package, such material must become available at the Computer Center and may not be purchased with Library fund. Software packages that are incompatible with existing hardware at the Computer Center will not be purchased. Faculty must comply with the Copyright Law governing the use of such material.

Michigan Technological University

J. ROBERT VAN PELT LIBRARY—COLLECTION MANAGE-
MENT DIVISION DRAFT: COLLECTION POLICY—COM-
PUTER-BASED RESOURCES

II. SELECTION CRITERIA

C. **Specific Concerns**

    9. *Computer-based Information*

        This section deals with a new area of library information which is
also affected by fast-changing technology. The section is necessarily more specific in order to speak to those issues which must be
considered in selection, collection building and information access.

    A) Definition: Electronic formats refer to materials/information which
require access through various kinds of computers ranging from
personal computer to mainframe.

    B) Scope: This section refers to materials selected for addition to the
collection. This section does not include pay-for-search databases
accessed online such as Dialog.

    C) Selection Criteria: Subject content and intellectual level of each
information resource will be reviewed in the context of the library's
established collection development policy.

        1) Selection Issues

        a. The priority issue in selection of an electronic product is
simultaneous use by multiple users.

        b. The issues below follow the priority issue and are to be consid-
ered separately and/or together in determining which electronic products will be selected. There is no priority order.

            (1) Use of multiple database access (MDAS) wherever pos-
sible.

            (2) Comprehensive abstracts and indexes have prior consid-
eration to individual specialized reference subject areas.

            (3) User need/demand.

            (4) Cost.

            (5) Level: research materials have prior consideration over
general and undergraduate materials.

            (6) Materials of current and previous three years. Earlier files
will be acquired if the data has significant importance to a
serially-issued database which has been already acquired.

(7) Significant overriding advantages to be gained with purchase of machine-readable form over the print form.

(8) Preservation and storage advantages.

(9) Recurring fees to be paid to the supplier/vendor.

(10) Custodial and special service considerations.

(11) Quality keyword searching, whether in MDAS, CD, or online.

(12) Number of disks per index.

2) Product Considerations

a. How does this product compare to existing print resources? What added value does it offer as opposed to the traditional format?

b. Does the product contain additional information over the traditional format?

c. Could an existing print subscription be canceled if this source were acquired?

d. Is the additional flexibility gained through automation significant for this particular resource?

e. Does usage of the print format merit an additional access point?

f. What is the coverage and scope of the information?

g. How frequently is the product updated?

h. Is the product capable of being accessed by simultaneous users?

i. Is the product available through another library?

j. Is the format the only one available for the product? Is it the most cost effective/user-friendly/accessible?

k. Can the vendor's claims be verified?

l. Is currency a factor?

3) Cost Analysis

a. CD-ROM

- one-time cost or initial subscription costs.
- annual subscriptions.
- costs to obtain backrun.
- equipment acquisition and maintenance.
- stafftime cost to configure new products.
- training costs.

b. Print Equivalent

- one-time cost or annual subscription costs.
- replacement costs.
- binding, storage, preservation costs.

c. Online equivalent

- one-time system fee or annual system subscription fees.
- database charges.
- telecommunications costs.
- equipment acquisition and maintenance costs.
- documentation costs.
- training costs (fees and stafftime).

4) Search/System Capabilities

a. Is there reasonable response time?

b. Can the searching and printing be interrupted?

c. Does the database provide desirable search features such as Boolean operators, truncation, and proximity searching?

d. Is downloading possible?

5) Vendor/Contract Considerations

a. Is a demonstration disk or trial account available?

b. Has the vendor demonstrated reliability, good performance, and production of high quality products with clear documentation?

c. Are software enhancements included in the purchase or lease price?

d. Is maintenance for hardware included in the subscription price?

e. Is there an easily accessible toll-free customer service?

f. Has the vendor produced other relevant databases?

g. Does the contract require restrictions such as:

- an obligation to return superseded disks.
- guarantee of limited access.
- restrictions on downloading.
- definitions of users and/or uses of the information.
- liability from patron use of information.
- restrictions on duplication of the documentation accompanying the product.

6) Hardware Considerations

   a. Is the hardware which is required currently available in the library?

   b. Are the storage and memory of currently available equipment sufficient?

   c. How does purchasing the hardware from the vendor affect the pricing of the subscription?

   d. If the vendor supplies customized hardware, does it provide significant enhancement of the use of the product that could not be achieved with existing library hardware?

   e. Does the vendor agreement require review by the University legal counsel prior to purchase?

D) Implementation

   The Collection Management Head, in consultation with the Reference Coordinator, the Systems Librarian and/or Computing Technology Services will assess the impact of the proposed acquisition on:

   1) Facilities: is additional hardware, wiring, furniture, etc. required?

   2) Location of product/space: will renovation or reconfiguration of space be required?

   3) Training: what are the requirements for staff and users? What is the quality of the search software?

   4) Will point-of-use manuals be required by the Bibliographic Instruction staff?

   5) Service: what will be the impact on other reference sources?

   6) Technical support: is adequate expertise available in the library or on campus to support use of the product?

E) Purchase and Budget

   Electronic formats, with the exception of online search charges, are to be included as line items in the Library materials' budget under both monographs (one-time purchases) and serials (subscriptions). This allows tracking of cost of the format, and makes visible to the administration and faculty the library's support.

   (Material for this document is compiled from ARL/OMS SPEC Kit Nos. 159 Nov/Dec 1989, 169 Nov/Dec 1990.)

Textbooks and Multiple Copies

Covenant College (Georgia)

On the matter of purchasing textbooks for the library collection, it is obvious that not all textbooks should be excluded from the library shelves. There are general textbooks in physics and accounting, to take but two examples, which are important for reference purposes. There are also desirable textbooks of a specialized nature which are monographic in nature. But ordering textbooks freely, particularly in multiple copies, should be avoided. Two or three introductory textbooks in recent editions should be sufficient in most subject areas. More than this can get very expensive without adding substantially new material to the collection.

Fairview Heights Public Library (Illinois)

Multiple Copies Policy

In order to provide the broadest possible range of materials for the support of the curriculum, the library will not usually purchase multiple copies of books, serials, or audio-visual items. Requests for multiple copies will be considered individually, according to present needs and the value of the resource as a part of the library's permanent collection. A librarian will contact faculty members who request multiple or duplicate copies in order to verify the actual need for such added titles. The criteria to be considered for the purchase of multiple copies for reserve required reading will include course enrollment and the nature and expected use of the reserve material. If a decision is made to purchase multiple copies, the additional copies will be acquired in the most economical format.

Hawaii Pacific University

The Library will not expend library funds for the purchase of generically classified textbooks except in those instances where the availability of substantive area literature is limited.

(a) A generically classified textbook is defined as a book created and written specifically for classroom use which serves as the principal vehicle of instruction. It is issued in successive editions, and contains review question sections.

The Library will not expend library funds to purchase books being used as textbooks in any specific class which are available in the University Bookstore.

Northwestern State University of Louisiana

Watson Library does not purchase textbooks which are used in the classes taught at Northwestern State University. The purpose of the Watson Library collections is to complement textbooks and lectures and to further coursework and research. The Library is unable to satisfy such a demand and expects that students will purchase the textbooks used in their classes. On occasion, textbooks may be accepted as gifts if they meet other criteria set forth in the Collection Development Policy. Textbooks not used in classes may be purchased in those areas which fall within the basic level of collection, or in those disciplines where textbooks provide the best overview.

Mount Wachusett Community College (Massachusetts)

Areas of Low Priority

Textbooks. "Textbooks," defined here as works whose published form clearly indicates its intended use as a principal teaching aid, are normally excluded from the library's permanent collection. There are, however, exceptions to the general exclusion of textbooks as noted below:

1. When a particular textbook is recognized as a classic by experts in the field.
2. When a textbook presents materials in a way which is especially valuable to users in the opinion of teaching faculty and librarians (as for example, "Case Studies" in Business and Literature) and whose usefulness to readers will probably outlive related course offerings.
3. When other kinds of monographic publications in a curricular area are sparse.
4. When a textbook treats an important extra-curricular subject not otherwise represented in the collection.

Periodicals

New City Library (New York)

A. General Statement

A wide range of popular magazines, scholarly journals, newspapers, business and investment serials, and other periodicals are purchased to provide information on current issues and events, recent research material for personal and scholastic study, and general and topical recreational reading. Several large-print magazines are also purchased. In addition, some periodicals are acquired to serve as materials selection aids and to provide professional reading for the staff of the Library.

B. Selection and Maintenance Process

The adult and young adult periodicals collections are reviewed annually by the Head of Reference and Audio-visual Services and a committee composed of other librarians on the Adult Services and Reference staffs. Materials acquired with Job Information Grant monies through the Ramapo Catskill Library System, such as Sunday editions of out-of-area newspapers, are reevaluated separately, when the grant is renewed. New periodicals, especially any indexed in the *Readers' Guide to Periodical Literature* and in *Magazine Index Plus*, are considered, as are all magazines, journals, business services, and newspapers that have been suggested by patrons and staff during the preceding year. Whenever possible, sample copies and/or critical reviews are read. All periodicals are evaluated relative to other publications in the same general subject area.

C. Selection Criteria

1. General criteria governing selection are: community interests; accuracy of presentation; accessibility of content through general and specific subject indexes; the need for such periodicals in reference work; editorial and design quality; and the representation of a variety of viewpoints.

2. Periodical acquisitions must meet the following standards:

- Be a general publication, of interest to the layperson
- If essentially informational (as opposed to recreational) in content, be indexed in at least one of the indexing services to which the library subscribes
- Have been in print for at least one year, to guard against the publication ceasing shortly after the library subscribes to it
- Have been favorably reviewed in the professional literature

- Be published by a known commercial or scholarly publisher or professional association, with a reputation for accuracy and authority

3. Other criteria used in the selection process include: Whether the journal or newspaper is available at other libraries in the Ramapo Catskill or the Southeastern New York library systems, and whether the library has other periodicals in its collection that substantially overlap or duplicate the subject area.

D. Periodicals on Microform

Microfilm and, less frequently, microfiche editions of newspapers and periodicals are purchased to provide permanent backfiles for reference purposes. The physical bulk of paper issues of periodicals and frequency of their use are the two principal criteria used in determining whether to obtain and retain issues of serials in microform. Materials no longer available in their original form, such as old Rockland County newspapers and federal and state census reports, are also purchased on microfilm.

Mount Wachusett Community College (Massachusetts)

Serials

Because of the importance of continuity in runs, the acquisition of each serial title usually results in budgetary commitment which is carried over from year to year. For this reason requests for any publication issued in successive parts at regular intervals which is intended to continue indefinitely will be reviewed with special care. For the purpose of this policy, newspapers, in addition to periodicals, annuals (reports, yearbooks, etc.), memoirs, proceedings and transactions of societies are considered serials.

Requests for serial title subscriptions, standing orders, and back files may be made by librarians and faculty on Request Forms. All such requests are considered by the library staff at staff meetings. In reviewing each serial request the staff considers the characteristics presented below. Those listed in Group A are of greater importance than those listed in Group B, and so forth. However, all characteristics in a given group are weighed equally.

Group A
- Appropriateness of the subject matter to the collection.
- Ability to access the title through an index which is available at the M.W.C.C. Library.

Group B

- Anticipated use as reflected by the title's relevance to courses frequently offered on campus.
- Favorable reviews.
- Reliable publisher.
- Predominance of articles written in English.

Group C

- High quality and appropriate physical format.
- High usage of similar titles already owned by the library.
- Cost which is justifiable based on the staff's perception of the title's value.

After approving a request the staff determines whether the library should keep all or only the latest year's issues. It also determines where non-periodical serial titles will be housed. In general, all periodical titles which are considered to be of lasting reference value, and are indexed, are acquired in microform whenever available.

Bay State College (Massachusetts)

Periodicals

Suggestions from faculty and students for new periodical subscriptions will be held until June of each year, at which time a general evaluation of all periodicals will be made. Additions to the holdings will be made on the basis of the following criteria:

- importance of recommended title to the curricula of the College
- ability of students to read and understand the material presented
- number of journals currently held in the subject area
- availability of adequate access to the contents through indexing media
- fiscal soundness of the publication

Clinch Valley College of the University of Virginia

Criteria for Material Selection

Periodicals and other serials. This includes journals, magazines, newspapers, conference proceedings, indexes, etc. The total periodical and other serials holdings and the retention or deletion of a title depend upon the Library's acquisitions budget and the extent of use. The following factors will be considered in the acquisition, retention, or deletion of a periodical/serial title or a periodical index:

1. The indexing/abstracting service(s) in which a periodical/serial is covered. A periodical/serial should be indexed in manual and/or computerized source(s) available in the Library;
2. The reputation of the chief editor, board of editors, and the publishing house;
3. The critical reviews from reputable selection tools and from preview copies. A complimentary copy for evaluation should be ordered from the publisher;
4. The justification for the new subscription submitted by the requestor to the Collection Development Librarian as to how the new title can serve the needs of both students and faculty;
5. The contribution of the title to existing or newer subject areas/ disciplines.

State University of New York, College of Technology at Farmingdale

Newspapers

Newspapers are added to the collection when they significantly supplement the quality or quantity of local, national, or international news available in those standard newspapers already available. If major changes occur in the quality or intent of those newspapers which have traditionally been part of the collection, they will be evaluated for possible discontinuation.

Serials

In general, the same criteria apply to the selection of serial titles as to the book collection. Since a relatively inexpensive journal title represents a continuing expense, titles are added very selectively. Backfiles on hard copy are kept for varying lengths of time depending on the discipline and the title involved. Microfilm are purchased to create backfiles for titles and are purchased in addition to hardcopy for specified titles which receive heavy use. The Serials Librarian periodically evaluates the serials collection and discontinues titles deemed least important. New titles are added to support college curricula and enrich the collection. Faculty and staff's input is sought and they are notified of changes related to their area of specialization.

Hawaii Pacific University

General

Criteria to be used in selecting periodicals include:

1. Importance of periodical, as indicated by its inclusion in standard bibliographies and/or "recommended lists."
2. Importance of periodical's subject matter in relation to the University's education goals and the curriculum.
3. Inclusion of periodical, and therefore access to its articles, in indexes and abstracts (both print and electronic) maintained by the Library.
4. Authoritativeness as reflected by recommendation or adverse criticism by respected authorities.
5. Reputation and standing of the publisher.
6. Price.

Northwestern State University of Louisiana

Serials

New subscription requests are collectively reviewed by the Serials Review Committee in May of each year. Serial selections are based on the same critieria as outlined for other materials in this policy statement. In addition to those guidelines, the following must be taken into account:

1. Indexing and availability of the index in Watson Library
2. Cost of the serial
3. Overall serials budget for the year
4. Requestor of the serial; requesting department; number of faculty members requesting the serial
5. Subject emphasis (see collection intensity levels); interdisciplinary nature of the publication (number of departments which might use the title); size of enrollments in requesting program; potential usage
6. Publisher: EBSCO/order direct
7. Foreign language/publisher
8. Frequency of publication

Whenever a new serial is selected a decision should be made concerning the retention of that serial, and if it is to be retained indefinitely, whether or not it should be bound or purchased in microformat. Serials cannot and will not be selected and dropped on a yearly basis: a commitment must be made to support new serials on an on-going basis.

Michigan Technological University

a. Guidelines for Periodical and Serial Selection

The following guidelines should be considered:

Does the journal support the curricula?
Has the journal been favorably reviewed?
Is the journal indexed?
Is the journal available in microform?
Does the journal offer enrichment or support material to university programs?

b. Core Lists

Undergraduate core titles (designated as "1" in the Serials Management File) must directly support the undergraduate curricula. These titles should be regularly reviewed by the Departments to ensure that they support all programs. These titles will be the last to be cancelled in the event of a budget reduction.

Research core titles ("2" in the Serials Management File) must directly support research efforts, either of individuals or of teams. These titles should be reviewed annually by the Departments to ensure that they support current research efforts. These titles will be the second group to be considered for cancellation in the event of a budget reduction.

Combined Research/Undergraduate titles ("3" in the Serials Management File) are research titles deemed necessary to maintain currency in teaching. These titles will be the third group to be considered for cancellation in the event of a budget reduction.

Non-core titles ("0" in the Serials Management File) are enrichment and support titles which will be the first to be cancelled in the event of a budget reduction.

Archives

State University of New York, College of Technology at Farmingdale

The college archives serve as the permanent memory of the institution. The purpose of the Archives is to collect, preserve and organize for convenient access materials which document significant activities and events in the history and development of SUNY Farmingdale. The following types of materials are collected.

1. College publications (catalogs, bulletins, schedules, directories, commencement and convocation programs).
2. Student publications (newspapers, magazines, yearbooks, handbooks).
3. Departmental publications (newsletters, programs of special events).
4. Faculty publications (books, journal reprints, bibliographies; items of a personal nature are usually excluded).
5. Manuscripts (when directly related to university matters; personal correspondence on a highly selective basis).
6. Alumni publications (published writings only, collected on a selective basis).
7. Governance and administrative documents.
8. Faculty Senate minutes.
9. Reports (Presidents', Deans' other reports of historic importance).
10. Brochures (issued by departments and campus offices).
11. Photographs (of significant events and persons).
12. Audio-visual materials (oral histories, video and sound recordings of major university events).
13. Memorabilia, newspaper clippings, leaflets, etc. (on a highly selective basis).

Queens College (North Carolina)

Guidelines for the Archives Collection

Appropriate Materials. The following shall serve as a checklist of materials appropriate for active collection in the Archives, and shall be reviewed annually.

College Materials

a. Minutes, memoranda, correspondence, and reports of the Board of Trustees and its committees.
b. Correspondence, subject files, and reports of the President.
c. Correspondence, subject files, and reports of the administrative heads of the four vice-presidents.
d. Contribution records from the Vice President for Development and College Relations.
e. Minutes, memoranda, correspondence, and reports of the academic divisions and departments, the general faculty, and regular, special, and ad hoc faculty committees.
f. Minutes, memoranda, correspondence, and reports of administrative and College-wide committees, regular, special, and ad hoc.
g. Official reports, periodic and special (including accreditation reports and supporting documentation, and auditors' reports).

h. Catalogs and bulletins, general and special, and recruiting materials.

i. Special publications (including press releases, calendars, posters, and notices of special events) and scrapbooks.

j. Records of student organizations and activities.

k. Student publications, including yearbooks and newspapers.

l. Records of the College Registrar, including class schedules, enrollment reports, graduation rosters, and other reports issued on a regular basis.

m. Records and publications of the Alumni Association and of the Alumni Affairs Office.

n. Reports of the Admissions Office.

o. Copies of successful grant proposals, following completion of project or termination of grant funding.

p. Schedules, programs and other publications of the Athletics Department.

q. Pictorial materials (including photographs, campus plans, building plans, renderings of campus buildings, and maps and plot plants) describing persons, buildings, and places relating to the College. NOTE: Individuals in photographs to be identified if possible, before transfer to the Archives.

r. Non-College publications, on a selective basis, including but not limited to newspaper clippings and scrapbooks, and pamphlets dealing wholly or in part with Queens College.

s. Theses that are a component of graduate degree programs, or major research projects that fulfill graduate degree of undergraduate program requirements.

t. Publications with a Queens College imprint.

u. Records of organizations associated with the College, such as advisory committees and Friends groups.

v. Audiovisual materials including those documenting the history and activities of the College, those produced by or for the College, and those accompanying theses.

w. Artifacts relating to the history of the College, as determined by the College Archivist.

x. Appropriate material from alumni and faculty, as determined by the College Archivist.

Inappropriate Materials. The following items are to be excluded unless their substance relates to the College.

a. Presbyterian materials, unless directly relating to the founding or operation of Queens College or the institutions from which it has evolved.

b. Regalia.

Loras College (Iowa)

Loras Archive & Center for Dubuque History

The Center for Dubuque History and the Loras College Archives share a facility inside the Wahlert Memorial Library. The Center for Dubuque History collects a wide range of current and retrospective material of historical value relating to the city and county of Dubuque and the lead mining region of the Upper Mississippi Valley. This includes, but is not limited to:

- books, periodicals, newspapers,
- manuscripts,
- government documents (city and county),
- maps and platbooks,
- census records,
- vertical file material,
- postcards,
- photographs,
- audio-visual materials (including oral histories).

The Center was founded in 1976 and relies mostly upon donations of materials for accession to the collections.

The Loras College Archives collects records, documents, and publications of historical, legal, fiscal, and administrative value to the college community. The collection includes, but is not limited to:

- annual catalogs, bulletins, baccalaureate and commencement programs,
- yearbooks, campus newsletters, and other serial publications produced by various members of the college community,
- alumnal newspapers and publications,
- student, staff, and alumnal directories and handbooks,
- records of students, faculty, and alumnal organizations and clubs,
- college charters, by-laws, and amendments,
- financial records, president's annual reports, audit reports,
- board of regents minutes and reports,
- faculty and staff biographical files,
- faculty, staff, and alumnal publications,
- physical environment records including blueprints and architectural plans,
- miscellaneous scrapbooks, clippings, programs, etc.,
- photographs.

Reference Collection

California State University, Chico

Abstracts and Indexes

Recognizing the value of reference materials in all defined areas of study the library attempts to acquire those abstracting and indexing services that support instruction and research. Those who request standing orders and subscriptions for indexes and abstracts should use the following criteria:

A. Duplication: significant overlap (50% or more) of coverage with other library index services indicates the need for considerable investigation before purchase.

B. Unique Indexing: while overlaps may be significant, there may be unique features that greatly enhance the use of the index such as short publication lag time, key word indexing, etc.

C. Subject Assessment: indexes should be purchased on a level appropriate to the patterns of collecting levels in the subject area.

D. Usage: realistic appraisal must be given to the probable use of the index and to the relationship of cost to use.

E. Electronic Access: many indexes are now available simultaneously on paper, CD-ROM, and online. Consideration should be given to price, added-value search capabilities, usage, and equipment requirements when choosing between the various formats.

Rosary College (Illinois)

Reference Collection Policy

I.   Objectives of the Reference Collection Policy

A. This policy shall define the type of material that will be collected by the Reference Department of the library, as well as establish the subject scope of the collection.

B. This policy shall also set standards for the withdrawal of reference works from the collection.

II. The Reference Collection

The reference collection at the Rebecca Crown Library shall provide information sources appropriate for the courses taught at Rosary College, as well as provide selective coverage of subjects not taught at the school.

III. Selection of Reference Works

    A. The Reference Librarian has the primary responsibility for selecting material for the reference collection. The following criteria shall be used when determining whether or not a book should be added to the collection:

       1. The usefulness of the publication, considering the existing reference and general collection.

       2. Favorable reviews in leading library or academic journals or inclusion in basic reference collection guides.

       3. Reputation of the author.

       4. Date of publication.

       5. Whether or not the library owns a previous edition of the work.

       6. Price of publication.

    B. The Reference Librarian will use a variety of sources to ensure the library acquires reference works appropriate for the collection.

       1. Professional literature will be scanned regularly. Such publications include *Booklist, Choice, Library Journal, RQ,* and *Wilson Library Bulletin.*

       2. Publishers' leaflets and catalogs will be perused.

       3. Standard reference collection guides such as Sheehy's *Guide to Reference Books* or Walford's *Guide to Reference Material* will be consulted to determine if older publications not in the current review literature should be added to the collection.

       4. Subject bibliographers will be consulted to help determine the worthiness of a publication in some specific fields.

       5. Faculty members will be consulted to determine if a publication not reviewed in the standard sources is a worthwhile addition to the reference collection.

IV. Types of Material in the Reference Collection

It is impossible to include every type of publication that is likely to be encountered in the reference collection in this policy. The major types of publications, however, are outlined below. This section will be used in conjunction with section V, "Subject Collection Levels," when determining the suitability of a publication for the reference collection—particularly for those with narrow subject scopes.

    A. *Almanacs.* The Reference Department shall collect at least two current editions of an American almanac, one of which shall be the

World Almanac and Book of Facts. Whitaker's Almanack, a British almanac, shall be purchased every even-numbered year and the *Canadian Almanac and Directory* every odd-numbered year.

B. *Bibliographies*. Subject and author bibliographies will be kept in the reference collection. The national bibliographies of America and Great Britain will be collected. The American trade bibliography *Books in Print* shall be purchased every year, as well as the equivalents for France, Germany, Great Britain, and Italy. No more than two years worth of these trade bibliographies will be retained at any time.

C. *Biographical Sources*. All major national biographies for the United States will be collected, as well as a representative collection of critically acclaimed biographical works for other countries. The *Who's Who* publications will be collected annually for the United States and Great Britain and shall be kept in the reference collection until the receipt of the *Who Was Who* volumes for those years, after which they shall be placed in storage. The extent of biographical sources collected for individual subjects will depend on the guidelines established for that subject in section V of this policy.

D. *Concordances*. At least two major biblical concordances shall be retained at all times by the reference department. Concordances of the works of individual authors will be collected only if the author is deemed important enough to warrant such a purchase.

E. *Corporate Manuals*. The *Moody's Bank and Finance, Industrial, OTC Industrial, Public Utilities,* and *Transportation* manuals shall be purchased every year and retained in the reference collection for two years, after which they shall be placed in storage. *Standard and Poor's Register of Corporations* shall also be purchased every year, retained for two in reference, and then placed in storage. *Moody's Bond Survey* and *Moody's Bond Record* shall have the current year plus the previous year kept in reference, then placed in storage. The *Million Dollar Directory* shall be kept for one year in reference, then withdrawn.

F. *Corporate Reports*. Annual reports and 10-K's from corporations listed on the annual *Fortune* magazine lists of the top 500 industrial and top 500 service companies shall be collected, as well as those from the corporations listed on the annual *Crain's Chicago Business* list of the 150 top publicly held firms in Chicago. These documents shall be retained for the current two years only, then discarded.

G. *Dictionaries*. All *major* English language dictionaries will be collected. The latest edition in the reference collection for a given title shall be no more than five years old, unless the work does not have a policy of continuous revision or the price of the work does not justify its purchase. Dictionaries shall also be collected for the major Romance languages and updated as needed. Bilingual dictionaries with English as one language shall be collected for as many major languages as possible. Slang dictionaries and etymological dictionaries will be collected for the English language only.

H. *Directories*. The library will purchase the manufacturing, industrial, and service directories for the state of Illinois at least every other years on a rotating basis depending on budgetary limitations. The Reference Department may also purchase manufacturing directories from other states should any cooperative purchase agreement be made with neighboring libraries in the Suburban Library System.

I. *Encyclopedias*. The Reference Department shall collect all major single volume and multivolume general encyclopedias. One set of *Collier's Encyclopedia, Encyclopedia Americana*, or *Encyclopedia Britannica* shall be purchased each year on a rotating basis if funds permit and so long as each work maintains a policy of continuous revision at an acceptable level (usually ten percent annually). Major general encyclopedias for other countries will be collected as funds permit. Encyclopedias devoted to specific subject areas will be collected depending on the guidelines established for that subject in section V.

J. *Geographical Sources*. Gazetteers and atlases will be collected by the Reference Department for all areas of the world. Maps will be kept in a separate map collection located near the vertical file. Topographic maps will not be intensively collected.

K. *Handbooks*. Current handbooks for all subjects collected by the Reference Department will be purchased and updated as frequently as possible. No handbook for any discipline shall be more than ten years old unless no other authoritative handbook has been written in the field.

L. *Indexes*. Periodical indexes and abstracts for various disciplines shall be collected to the extent necessary to maintain the level of study indicated for that discipline in section V. The library shall always collect at least the *general* periodical indexes for art, business, the humanities, the social sciences, and the sciences.

M. *Legal Materials*. Only the general legal dictionaries or encyclopedias will be collected by the Reference Department. The latest edition of the statutes of the state of Illinois will be collected. Many federal materials, such as the *U.S. Code*, are in the government documents collection. No indexes to court cases below the level of the United States Supreme Court will be collected. The *Standard Federal Tax Reporter* will be updated each year, with the Index volume kept for the current year plus the previous year.

N. *Plot Summaries*. Major collections of plot summaries, such as *Masterplots*, will be collected. Single works, such as *Cliffs' Notes* or *Monarch Notes*, will not be collected.

O. *Style Manuals*. Current editions of the style manuals issued by the University of Chicago and the Modern Language Association of America will be collected. The style manual currently assigned by the majority of the undergraduate instructors shall also be purchased if it is not one of these. Style manuals from individual scholarly associations will be purchased only if assigned by a department for classes.

P. *Telephone Directories*. The telephone directories for the thirty largest Standard Metropolitan Statistical Areas as established by the U.S. Census Bureau will be collected as will the directories for Chicago, the Chicago area, and Springfield, Illinois. Telephone directories from one or more other states will also be collected as part of a cooperative agreement with other area libraries in the Suburban Library System.

Q. *Travel Books*. Travel books for various countries will be collected to serve only as representative samples of such works. These books will include the publications from the more popular publishers such as Baedeker, Fodor's, and Michelin.

R. *Yearbooks*. Yearbooks connected with sets of encyclopedias are not collected and shall be retained only when included with the purchase of an entire set. Other yearbooks from various organizations shall be kept in the reference collection for two years, unless it is determined that they have historical value and will be referred to often. The disposition of a yearbook after two years (i.e. being placed in storage or withdrawn) will depend on whether or not information in the yearbook is entirely superseded by the next year's edition. If information in a yearbook is superseded by the next edition, it will generally be withdrawn from the collection.

Foreign Language Materials

Naval War College (Rhode Island)

Scope

Foreign language publications. On a highly selective basis, significant scholarly monographs in the original and foreign language periodicals and newspapers are acquired in those spheres of particular relevance to the collection. Normally, only titles in major foreign languages, i.e., French, German, Russian and Spanish will be selected. However, titles in other languages will be considered if their subject matter is such to be of prime importance to the mission of the Naval War College.

Northern Arizona University

Foreign Language Material: The Cline Library will collect materials primarily in the English language. Translations of foreign language materials to English will normally be preferred. Materials will be acquired in other languages when needed by academic programs. Literary classics may be acquired in major European languages. Navajo. Hopi, and other native American language materials related to the Colorado Plateau area will be acquired. Some major foreign language newspapers and periodicals will be included. Major reference works and dictionaries in foreign languages will be added to the collection.

Doane College (Nebraska)

Foreign language materials: With the exception of materials acquired primarily for use of students and faculty in the study of modern languages, books and other materials printed or recorded in languages other than English will not be purchased. Exceptions to this policy will be foreign language dictionaries for reference use and other foreign language material which might be determined to be appropriate by the librarian in consultation with the faculty concerned.

APPENDIXES

A P P E N D I X
1

❋ ❋ ❋ ❋ ❋ ❋ ❋ ❋

Library Bill of Rights

The American Library Association affirms that all libraries are forums for information and ideas, and that the following basic policies should guide their services.

1. Books and other library resources should be provided for the interest, information, and enlightenment of all people of the community the library serves. Materials should not be excluded because of the origin, background, or views of those contributing to their creation.

2. Libraries should provide materials and information presenting all points of view on current and historical issues. Materials should not be proscribed or removed because of partisan or doctrinal disapproval.

3. Libraries should challenge censorship in the fulfillment of their responsibility to provide information and enlightenment.

4. Libraries should cooperate with all persons and groups concerned with resisting abridgment of free expression and free access to ideas.

5. A person's right to use a library should not be denied or abridged because of origin, age, background, or views.

6. Libraries which make exhibit spaces and meeting rooms available to the public they serve should make such facilities available on an equitable basis, regardless of the beliefs or affiliations of individuals or groups requesting their use.

Adopted June 18, 1948.
Amended February 2, 1961, June 27, 1967, and January 23, 1980,
by the ALA Council.

APPENDIX
2

❖ ❖ ❖ ❖ ❖ ❖ ❖ ❖

The Freedom to Read

The freedom to read is essential to our democracy. It is continuously under attack. Private groups and public authorities in various parts of the country are working to remove books from sale, to censor textbooks, to label "controversial" books, to distribute lists of "objectionable" books or authors, and to purge libraries. These actions apparently rise from a view that our national tradition of free expression is no longer valid; that censorship and suppression are needed to avoid the subversion of politics and the corruption of morals. We, as citizens devoted to the use of books and as librarians and publishers responsible for disseminating them, wish to assert the public interest in the preservation of the freedom to read.

We are deeply concerned about these attempts at suppression. Most such attempts rest on a denial of the fundamental premise of democracy: that the ordinary citizen, by exercising critical judgment, will accept the good and reject the bad. The censors, public and private, assume that they should determine what is good and what is bad for their fellow-citizens.

We trust Americans to recognize propaganda, and to reject it. We do not believe they need the help of censors to assist them in this task. We do not believe they are prepared to sacrifice their heritage of a free press in order to be "protected" against what others think may be bad for them. We believe they still favor free enterprise in ideas and expression.

We are aware, of course, that books are not alone in being subjected to efforts at suppression. We are aware that these efforts are related to a larger pattern of pressures being brought against education, the press, films, radio and television. The problem is not only one of actual censorship. The shadow of fear cast by these pressures leads, we suspect, to an even larger voluntary curtailment of expression by those who seek to avoid controversy.

Such pressure toward conformity is perhaps natural to a time of uneasy change and pervading fear. Especially when so many of our apprehensions are directed against an ideology, the expression of a dissident idea becomes a thing feared in itself, and we tend to move against it as against a hostile deed, with suppression.

And yet suppression is never more dangerous than in such a time of social tension. Freedom has given the Untied States the elasticity to endure strain. Freedom keeps open the path of novel and creative solutions, and enables change to come by choice. Every silencing of a heresy, every enforcement of an orthodoxy, diminishes the toughness and resilience of our society and leaves it the less able to deal with stress.

Now as always in our history, books are among our greatest instruments of freedom. They are almost the only means for making generally available ideas or manners of expression that can initially command only a small audience. They are the natural medium for the new idea and the untried voice from which come the original contributions to social growth. They are essential to the extended discussion which serious thought requires, and to the accumulations of knowledge and ideas into organized collections.

We believe that free communication is essential to the preservation of a free society and a creative culture. We believe that these pressures towards conformity present the danger of limiting the range and variety of inquiry and expression on which our democracy and our culture depend. We believe that every American community must jealously guard the freedom to publish and to circulate, in order to preserve its own freedom to read. We believe that publishers and librarians have a profound responsibility to give validity to that freedom to read by making it possible for the readers to choose freely from a variety of offerings.

The freedom to read is guaranteed by the Constitution. Those with faith in free people will stand firm on these constitutional guarantees of essential rights and will exercise the responsibilities that accompany these rights.

We therefore affirm these propositions:

1. *It is in the public interest for publishers and librarians to make available the widest diversity of views and expressions, including those which are unorthodox or unpopular with the majority.*

   Creative thought is by definition new, and what is new is different. The bearer of every new thought is a rebel until that idea is refined and tested. Totalitarian systems attempt to maintain themselves in power by the ruthless suppression of any concept which challenges the established orthodoxy. The power of a democratic system to adapt to change is vastly strengthened by the freedom of its citizens to choose widely from among conflicting opinions offered freely to them. To stifle every nonconformist idea at birth would mark the end of the democratic process. Furthermore, only through the constant activity of weighing and selecting can the democratic mind attain the strength demanded by times like these. We need to know not only what we believe but why we believe it.

2. *Publishers, librarians and booksellers do not need to endorse every idea or presentation contained in the books they make available. It would conflict with the public interest for them to establish their own political, moral or aesthetic views as a standard for determining what books should be published or circulated.*

Publishers and librarians serve the educational process by helping to make available knowledge and ideas required for the growth of the mind and the increase of learning. They do not foster education by imposing as mentors the patterns of their own thought. The people should have the freedom to read and consider a broader range of ideas than those that may be held by any single librarian or publisher or government or church. It is wrong that what one who can read should be confined to what another thinks proper.

3. *It is contrary to the public interest for publishers or librarians to determine the acceptability of a book on the basis of the personal history or political affiliations of the author.*

A book should be judged as a book. No art or literature can flourish if it is to be measured by the political views or private lives of its creators. No society of free people can flourish which draws up lists of writers to whom it will not listen, whatever they may have to say.

4. *There is no place in our society for efforts to coerce the taste of others, to confine adults to the reading matter deemed suitable for adolescents, or to inhibit the efforts of writers to achieve artistic expression.*

To some, much of modern literature is shocking. But is not much of life itself shocking? We cut off literature at the source if we prevent writers from dealing with the stuff of life. Parents and teachers have a responsibility to prepare the young to meet the diversity of experiences in life to which they will be exposed, as they have a responsibility to help them learn to think critically for themselves. These are affirmative responsibilities, not to be discharged simply by preventing them from reading works for which they are not yet prepared. In these matters taste differs, and taste cannot be legislated; nor can machinery be devised which will suit the demands of one group without limiting the freedom of others.

5. *It is not in the public interest to force a reader to accept with any book the prejudgment of a label characterizing the book or author as subversive or dangerous.*

The ideal of labeling presupposes the existence of individuals or groups with wisdom to determine by authority what is good or bad for the citizen. It presupposes that individuals must be directed in making up their minds about the ideas they examine. But American do not need others to do their thinking for them.

6. *It is the responsibility of publishers and librarians, as guardians of the people's freedom to read, to contest encroachments upon that freedom by individuals or groups seeking to impose their own standards or tastes upon the community at large.*

It is inevitable in the give and take of the democratic process that the political, the moral, or the aesthetic concepts of an individual or group will occasionally collide with those of another individual or group. In a free society individuals are free to determine for themselves what they wish to read, and each group is free to determine what it will recommend to its freely associated members. But no group has the right to take the law into its own hands, and to impose its own concept of politics or morality upon other members of a democratic society. Freedom is no freedom if it is accorded only to the accepted and the inoffensive.

7. *It is the responsibility of publishers and librarians to give full meaning to the freedom to read by providing books that enrich the quality and diversity of thought and expression. By the exercise of this affirmative responsibility, they can demonstrate that the answer to a bad book is a good one, the answer to a bad idea is a good one.*

The freedom to read is of little consequence when expended on the trivial; it is frustrated when the reader cannot obtain matter fit for that reader's purpose. What is needed is not only the absence of restraint, but the positive provision of opportunity for the people to read the best that has been thought and said. Books are the major channel by which the intellectual inheritance is handed down, and the principal means of its testing and growth. The defense of their freedom and integrity, and the enlargement of their service to society, requires of all publishers and librarians the utmost of their faculties, and deserves of all citizens the fullest of their support.

We state these propositions neither lightly nor as easy generalizations. We here stake out a lofty claim for the value of books. We do so because we believe that they are good, possessed of enormous variety and usefulness, worthy of cherishing and keeping free. We realize that the application of these propositions may mean the dissemination of ideas and manners of expression that are repugnant to many persons. We do not state these propositions in the comfortable belief that what people read is unimportant. We believe rather that what people read is deeply important; that ideas can be dangerous; but that the suppression of ideas is fatal to a democratic society. Freedom itself is a dangerous way of life, but it is ours.

This statement was originally issued in May of 1953 by the Westchester Conference of the American Library Association and the American Book Publishers Council, which in 1970 consolidated with the American Educational Publishers Institute to become the Association of American Publishers.

Adopted June 25, 1953; revised January 28, 1972, January 16, 1991, by the ALA Council and the AAP Freedom to Read Committee.

A Joint Statement by:
American Library Association
Association of American Publishers

Subsequently Endorsed by:
American Booksellers Association
American Booksellers Foundation for Free Expression
American Civil Liberties Union
American Federation of Teachers AFL-CIO
Anti-Defamation League of B'nai B'rith
Association of American University Presses
Children's Book Council
Freedom to Read Foundation

International Reading Association
Thomas Jefferson Center for the Protection of Free Expression
National Association of College Stores
National Council of Teachers of English
P.E.N. - American Center
People for the American Way
Periodical and Book Association of America
Sex Information and Education Council of the U.S.
Society of Professional Journalists
Women's National Book Association
YWCA of the U.S.A.

APPENDIX
3

❀ ❀ ❀ ❀ ❀ ❀ ❀ ❀

Intellectual Freedom Statement

AN INTERPRETATION OF THE LIBRARY BILL OF RIGHTS

The heritage of free men is ours.

In the Bill of Rights to the United States Constitution, the founders of our nation proclaimed certain fundamental freedoms to be essential to our form of government. Primary among these is the freedom of expression, specifically the right to publish diverse opinions and the right to unrestricted access to those opinions. As citizens committed to the full and free use of all communications media and as professional persons responsible for making the content of those media accessible to all without prejudice, we, the undersigned, wish to assert the public interest in the preservation of freedom of expression.

Through continuing judicial interpretations of the First Amendment to the United States Constitution, freedom of expression has been guaranteed. Every American who aspires to the success of our experiment in democracy who has faith in the political and social integrity of free men—must stand firm on those Constitutional guarantees of essential rights. Such Americans can be expected to fulfill the responsibilities implicit in those rights.

We, therefore, affirm these propositions:

1. *We will make available to everyone who needs or desires them the widest possible diversity of views and modes of expression, including those which are strange, unorthodox or unpopular.*

   Creative thought is, by its nature, new. New ideas are always different and, to some people, distressing and even threatening. The creator of every new idea is likely to be regarded as unconventional—occasionally heretical—until his idea is first examined, then refined, then tested in its political, social or moral applications. The characteristic ability of our governmental system to adapt to necessary change is vastly strengthened by the option of the people to choose freely from among conflicting opinions. To stifle nonconformist ideas at their inception would be to end the democratic process. Only through continuous weighing and selection from among opposing views can free individuals obtain the strength needed for intelligent, constructive decisions and actions. In short, we need to understand not only what we believe, but why we believe as we do.

2. *We need not endorse every idea contained in the materials we produce and make available.*

We serve the educational process by disseminating the knowledge and wisdom required for the growth of the mind and the expansion of learning. For us to employ our own political, moral, or esthetic views as standards for determining what materials are published or circulated conflicts with the public interest. We cannot foster true education by imposing on others the structure and content of our own opinions. We must preserve and enhance the people's right to a broader range of ideas than those held by any librarian or publisher or church or government. We hold that it is wrong to limit any person to those ideas and that information another believes to be true, good, and proper.

3. *We regard as irrelevant to the acceptance and distribution of any creative work the personal history or political affiliations of the author or others responsible for it or its publication.*

A work of art must be judged solely on its own merits. Creativity cannot flourish if its appraisal and acceptance by the community is influenced by the political views or private lives of the artists or the creators. A society that allows blacklists to be compiled and used to silence writers and artists cannot exist as a free society.

4. *With every available legal means, we will challenge laws or governmental action restricting or prohibiting the publication of certain materials or limiting free access to such materials.*

Our society has no place for legislative efforts to coerce the taste of its members, to restrict adults to reading matter deemed suitable only for children, or to inhibit the efforts of creative persons in their attempts to achieve artistic perfection. When we prevent serious artists from dealing with truth as they see it, we stifle creative endeavor at its source. Those who direct and control the intellectual development of our children—parents, teachers, religious leaders, scientists, philosophers, states-men—must assume the responsibility for preparing young people to cope with life as it is and to face the diversity of experience to which they will be exposed as they mature. This is an affirmative responsibility that cannot be discharge easily, certainly not with the added burden of curtailing one's access to art, literature, and opinion. Tastes differ. Taste, like morality, cannot be controlled by government, for govern-mental action, devised to suit the demands of one group, thereby limits the freedom of all others.

5. *We oppose labeling any work of literature or art, or any persons responsible for its creation, as subversion, dangerous, or otherwise undesirable.*

Labeling attempts to predispose users of the various media of communication, and to ultimately close off a path to knowledge. Labeling rests on the assumption that persons exist who have a special wisdom, and who, therefore, can be permitted to determine what will have good and bad effects on other people. But freedom of expression rests on the premise of ideas vying in the open marketplace for acceptance, change or rejection by individuals. Free men choose this path.

6. *We, as guardians of intellectual freedom, oppose and will resist every encroachment upon the freedom by individuals or groups, private or official.*

It is inevitable in the give-and-take of the democratic process that the political, moral and esthetic preferences of a person or group will conflict occasionally with those of others. A fundamental premise of our free society is that each citizen is privileged to decide those opinions to which he will adhere or which he will recommend to the members of a privately organized group or association. But no private group may usurp the law and impose its own political or moral concepts upon the general public. Freedom cannot be accorded only to selected groups for it is then transmuted into privilege and unwarranted license.

7. *Both as citizens and professionals, we will strive by all legitimate means open to us to be relieved of the threat of personal, economic, and legal reprisals resulting from our support and defense of the principles of intellectual freedom.*

Those who refuse to compromise their ideals in support of intellectual freedom have often suffered dismissals from employment, forced resignations, boycotts of products and establishments, and other invidious forms of punishment. We perceive the admirable, often lonely, refusal to succumb to threats of punitive action as the highest form of true professionalism: dedication to the cause of intellectual freedom and the preservation of vital human and civil liberties.

In our various capacities, we will actively resist incursions against the full exercise of our professional responsibility for creating and maintaining an intellectual environment which fosters unrestrained creative endeavor and true freedom of choice and access for all members of the community.

We state these propositions with conviction, not as easy generalizations. We advance a noble claim for the value of ideas, freely expressed, as embodied in books and other kinds of communications. We do this in our belief that a free intellectual climate fosters creative endeavors capable of enormous variety, beauty, and usefulness, and thus worthy of support and preservation. We recognize that application of these propositions may encourage the dissemination of ideas and forms of expression that will be frightening or abhorrent to some. We believe that what people read, view, and hear is a critically important issue. We recognize, too, that ideas can be dangerous. It may be, however, that they are effectually dangerous only when opposing ideas are suppressed. Freedom, in its many facets, is a precarious course. We espouse it heartily.

Adopted by the ALA Council, June 25, 1971, Endorsed by the Freedom to Read Foundation, Board of Trustees, June 18, 1971.

A P P E N D I X
4

❋ ❋ ❋ ❋ ❋ ❋ ❋ ❋ ❋

Freedom to View

The Freedom to View, along with the freedom to speak, to hear, and to read, is protected by the First Amendment to the Constitution of the United States. In a free society, there is no place for censorship of any medium of expression. Therefore these principles are affirmed:

1. To provide the broadest possible access to film, video, and other audiovisual materials because they are a means for the communication of ideas. Liberty of circulation is essential to insure the constitutional guarantee of freedom of expression.
2. To protect the confidentiality of all individuals and institutions using film, video, and other audiovisual materials.
3. To provide film, video, and other audiovisual materials which represent a diversity of views and expression. Selection of a work does not constitute or imply agreement with or approval of the content.
4. To provide a diversity of viewpoints without the constraint of labeling or prejudging film, video and other audiovisual materials on the basis of the moral, religious, or political beliefs of the producer or filmmaker or on the basis of controversial content.
5. To contest vigorously, by all lawful means, every encroachment upon the public's freedom to view.

This statement was originally drafted by the Freedom to View Committee of the American Film and Video Association (formerly the Educational Film Library Association) and was adopted by the AFVA Board of Directors in February 1979. This statement was updated and approved by the AFVA Board of Directors in 1989. Additional copies may be obtained for $1.00 (to cover postage and handling) from: American Film & Video Association, 920 Barnsdale Road, Suite 152, La Grange Park, Illinois 60525, (312) 482-4000.

Endorsed by the ALA Council January 10, 1990

A P P E N D I X
5

* * * * * * * * *

Challenged Materials

AN INTERPRETATION OF THE LIBRARY BILL OF RIGHTS

The American Library Association declares as a matter of firm principle that it is the responsibility of every library to have a clearly defined materials selection policy in written form which reflects the Library Bill of Rights, and which is approved by the appropriate governing authority.

Challenged materials which meet the criteria for selection in the materials selection policy of the library should not be removed under any legal or extra-legal pressure. The Library Bill of Rights states in Article 1 that "Materials should not be excluded because of the origin, background, or views of those contributing to their creation," and in Article 2, that "Materials should not be proscribed or removed because of partisan or doctrinal disapproval." Freedom of expression is protected by the Constitution of the United States, but constitutionally protected expression is often separated from unprotected expression only by a dim and uncertain line. The Constitution requires a procedure designed to focus searchingly on challenged expression before it can be suppressed. An adversary hearing is a part of this procedure.

Therefore, any attempt, be it legal or extra-legal, to regulate or suppress materials in libraries must be closely scrutinized to the end that protected expression is not abridged.

Adopted June 25, 1971; amended July 1, 1981; amended January 10, 1990, by the ALA Council.

A P P E N D I X
6

❋ ❋ ❋ ❋ ❋ ❋ ❋ ❋ ❋

Statement on Labeling

AN INTERPRETATION OF THE LIBRARY BILL OF RIGHTS

Labeling is the practice of describing or designating materials by affixing a prejudicial label and/or segregating them by a prejudicial system. The American Library Association opposes these means of predisposing people's attitudes toward library materials for the following reasons:

1. Labeling is an attempt to prejudice attitudes and as such, it is a censor's tool.
2. Some find it easy and even proper, according to their ethics, to establish criteria for judging publications as objectionable. However, injustice and ignorance rather than justice and enlightenment result from such practices, and the American Library Association opposes the establishment of such criteria.
3. Libraries do not advocate the ideas found in their collections. The presence of books and other resources in a library does not indicate endorsement of their contents by the library.

A variety of private organizations promulgate rating systems and/or review materials as a means of advising either their members or the general public concerning their opinions of the contents and suitability or appropriate age for use of certain books, films, recordings, or other materials. For the library to adopt or enforce any of these private systems, to attach such ratings to library materials, to include them in bibliographic records, library catalogs, or other finding aids, or otherwise to endorse them would violate the Library Bill of Rights.

While some attempts have been made to adopt these systems into law, the constitutionality of such measures is extremely questionable. If such legislation is passed which applied within a library's jurisdiction, the library should seek competent legal advice concerning its applicability to library operations.

Publishers, industry groups, and distributors sometimes add ratings to material or include them as part of their packaging. Librarians should not endorse such practices. However, removing or obliterating such ratings—if placed there by or with permission of the copyright holder—could constitute expurgation, which is also unacceptable.

The American Library Association opposes efforts which aim at closing any path to knowledge. This statement, however, does not exclude the adoption of organizational schemes designed as directional aids or to facilitate access to materials.

Adopted July 13, 1951. Amended June 25, 1971; July 1, 1981; June 26, 1990, by the ALA Council.

A P P E N D I X
7

❋ ❋ ❋ ❋ ❋ ❋ ❋ ❋

Policy on Confidentiality of Library Records

The Council of the American Library Association strongly recommends that the responsible officers of each library in the United States:

1. Formally adopt a policy which specifically recognizes its circulation records and other records identifying the name of library users to be confidential in nature.*
2. Advise all librarians and library employees that such records shall not be made available to any agency of state, federal, or local government except pursuant to such process, order, or subpoena as may be authorized under the authority of, and pursuant to, federal, state, or local law relating to civil, criminal, or administrative discovery procedures or legislative investigative power.
3. Resist the issuance or enforcement of any such process, order, or subpoena until such time as a proper showing of good cause has been made in a court of competent jurisdiction.**

Adopted January 20, 1971; revised July 4, 1975, by the ALA Council.

---

*Note: See also ALA Policy Manual 54.15, Code of Ethics, point 3: "Librarians must protect each user's right to privacy with respect to information sought or received, and materials consulted, borrowed, or acquired."

**Note: Point 3, above, means that upon receipt of such process, order, or subpoena, the library's officers will consult with their legal counsel to determine if such process, order, or subpoena is in proper form and if there is a showing of good cause for its issuance; if the process, order, or subpoena is not in proper form or if good cause has not been shown, they will insist that such defects be cured.

BIBLIOGRAPHY

❋ ❋ ❋ ❋ ❋ ❋ ❋ ❋

Bostic, Mary J. "A Written Collection Development Policy: To Have and Have Not," *Collection Management* 10, No. 3/4 (1988): 89–103.

Cassell, Kay and Elizabeth Futas. *Developing Public Library Collections, Policies and Procedures*. New York: Neal-Schuman, 1991.

Collection Development Policies. Chicago: American Library Association, Association of College and Research Libraries (CLIP Notes #2), 1981.

Collection Development Policies for College Libraries. Chicago: American Library Association, Association of College and Research Libraries (CLIP Notes #11), 1989.

Disaster Readiness, Response and Recovery Manual. Washington, D.C.: Rhode Island Council for the Preservation of Research Resources, [1993].

Donohue, Mary Kay, Deborah Brown, and Suzanne Gyeszly. "Collection Development Policy Making: Research, Design, and Implementation at Texas A & M University," *Collection Building* 6, No. 3 (Fall, 1984): 18–21.

Dowd, Shella T. "The Formulation of a Collection Development Policy Statement." In *Collection Development in Libraries: A Treatise* edited by Robert D. Stueart and George B. Miller, Jr. Greenwich, CT: JAI Press, 1980: 67–87.

Futas, Elizabeth. *Library Acquisition Policies and Procedures*. Phoenix, AZ: Oryx Press, 1977.

Futas, Elizabeth. *Library Acquisition Policies and Procedures*. 2nd ed. Phoenix, AZ: Oryx Press, 1984.

Guide for Written Collection Policy Statements. Chicago: American Library Association, Resources and Technical Services Division (Collection Management and Development Guide #3), 1989.

Guide to Review of Library Collections: Preservation, Storage, and Withdrawal. Chicago: American Library Association, Association for Library Collections & Technical Services (Collection Management and Development Guides #5), 1991.

Guide to the Evaluation of Library Collections. Chicago: American Library Association, Resources and Technical Services Division (Collection Management and Development Guide #2), 1989.

Jacob, Merle. "Get It in Writing: A Collection Development Plan for the Skokie Public Library," *Library Journal* 115 (September 1, 1990): 166–169.

Librarians Collection Letter: A Monthly Newsletter for Collection Development Staff ed. by Regan Robinson, Westerly, RI, 1990- .

Perkins, David L. "Writing the Collection Development Manual," *Collection Management* 4 (Fall 1982): 37–47.

PLA Handbook for Writers of Public Library Policies. Chicago: American Library Association, Public Library Association, 1993.

A Primer on Disaster Preparedness, Management and Response: Paper-Based Materials. Washington, D.C.: Smithsonian Institution et. al., October 1993.

Slote, Stanley. *Weeding Library Collections: Library Weeding Methods*, 3rd ed. Littleton, CO: Libraries Unlimited, 1989.

INDEX

* * * * * * * *

Compiled by James Minkin

Elizabeth Futas, Ph.D., is a professor and director of the Graduate School of Library and Information Studies at the University of Rhode Island. Over the past 27 years, she has acquired a wide variety of teaching and library experience, having served as reference librarian, cataloguer, and bibliographer at a variety of academic and public libraries, in addition to holding professor and lecturer positions at several universities. Dr. Futas also provides consulting services for collection evaluation and policy formation. A former editor of the ALA *SRRT Newsletter*, she is the author or editor of numerous publications, including *Library Acquisitions Policies and Procedures, Second Edition*, also published by Oryx Press.

ISBN 0-89774-797-6

90000

9 780897 747974